Word Phonology in a Systemic Functional Linguistic Framework

Key Concepts in Systemic Functional Linguistics

Series Editors
Gerard O'Grady, Cardiff University
Rebekah Wegener, University of Salzburg
Tom Bartlett, University of Glasgow

Books in this series provide monographic treatments of core theoretical concepts within Systemic Functional Linguistics, together with coverage of more recent concerns in Systemic Functional Linguistic theory and important areas of application and trans-disciplinary collaboration.

Each monograph is organized around a description of the historical factors that led to the emergence of the concept within Systemic Functional Linguistics and a detailed theoretical description of the concept within the overall architecture of the theory.

Published

Neo-Firthian Approaches to Linguistic Typology
William B. McGregor

System in Systemic Functional Linguistics: A System-based Theory of Language
Christian M.I.M. Matthiessen

Systemic Functional Translation Studies: Theoretical Insights and New Directions
Bo Wang and Yuanyi Ma

Verbal Art and Systemic Functional Linguistics
Donna R. Miller

Word Phonology in a Systemic Functional Linguistic Framework

Phonological Studies in English, German, Welsh and Tera (Nigeria)

Paul Tench

UNIVERSITY OF TORONTO PRESS
Toronto Buffalo London

Published by University of Toronto Press in 2024
Toronto Buffalo London
utorontopress.com
Printed in the USA

ISBN 978-1-4875-6652-4 (cloth)
ISBN 978-1-4875-6653-1 (paper)
ISBN 978-1-4875-6655-5 (EPUB)
ISBN 978-1-4875-6654-8 (PDF)

Publication cataloguing information available from Library and Archives Canada.

Cover design: Mark Lee / hisandhers.design

We wish to acknowledge the land on which the University of Toronto Press operates. This land is the traditional territory of the Wendat, the Anishnaabeg, the Haudenosaunee, the Métis, and the Mississaugas of the Credit First Nation.

University of Toronto Press acknowledges the financial support of the Government of Canada, the Canada Council for the Arts, and the Ontario Arts Council, an agency of the Government of Ontario, for its publishing activities.

Canada Council for the Arts Conseil des Arts du Canada

ONTARIO ARTS COUNCIL
CONSEIL DES ARTS DE L'ONTARIO
an Ontario government agency
un organisme du gouvernement de l'Ontario

Funded by the Government of Canada Financé par le gouvernement du Canada Canada

Contents

List of Tables

List of Figures

Preface

This study has grown out of the idea that the principles and procedures of Systemic Functional Linguistics (SFL) could apply at the level of word phonology. They have successfully been applied to all levels of lexicogrammar and discourse, and indeed in phonology, but only at the levels of rhythm and intonation. The principal concern of SFL is to show the options that a language user has to express meaning and the functions that those options perform (see e.g. Halliday 1985, 2002). That is less appropriate at the level of word phonology, because individual sounds and features are not normally associated directly with meaning. Nevertheless, the whole apparatus of SFL might be appropriate if it can only be shown to be so; this study is therefore an attempt to identify the function of phonology in words and show how system networks in phonology can operate at word level.

Chapter 1 is an introduction to phonology by way of brief comparisons with a general public awareness of pronunciation and an overview of phonetics. Phonology is then distinguished from phonetics and shown to be relevant to all levels of lexicogrammar and discourse in terms of its various functions and its hierarchy of units, before focussing on the topic of this book, the phonology of words. The chapter continues with an outline of how principles of SFL can be applied to phonology below the level of intonation and concludes with comparisons with other presentations of phonology from other theoretical perspectives.

Chapter 2 applies the SFL principles in phonology first of all to simple, basic, word forms in English and guides the reader through the mechanisms of system networks. Chapter 3 follows with a description of the complex word formations of inflexions, derivations and compounding. Chapters 4, 5 and 6 take the reader through SFL descriptions of word phonology in

- German, a language close to English;
- Welsh, a Celtic language, from a different branch of Indo-European languages; and then
- Tera, spoken in Northern Nigeria, a non-Indo-European language.

In each case, different aspects of a SFL presentation of phonology come to the fore and SFL word phonology is shown to be appropriate.

*

I wish to acknowledge the encouragement of Professors Gerard O'Grady and Tom Bartlett in recommending me to engage in this study, both at that time at Cardiff University, and Gerard O'Grady's subsequent advising, and Dr Lucy Chrispin of Cardiff University for her invaluable help in drawing system networks; and Prof. Dr Petr Rösel, Mainz University, for helping me to think out degrees of word stress in German, and Dr Dörthe Schilken, Summer Institute of Linguistics, for her occasional help in German also; Dr Iwan Rees of the Welsh Department at Cardiff University for his advice, and Gareth Clee of *Learn Welsh Glamorgan*, at the University of South Wales, for an enormous amount of help in developing the data charts for Welsh; and Dr Rebecca Ishaku Musa, Newcastle University, for her responses to frequent requests for help in Tera, and especially to Babayo Mahdi, now of Language Developers and Bible Translators, Bauchi, Nigeria, for his enthusiastic involvement with me in developing an orthography for Tera in Luke Partnership workshops and the Introductory Course in Applied Linguistics (ICAL) in Nigeria and, subsequently, his supply of a great deal of data and advice. And finally, I wish to thank Cheryl Merritt for her patience and perseverance with a tricky typescript with all its symbols and changes of font!

Paul Tench
Honorary Research Associate
Cardiff University

Chapter 1

Towards a Systemic View of Phonology

People are aware of pronunciation, if not phonology and phonetics. Phonetics is the study of the production, transmission and reception of sounds in human speech and is the subject of careful, informed, scientific investigation. Phonology is the study of the usage of speech sounds in language in general and languages in particular and is the subject of careful, informed, linguistic investigation. Pronunciation, on the other hand, is everyone's activity in spoken communication; that is what we hear and what we produce in talk; it is everyone's experience and hence is part of everyone's business.

1.1 Pronunciation

Everyone engages in pronunciation (unless, of course, they are unable to talk). Most of the time, we are not aware of how we are pronouncing words, phrases, clauses, sentences and whole discourses, because we are more aware of the messages that we are seeking to convey. We usually take no notice of our pronunciation because it is not the focus of our attention when we talk. But sometimes we do. That usually happens when something unusual happens or when something different from our usual expectations happens. It is similar to people taking their breathing for granted because their attention is focussed on what they are doing, until something unusual or different happens.

Very briefly, people become aware of pronunciation when they hear a different **accent** from what they are used to. Accents vary by region, nation, ethnic groups, social class and generation. We also become aware of **pathological** conditions of voice, like lisping, stammering and stuttering. We are also aware of the expression of **emotions**, moods and attitudes: 'it's not what they said, but the way they said it'. We are also aware of different **styles.** We tend to adapt our speech according to norms for different situations; sometimes very formal, sometimes more casual and sometimes very colloquial and intimate.

Some people are concerned about **normative** issues: how they should pronounce a word; or why businesses use 'pop spelling' like *Back to Skool* and *lite* (meaning 'reduced'), and hundreds of others. Normative issues also include learning the pronunciation of another language. Many people enjoy pronunciation games for **entertainment**: puns, puzzles, tongue twisters, jokes, etc. We are also aware of the **poetic** effect of pronunciation in literature: *rhythmicality* in recitals, and *rhyme*, *alliteration*, and other strategies that make some discourse or a phrase memorable.

Less obvious maybe are cultural preferences of **euphony**, an awareness of words that sound pleasant, and also, at least in British culture, first names given to children that sound either more feminine or masculine.

Another obvious point of awareness of pronunciation is the imitative effect of pronunciation in **onomatopoeia**: that is, the attempt to reproduce natural sounds in pronunciation, like *whoosh, bang, moo, hoot, plop, tinkle*, etc. Also, as 'secondary onomatopoeia', sounds may have a particular association, e.g. words with initial *sl-* having a negative connotation. More will be said below under **1.5 Phonology and Words.**

Finally, and perhaps most obviously, we are aware of the **indexical function** of pronunciation by which we recognize people by their voices – acquaintances and strangers alike when we cannot see them; we do so from their voice, say, on the phone or on the radio or from an audio recording. As for strangers, we guess a person's gender, age range, state of health, mood, personality, where they come from and their social class and level of education.

Generally speaking, people are *not* aware of the physical mechanisms in producing, transmitting and receiving speech sounds, nor are they aware of the patterns of sounds that operate in a language. It is to these two issues that we now turn very briefly. First, to phonetics.

1.2 Phonetics

Phonetics is the specialized scientific study of the physiological mechanisms for producing speech sounds within the human anatomy, then transmitting those sounds through the air and receiving them, again, within the human anatomy. These three phases are usually designated articulatory, acoustic and auditory phonetics respectively.

In the study of phonetics, the lion's share of attention is usually given to the articulatory aspect because people find it relatively easier to follow the descriptive apparatus kinaesthetically, whereas we have no direct sense of what happens in the transmission of sound through the air or the reception of sound by the ear – we have to depend on technical apparatus to do so.

A cursory glance at the IPA chart might suggest that articulation is confined to physical activity in the throat and mouth, but a closer inspection will indicate that in addition to the details of the production of consonants and vowels ('segments'), there are also suprasegmental features, often also referred to as 'prosodic features', because they accompany the 'segments' (or, literally, 'sung with' them). The study of phonetics includes handling stress ('loudness'), length ('duration') and pitch ('tone'), which feature in the description of syllables, rhythm and intonation; in other words, phonetics is the study of the total physical production of all the mechanisms that compose spoken discourse, from the minute specifications of consonants and vowels to the effect of rhythm and intonation on whole discourses.

Phonetics can be viewed in general terms irrespective of particular languages, or indeed, in terms of particular languages, e.g. English, German, Welsh, Tera (Nigeria), etc. Just as phonetics is the specialized scientific study of speech sounds, phonology is the specialized linguistic study of the patterns of speech sounds utilized by languages for the expression of units of meaning. Again, most people have little awareness of these patterns.

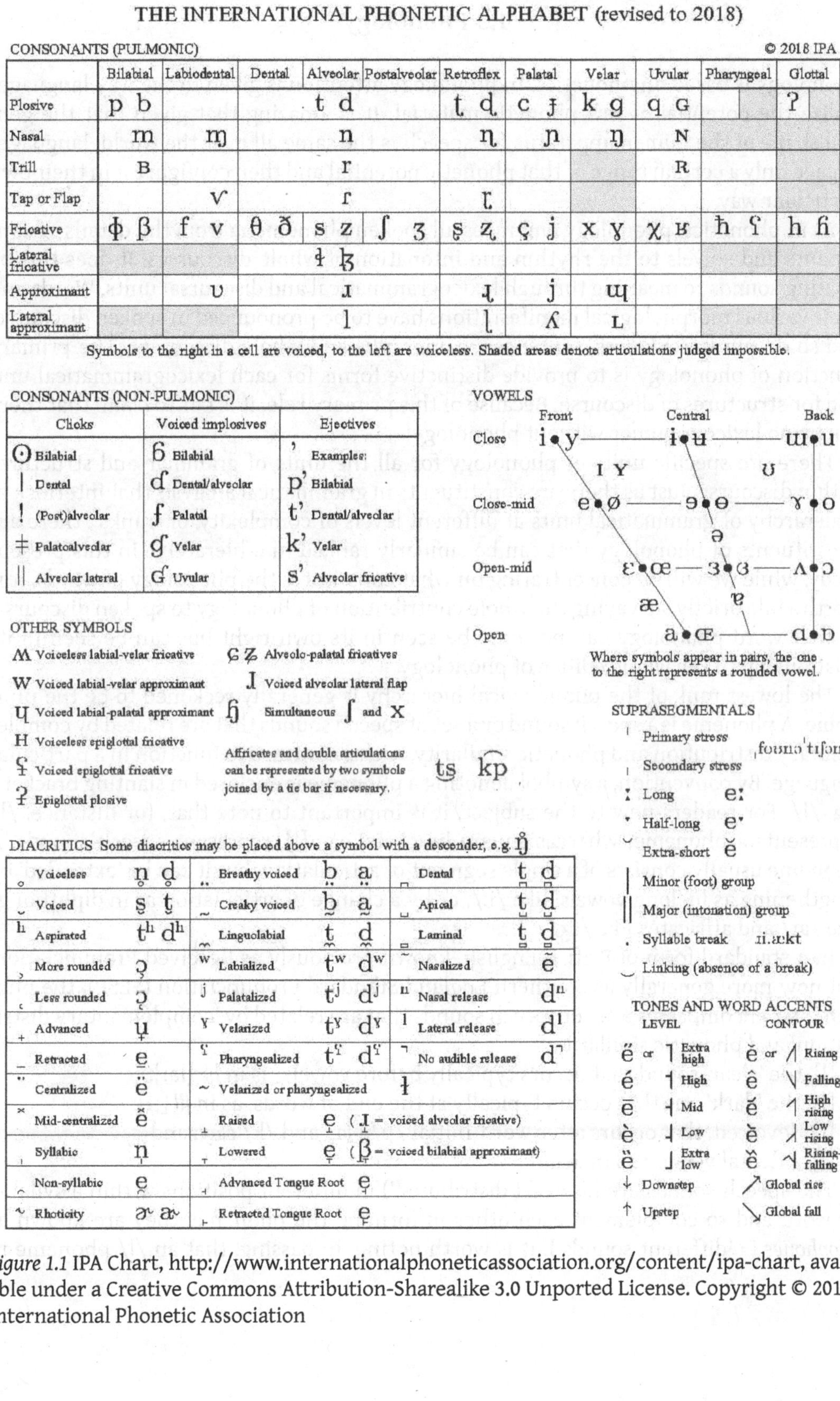

Figure 1.1 IPA Chart, http://www.internationalphoneticassociation.org/content/ipa-chart, available under a Creative Commons Attribution-Sharealike 3.0 Unported License. Copyright © 2015 International Phonetic Association

1.3 Phonology

Phonology is based on phonetics. In phonology attention is given to the way languages utilize the potential of raw phonetic material. It is amazing that given that the general shape of the human apparatus for speech is the same all over the world, languages engage only a certain range of that phonetic potential and then configure it in their own particular way.

As in phonetics, phonology embraces all spoken phenomena from the details of consonants and vowels to the rhythm and intonation of whole discourses. It does this by relating sounds to meaning through lexicogrammatical and discoursal units. Words and their various morphological manifestations have to be pronounced in spoken discourse, and so do phrases, clauses, sentences, paragraphs and whole discourses. The primary function of phonology is to provide distinctive forms for each lexicogrammatical unit and for structures of discourse. Because of this primary role, it is fair to claim that there can be no lexicogrammar without phonology!

There are specific units of phonology for all the units of grammar and structures within discourse. Just as there are constituents in grammatical analysis that interlock in a hierarchy of grammatical units at different levels of complexity, or 'ranks', there are constituents of phonology that can be similarly ranked in a hierarchy. In this present study, while we will be concentrating on what constitutes the phonology of words, it is worthwhile briefly surveying the whole contribution of phonology to spoken discourse, so that word phonology can not only be seen in its own right but can be seen in its relationship to the whole edifice of phonology.

The lowest rank of the phonological hierarchy is generally reckoned to be the **phoneme**. A phoneme is a speech sound or a set of speech sounds that are related by complementary distribution and phonetic similarity, with a contrastive function in a particular language. By convention, a symbol denoting a phoneme is enclosed in slanting brackets, e.g. /l/. For readers new to the subject, it is important to note that, for instance, /l/ represents a phoneme, whereas square brackets, e.g. [l], represent speech sounds. A phoneme usually consists of a single segment of articulation, but it can be 'extended' by lengthening as in 'long vowels' like /iː/, or by a change of articulation as in diphthongs like /aɪ/ and affricates like /ʤ/.

In a standard form of British English, known previously as Received Pronunciation, but now more generally as Southern England Standard Pronunciation (SESP), the phoneme /l/ encompasses a set of speech sounds that are related by 'complementary distribution' and phonetic similarity:

[l], the 'clear' sound that occurs typically before vowels, as in *lie* [laɪ];
[ɫ], the 'dark' one that occurs typically at the end of words, as in *ill* [ɪɫ];
[l̥], devoiced, that occurs after word-initial /p/ *play* and /k/ *clay*; and
[ɫ̪], a dental version as in *wealth*.

The speech sounds are located ('distributed') in different positions within a syllable or word and so complement each other in forming the phoneme; they are known as *allophones* (= 'different sounds'). It is worth noting, in passing, that an /l/ phoneme in one language is unlikely to have the same range of allophones as in another, like English; allophonic variation is specific to the phonology of a given language.

There is, however, yet another instance of /l/ in English (SESP). In all the English examples given so far, /l/ appears as a consonant either before or after a vowel, but in words like *middle*, the /l/ itself functions as the realization of the second syllable: [mɪdɫ̩], /mɪdl̩/. The /l/ is said to be 'syllabic', i.e. functioning as the realization of the centre of a syllable; this is indicated by the symbol [̩]. This situation alerts us to the different perspectives of phonetics and phonology in the definition of the terms consonant and vowel. From a phonetic point of view, a consonant is a speech sound that is produced with some degree of interference to the flow of air through the pharyngeal and oral cavities; and a vowel is produced with no such interference, but with a smooth uninterrupted flow of air. On the other hand, from a phonological point of view, a vowel sound typically functions as the nucleus (centre, or peak) of a syllable and a consonant sound as a margin of a syllable. However, it sometimes happens that an articulation that is phonetically consonantal functions as the centre of a syllable, such as the syllabic /l̩/ in English *middle*, and that an articulation that is phonetically a vowel functions as a margin; English /j/ (usually spelled as <y>) as in *yet* has, like the vowel [i], no consonant-like interruption to the flow of air and yet functions as an initial margin; similarly, English /w/ as in *wet* is articulated like the vowel [u] but functions as a consonant at a margin. /j/ and /w/ are therefore traditionally called 'semi-vowels': vowel by nature, but not by function.

The operative words in the above discussion are, therefore, 'production' in phonetics and 'function' in phonology. Vowels and syllabic consonants function as the centre ('peak' or 'nucleus') of syllables; in fact, they constitute the basis of syllables as a consequence of their greater sonority (see below). Consonants function as the initial or final margins of syllables, unless, of course, they are syllabic. Margins include the so-called 'semi-vowels', which are now usually classified with 'approximants'.

Phonemes have functions within syllables, largely as a consequence of degrees of sonority. A **syllable** is either a single phoneme or a sequence of phonemes, one of which has a relatively high level of sonority. The notion of sonority has an honourable tradition since Jespersen (e.g. 1932). In laymen's terms, relative sonority refers to the inherent capacity of a speech sound to 'travel' and be heard at a distance. Compare, for instance, how far a vowel sound like [a] can be heard in contrast to [p]; [a] has a high degree of sonority, and [p] has low, and there are degrees of sonority in between.

Jespersen (1932: 190–193) proposed a scale or hierarchy of sonority that has been confirmed by linguists since, although with slight variations. Jespersen maintained that vowels have greater sonority (*Schallfülle*) than consonants, and that there are degrees of sonority among the consonants. Resonant consonants have articulations with no plosion of friction and are typically accompanied by voice; obstruents do involve plosion and friction, with voiceless possibilities that are less sonorous. A scale of sonority emerges as follows and is applied to the word *English*:

1. Vowels
2. Approximants
3. Trills and flaps
4. Lateral resonants
5. Nasal resonants
6. Voiced fricatives
7. Voiced plosives
8. Voiceless sibilants
9. Voiceless non-sibilant fricatives
10. Voiceless plosives

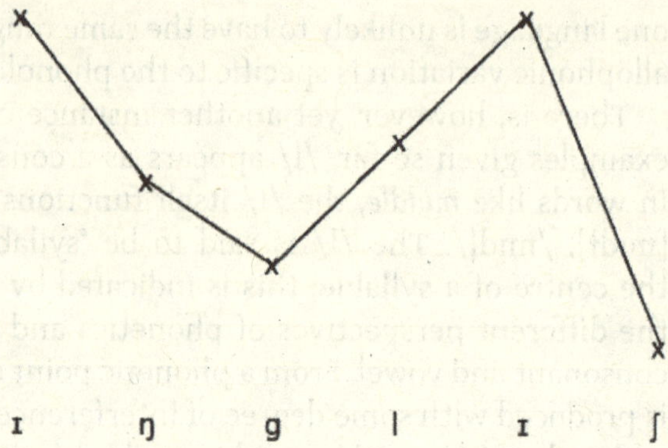

Figure 1.2 The sonority hierarchy

Two peaks of sonority emerge, which tallies with a native speaker's intuition that *English* consists of two syllables. From a phonological perspective, however, not all peaks of sonority constitute syllables. Here is a well-known example, the word *extra*, that shows that peaks do not always coincide with a native speaker's intuition. If each segment is graded according to Jespersen's scale of sonority, *extra* has the following sequence of sonorous segments:

1. Vowels
2. Approximants
3. Trills and flaps
4. Lateral resonants
5. Nasal resonants
6. Voiced fricatives
7. Voiced plosives
8. Voiceless sibilants
9. Voiceless non-sibilant fricatives
10. Voiceless plosives

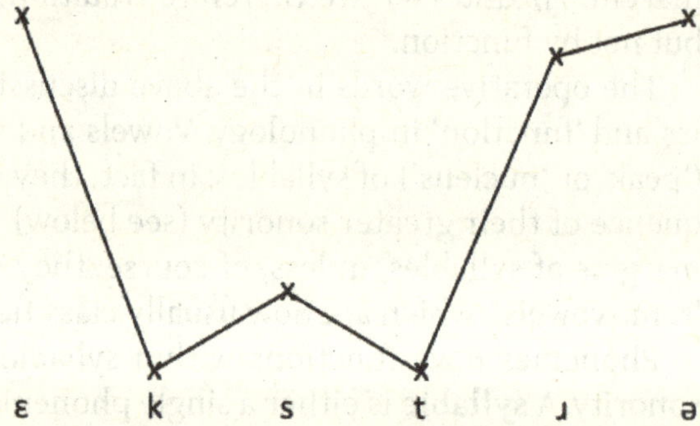

Figure 1.3 The sonority of *extra*

with peaks at /ɛ/, /s/ and /ə/; in other words, three phonetic syllables, but this defies a native speaker's intuition.

This discrepancy can be resolved by recognizing a difference between 'phonetic' syllables – the observation that *extra* has three syllables; and 'phonemic' syllables – native speakers will readily identify just two syllables, even if they might not agree where exactly the division between the two syllables comes. In English phonology, it seems that the distinctions in sonority among voiceless consonants are not significant; that means that the grades 8, 9 and 10 merge into one, resulting in a flat 'line' for /-kst-/. So, just as linguists distinguish between *phonetic* speech sounds and *phonological* phonemes, they also distinguish (see e.g. Pike 1947: 65, 90, 246) between *phonetic* syllables that are based on their production and *phonological* syllables that, we will now see, are based on their function.

However, first a note on the *structure* of syllables as it varies from language to language. In some languages, consonants cannot combine, and so the syllable structure can be depicted as either V (= any vowel) or CV (C = any consonant). Such syllable structures are known as 'open', but they can be 'extended' with a 'closing' consonant. Many languages allow consonant combinations as English does, in both open and closed structures, e.g. CCV, VCC, CCCV, etc. Sequences of vowels and consonants may sometimes be restricted in a language. The permissible combinations of consonants with consonants, and of vowels with consonants is known as *phonotactics*; since the phonotactics of languages varies, it has to be regarded as a significant feature of the phonology of a language. The effect of one phoneme on another is often the result of *simplifications* in articulation; simplification processes also vary from language to language, and hence are also an appropriate dimension of phonology.

As for the *functions* of syllables, there is in many languages a contrastive choice of degrees of stress as part of the identification of a word, as a lexicogrammatical item; this is true for English, German and Welsh. In other languages, there is a contrastive choice of pitch level to help identify words, and this is true for Chinese and many other languages not only in Asia, but also across South America and Africa, including Tera in Nigeria; a phonological unit of pitch is known as a 'tone' (or 'lexical tone' when it is necessary to distinguish between pitch choices in words and in intonation). There are also languages that use timing as a feature for identifying words, such as Japanese and Chadic languages in Africa, again including Tera; a phonological unit of timing is known as a 'mora'.

The function of phonological syllables then is to carry the distinctive degrees of suprasegmental ('prosodic') features of a given language. For instance, English is usually reckoned (see e.g. Roach 2000: 95–96) as having three distinctive degrees of stress: primary, secondary and no stress. In the example of *extra* above, the first syllable peaking on /ɛ/ has primary stress and the final syllable peaking on /ə/ is unstressed, whereas the middle 'syllable' peaking with /s/ has no suprasegmental function at all. Although that /s/ has a 'phonetic' peak, it carries no phonological function of stress.

Similarly, syllables carry phonologically distinctive degrees of pitch (*tone*) in tone languages; and distinctive degrees of timing that operate with moras, often also referred to as *heavy* and *light syllables*. Descriptions of phonologically distinctive degrees of stress, pitch and moras appear in the following chapters on English, German, Welsh and Tera.

Furthermore, syllables lay the base of what is termed syllable timed rhythm. In a great many languages, though not Germanic or Celtic, the rhythm of speech is created by a more or less equal sense of timing for each successive syllable in an utterance (see e.g. Roach 2000: 134–138). This is noticeably the case of Romance languages and many other language families, including Chadic languages like Tera.

Just as consonants and vowels have specific functions in the structure of syllables, as nuclei and margins, so different kinds of syllables have different functions in the phonology of the foot or 'rhythm wave' (Pike 1962). A **foot** is a phonological unit that consists of a relatively prominent syllable and, optionally, a number of weaker syllables; for instance, a stressed syllable functions as the nucleus of the foot and is referred to as a 'strong' syllable (symbol = s, /ˈ/), whereas accompanying syllables are known as 'weak' (symbol = w, unmarked). Like phonemes and syllables, feet may also be 'extended' with a syllable with secondary degree of stress (symbol = s^2, /ˌ/), e.g. *locomotive* /ˌləʊkəˈməʊtɪv/, *engine driver* /ˈɛndʒɪnˌdɹaɪvə/; see also Tench (1976). These phonological units – phonemes, syllables and feet – constitute the phonology of words in English, and by virtue of their interrelationships of structure and function form a kind of hierarchy:

Foot
Syllable
Phoneme

However, phonology, as we have said, relates to more than words, and for the sake of completing the full scope of phonology, we briefly cover another aspect of rhythm and intonation in relation to higher levels of lexicogrammar and discourse.

Just as syllables lay the foundation of syllable timed rhythm, feet lay the foundation of stress timed rhythm. Abercrombie (1967), Halliday et al. (1964) and many others claimed that English speech employs feet that begin with a strong syllable (the 'beat'), and that rhythm is stressed timed, so that the interval of time from one strong syllable to the next is more or less isochronous ('same time'). Abercrombie's famous example was

Which is the train for Crewe please
s ww|s w|s |s

consisting of four feet of differing structure but of more or less identical timing. That timing is maintained even if we substitute *Manchester* with its three syllables for *Crewe*'s single syllable.

Which is the train for Manchester please
s ww|s w|s w w|s

The notion of stress timing in English has been disputed, but allowance has to be made for styles of delivery and degrees of fluency. Stress-timed rhythm in conversation is certainly not as regular as in traditional poetry, but there is tendency towards it in single paratones ('phonological paragraphs'). It explains the prevalence of weak forms of grammatical items with the deletion of weak syllables in some contexts.

Abercrombie and Halliday et al. also posited silent stresses to account for initial weak syllables before the first strong one in an utterance, marked as (^), as in

Delighted to meet you
^w|s w w|s w

However, this view of the foot is somewhat artificial, unduly dependent on what is referred to as 'poetic metre'. In traditional poetry, each line has a set number of beats, i.e. stressed syllables, and each foot is measured from a strong beat. Typically, the foot in English poetry is one of the following:

Spondee: a foot with a single strong syllable	*love*	*life*
Trochee: a foot consisting of a strong syllable followed by a weak one	*love it*	*lively*
Dactyl: a foot consisting of a strong syllable followed by two weak ones	*love of it*	*livelihood*

But this 'poetic' description of the foot does not distinguish between the accelerating unstressed syllable preceding the stressed syllable and the decelerating syllables that follow. It also ignores the great variety of foot structures of single words in citation form in English (see **2.1 The foot and syllable count**). Poetic metre, nevertheless, does, of course, exist, but it belongs to particular cultural styles of speaking, like poetry recitals and the singing of songs, hymns, etc.

The foot, whether it is basically trochaic in one language or iambic in another, is also basic to the structure of units of intonation. **Intonation** is the sounding of clauses and sentences, as Matthiessen (2021) put it. Halliday (1967; 1970) provided the basis of a phonological description of intonation in (British) English, which has been widely accepted. In an intonation unit, the most prominent foot is the nucleus; its prominence is typically detected by being louder, longer and more displaced from a median pitch level and carrying a significant movement of pitch. This nucleus of the intonation unit is commonly called the tonic foot; hence the term tonicity. In all four languages of this study there is a strong tendency for the tonic foot to occur as the final foot in an intonation unit; in Tera, however, it is always, and obligatorily, final; this might be true of all Chadic languages (see Tench and Miller 1980: 62–63 on Hausa). But in the three European languages the tonic foot can be located elsewhere for the sake of alternative meanings. Since there are meaning alternatives, a speaker can choose; meaningful choices constitute a system – but this is not possible in Tera or Hausa.

Intonation features in every language, but its functions and forms vary considerably from language to language. For instance, every language engages in tonality, the 'segmentation' of discourse into discrete intonation units, but the 'rules' and the functions of tonality differ from language to language; German rules of tonality differ from those of English, for instance (Tench 1996b). Likewise, every language engages in tonicity, but the rules and functions of tonicity differ from language to language, even to the extent that it may not have any phonological function, as in Tera and Hausa. And every language engages in intonational tone, and each language 'selects' its inventory of tones for its own range of functions.

Intonation units combine into **paratones** (or 'increments', 'pitch sequences' or 'phonological paragraphs'). One unit functions as the nucleus of the paratone, often designated as the 'major' unit, which may be accompanied by 'minor' units before it and after. There is a characteristic pitch pattern to a paratone, but languages may well exploit deviations from that pattern (see Brazil 1978; 1985; O'Grady 2010).

Finally, paratones combine to form larger units of complete, whole, discourses, like progressive stages in a narrative or talk. The distinctive features of different genres of discourse derive from the exploitation of prosodic compositions (Tench 1990: 476–514) and may well be better determined in terms of culture rather than language.

We conclude this section with a summary of phonological units described in a hierarchy of structure and function. This two-way relationship within each level, or 'rank', in the hierarchy was first noted by Pike (1955) and adopted by Halliday (1967: 12–15), although the latter did not acknowledge any rank above intonation.

Paratones are the largest units and consist of one intonation unit or more, in which case one of the intonation units functions as the major (or 'nuclear') unit. Intonation units consist of one foot or more, in which case one foot functions as the tonic (or 'nuclear') foot. However, in non-stress languages an intonation unit consists of a 'rhythm wave' of lexical tone or timing. A foot, or 'rhythm wave', consists of one syllable or more, in which case the most prominent syllable functions as its nucleus. A syllable consists of one phoneme or more, in which case a vowel or syllabic consonant functions as its nucleus and consonants as margins. The phoneme is generally regarded as the smallest unit of phonology. However, we noted in passing that the allophonic variations of a phoneme are specific to a language and have therefore a minor phonological status.

A phonological hierarchy must reflect the phonological features that characterize specific languages; hence, phonological hierarchies may differ across languages. Halliday (1992) argued that the basic unit in the phonology of the 'Peking' variety of Mandarin Chinese was, in fact, the syllable, consisting basically of a single set of consonants as 'initials' and vowels with or without nasal closure as 'finals'. In the four languages of this present study, the composition of syllables necessitates the designation of the phoneme as the basic unit in their hierarchies. English, German and Welsh require the level of foot because their syllables exhibit degrees of stress, whereas Tera does not. All languages have intonation units, although as we have seen, Tera does not require a specific system of tonicity. All languages have paratones as a necessary precursor to whole discourses.

1.4 Phonology for Lexicogrammar

As we briefly reviewed the range and features of phonology, we drew particular attention to the notion of function in the units of phonology. However, the primary function of phonology itself is to provide a distinctive spoken form for every single unit in the lexicogrammar of a language; the lexicogrammar is the total set of words in the vocabulary of a language (its lexis) and grammatical forms and structures (the morphology and syntax of a language), which includes affixes to words, the grouping of words into groups, phrases, clauses, sentences and paragraphs. Each unit requires its own distinctive form to be identified from all the others. As we claimed above, there can be no lexicogrammar without phonology!

In a rather simplistic manner, we can state that phonology is in the mind, whereas phonetics is in the body and the air. A person's competence in the lexicogrammar of the language(s) they know is also in the mind. Phonology provides the specific spoken form of all the lexicogrammatical units that a person knows, so that they can use them in speech. Similar statements can be made for the orthography and script that are in the mind of a literate person which they use for their lexicogrammar in reading and writing; and for the sign language that deaf people use likewise in communication.

Phonology not only provides the spoken form of words, but also of affixes, groups, phrases, clauses, sentences and paragraphs. The main focus of this book is the phonology of words and their affixes; but in this section, the systems of phonology for the rest of the lexicogrammar will be briefly outlined, to show the whole 'task' of phonology and to show the place of word phonology within that whole 'task'.

Just as the range of phonology can be portrayed in the form of a hierarchy of units that interlock with each other in terms of structure and function, so can the units of the lexicogrammar of a language. The levels, or ranks, of the lexicogrammar will vary from language to language, as does the phonological hierarchy. We will take a typical statement of the lexicogrammatical hierarchy of English to illustrate.

The most basic unit of lexicogrammatical meaning is the morpheme, whether it is a minimum free form, a stem or an affix. The morpheme *delight* is a minimum free form in English lexicogrammar; the morpheme *-ed* is not, but a bound affix. *Delect-* is not a free form, but it does act as the stem for the affix *-able*; *delic-* likewise is a stem which is not free, but takes the affix *-ious* and, with changes of pronunciation, the affixes *-ate*, *-acy*, *-atessen*.

The morphemes make up words. An ordered amalgamation of these morphemes produces words as free-standing lexical items: *delight, delighted, delectable, delicious, delicate, delicacy* and *delicatessen*, this last one forming a kind of quasi-compound. Such words are classified into the main 'content' word classes: nouns, verbs, adjectives and adverbs (e.g. *delicately*). Other words are classified as grammatical items in English: articles, prepositions, pronouns, auxiliary and modal verbs, or conjunctions. Although they are usually spoken with unstressed syllables, they are nevertheless free-standing grammatical words.

Words make up groups and phrases. A group is a single word or a collection of words that 'group together' around a head word, that performs a function in a clause. A phrase is a group of words that takes a preposition as head followed by a group; hence, the alternative term 'prepositional group'. As a general rule, the four content word classes provide the heads of groups and the grammatical items cluster around them, but this is not always the case as is observable in *[Which] [is] [the train] [for Crewe] [please]* where the groups are enclosed in square brackets. *Which* is a single grammatical item functioning as the Subject; *is* is also a single grammatical item functioning as Predicator; *the train* has *train* as the head of the group functioning as Complement; *for Crewe* is a prepositional phrase/group functioning as an Adjunct to the Complement; and *please* is a single word acting as a group as a discourse item of politeness.

The groups and phrases make up clauses. They function as the different elements in the structure of clauses: Subject, Predicator, Complement and Adjunct, which themselves fulfil the functions of Participants, Processes and Circumstances of the propositions that clauses express. The Participants of this question are *which* and *the train*, the Process is relational with *is*, the Circumstance is *for Crewe*; *please* is external to the basic structure of the clause because it is a discourse marker.

Furthermore, clauses are either independent ('main'), co-ordinating or dependent ('subordinate'). This can be illustrated in a typical train announcement: *The train for Crewe is standing at platform 3 but its departure is delayed because a connecting service has not yet arrived*: independent clause + co-ordinating clause + dependent clause. Such a sequence of clauses justifies the term 'clause complex' besides the more traditional term 'sentence'.

A single clause complex or a combination of them makes up turns in dialogues or paragraphs in long turns or monologues. Turns make up whole dialogues, and paragraphs make up whole discourses. As we conceded in our discussion of the phonological constituents of discourse, this highest level might be perceived in terms of cultural norms rather than linguistic. For instance, a recipe is a distinctive genre of discourse, but while it takes a distinctive shape in European culture, it might well sound, or look, very different in other cultures.

We have described the range of units in English lexicogrammar, very briefly and in rather simplistic terms – deliberately so, for the sake of space and relevance. The range of units can be arranged in hierarchical form as in phonology and phonetics; words consist of morphemes and have specific functions in groups/phrases; groups/phrases consist of words and have specific functions in clauses; clauses consist of groups/phrases and have a variety of statuses in clause complexes, or sentences, and these form turns and/or paragraphs. A traditional presentation of the English grammar hierarchy has the following 'ranks' (Berry 1975: 104):

Sentence
Clause
Group/phrase
Word
Morpheme

Others, however, dispense with 'sentence', regarding it as redundant, being equivalent to 'clause complex' (Young 1980: 11–12, 224–227; Halliday 1985: 192–193; Thompson 1996: 194–195; Fontaine 2013: 19–22), or as irrelevant because it is usually regarded as a unit in written language only (e.g. Halliday et al. 1964: 51).

The question now arises, how might the phonological and grammatical hierarchies relate to each other? The question is important because, as we said at the head of this section, 'the primary function of phonology ... is to provide a distinctive spoken form for every single unit in the lexicogrammar of a language', including words and their affixes, the grouping of words into groups, phrases, clauses, sentences and paragraphs. Each unit requires its own distinctive form to be identified from all the others.

One answer to the question was that they should not relate at all; this was the view of American structuralists like Harris (1951) in the middle of the twentieth century; they advocated strict compartmentalization in their methodology, i.e. phonological units should not be defined by grammatical criteria, or vice versa. On the other hand, at the same time British linguists following Firth and promoting Prosodic Analysis unashamedly used grammatical units as 'domains' of phonological features (see Palmer 1970); their units included

Sentence
Sentence part
Word
Word part
Syllable
Syllable part
Phonematic unit

In other words, a sentence might be the domain of a phonological feature that extended through the whole or part of it; this was a notion that Halliday (1967) exploited in his intonational theory. A phonological feature such as vowel harmony, nasalization, palatalization, pharyngealization, etc. might run through the whole or part of a word, or through the whole or part of a syllable. Such extended features were known as 'prosodies'; a phonematic unit was a consonantal or vocalic segment that carried a 'prosody'. A simple example of a part-syllable prosody in English is labialization (rounding) of a consonant before /w/ or a rounded vowel: the /k/ of *quit* and of *coot* is rounded in anticipation of the following /w/ or rounded vowel; labialization is the prosody, /k/ is the phonematic unit. Another well-known but more complicated example is vowel harmony in a language like Turkish: if a word begins with a front vowel, then all the other vowels in that word must be front; if a word begins with a close back rounded vowel like /u/, then all the other vowels in that word must be back and rounded; in these cases the prosody is vowel harmony, the domain is the word, and the vowels would be the phonematic units.

Others, such as Young (1980: 9) suggested parallel hierarches, such as (in part):

grammar	*phonology*
clause	tone group
group	foot
word	syllable
morpheme	phoneme

However, he admitted that there is no easy and direct correspondence between the units of grammar and phonology, but he did suggest that there is a close correspondence between clause and tone group and a discourse 'act'. Halliday et al. (1964: 51) had proposed something similar (in part):

PHONOLOGY	FORM (Grammar)
Paratone	Clause complex
Tone group	Clause
Foot	Group Word
Syllable Phoneme	Morpheme

Halliday et al. had used the notion of 'co-extensiveness': tone group and clause are 'most frequently co-extensive' (1964: 51), but foot could be co-extensive with both group and word, and syllable with morpheme.

The frequent co-extensiveness of tone group and clause led Halliday (1967) further to postulate a sense of congruence between tone group, clause and unit of information. The unit of information referred to a state or happening that comprises a Process, Participants and Circumstances, which are encapsulated in the grammar of the clause as Subject, Predicator, Complement and Adjunct; this congruence of semantic and grammatical units in speech is matched by the phonological unit of the tone group (or our preferred term intonation unit[1]). Halliday (1967) called such congruence 'neutral tonality'.

The foot is the phonological unit that contains a syllable with stress. It is usually co-extensive with both group/phrase and word as a lexical item in citation form. If we take the train announcement and mark the groups/phrases within square brackets:

||[The train] [for Crewe] [is standing] [at platform 3] || but [its departure] [is delayed] ||
because [a connecting service] [has not yet arrived]|||

most of them contain a single lexical item accompanied by grammatical words, but not all of them: [at platform 3] contains two lexical items; [a connecting service] is best considered as containing a single compound noun.

Each of the lexical items can also be viewed as items in the lexicon: *train, Crewe, standing, platform, 3, departure, delayed, connecting service, arrived*; they each have one primary stress. (The fact that *platform* and *connecting service* also have a secondary stress does not invalidate this claim.) Most items in the lexicon are pronounced as one foot, but certain items like titles and names have more than a single foot: *Director-General, archbishop, queen mother, Abraham Lincoln, Captain Cook, M.A.K. Halliday, Red Rum*, etc., are clearly single items, but with more than foot (!). Similarly, single groups/phrases may often contain more than one foot, e.g. *platform 3*; *men and women*; *hop, skip and jump*; etc.

The foot is also the basis of stress-timed rhythm. In stress-timed languages like English, lexical items ('content words') such as nouns, verbs, adjectives and adverbs of manner tend to keep their foot structure, whereas grammatical items do not, but become unstressed, as can be seen in the examples below. However, the practice of designating the foot as consisting first of a stressed syllable followed perhaps by a number of unstressed syllables until the next stressed syllable is misleading. To transcribe the feet in *Which is the train for Crewe please* as Abercrombie and Halliday would (p. 8)

Which is the train for Crewe please
s ww|s w|s |s

disregards the group/phrase structure

[Which is] [the train] [for Crewe] [please]

and the actual phonetics of the foot (p. 9).

Similarly, transcribing the foot structure as (p. 8)

Delighted to meet you
^w|s w w|s w

seems counter-intuitive as well as misleading.

Better to retain the group/phrase structure and let the foot take its more natural form:

['Which is] [the 'train] [for 'Crewe] ['please]
'wɪʧ ɪz ðə 'treɪn fə 'kru: 'pli:z
[de'lighted] [to 'meet you]
dɪ'laɪtəd tə 'mi:t ju

These transcriptions preserve the locations of the stresses and therefore also the beats of the rhythm, without forcing an unnatural foot structure. In this way, it is possible to better preserve the co-extensiveness of group/phrase and foot, with its 'accelerating' initial unstressed syllables and 'decelerating' unstressed syllables following. It also dispenses with the need to posit silent beats before unstressed syllables as proposed for *delighted* /^dɪˈlaɪtəd/.

But there is a need for positing silences elsewhere in groups. To take one simple and well-known example, a contrast is possible between *old men and women* and *old men ^ and women.* In the former, the adjective *old* describes both the men and the women, but in the latter, the extra silent beat, or pause, limits the range of *old* to just the men. One can imagine a situation where priorities are announced: *old men ^ and women* would exclude men who are not old, but would include all women, whereas the former would exclude all men and all women who are not old. The group structure would then be indicated as either

[old men and women]
or
[old men] [^ and women]

with consequent variations in rhythm.

One other feature of the phonology of groups/phrases is the processes of simplification, which bind words together. They include assimilation, by which a segment adjusts to a phonetic feature of an adjacent segment as the /d/ of *good* takes on the bilabial articulation of /m/ in *good morning* /ˈgʊb ˈmɔːnɪŋ/; elision, by which a segment is deleted in certain phonetic environments, as the /d/ of *old* is usually deleted before another consonant as in *old men* /ˈəʊl ˈmɛn/ (and *Ole King Cole*); and linking, by which a segment is added to ease transition between very different segments, such as /r/ as in SESP *law and order* /ˈlɔːr ən ˈɔːdə/ and the more regular ˈlinking /r/ of *far away.* Such simplification processes do not usually occur between groups/phrases but only within them as a binding factor.

Morphemes are matched against syllables. Again, this can only be approximate even though frequent. In this particular context, it would be best to regard 'morpheme' as referring primarily to affixes, since words as lexical items in citation form are matched by feet. For instance, *depart* is a foot, but the affix *-ure* of *departure* is a syllable that could never constitute a foot in English. Other affixes attached to *depart* include

-ment as in *department*
-ing as in *departing*
-ed as in *departed*

which are all syllables, albeit unstressed. This would also have been true in Early Modern English:

-eth as in *departeth*
-est as in *(thou) departest*

However, the affix

-s as in *departs*

is not a syllable in modern English, but a single consonant phoneme. This is true for the affixes in the following: *arrived, gone, trains, Crewe's, fourth,* etc. Hence, the grammatical unit 'morpheme' ought to stand midway between 'syllable' and 'phoneme'.

One further consideration that Halliday et al. (1964) declined to include was the co-extensiveness between 'clause complex' and 'paratone'. We could then extend their matching hierarchies of grammar and phonology to show frequent co-extensiveness as:

PHONOLOGY	FORM (Grammar)
Paratone	Clause complex
Tone group	Clause
Foot	Group Word
Syllable Phoneme	Morpheme

This section has attempted to show that features of phonology accompany all levels of the lexicogrammar of a language and of discourse in different cultures. And now it is time to focus on the phonology of words.

1.5 Phonology and Words

Words are the basic free-standing lexicogrammatical units of language that bear meaning and grammatical form and are identified by phonological and/or orthographical form. They are semantic units that represent our experience of the world, and in many languages fall into two categories: thousands upon thousands of *lexical* items that represent the whole range of things, qualities, activities and states that we know about, and a relatively small number of *grammatical* items that represent relationships between those things, qualities, activities and states. The lexical items are said to belong to 'open systems' because of the sheer size of the number of choices they offer; grammatical items are said to belong to 'closed sets' because of the limited number of items a speaker can choose from. Grammatical meaning may include notions like definiteness and indefiniteness, quantity, tense, mood, comparison and other such categories. Lexical items are often called 'content' words because they bear the main semantic force of a proposition; in many languages they are classified as nouns, verbs, adjectives and adverbs.

Each word has a distinct, unique, form that is expressed in phonology and orthography; there are exceptions to this general statement, but they are relatively few in comparison to the vastness of the lexical stock. The exceptions are usually identified as homonyms and occur as a rule by historical accident. In *delighted to meet you*, the verb *meet* in modern English is distinct orthographically from *meat* and *mete*, but not phonologically as all three are pronounced as /mi:t/. But this is a historical accident, since at an earlier stage of the English language they were all distinct phonologically as well: *meet* as Early Modern English /me:t/, *meat* as /mɛ:t/, and *mete* as /metə/. However, as a result of the so-called Great Vowel Shift of the fifteenth and sixteenth centuries in England, the three different vowels coalesced. There happen to be quite a number of homonyms in English, but still they amount to a very small percentage of the total stock of lexical items in the language.

Words are in the mind and the totality of them forms a personal mental lexicon. That mental lexicon contains all a word's meanings and usage patterns, collocations, semantic networks, connotations and morphology, but also its phonology and orthography. The mind also recognizes words as conventions in the sense that, when another person wishes to use a particular word, they have to 'agree' to use it with the same meaning, usage patterns, collocations, semantic networks, connotations, morphology, phonology and orthography as everybody else in their language community. Simply put, one person's lexicon has to more or less match another's in that same language community for mutual comprehension. However, everyone's voices are different, and so the mind has to make allowances for a measure of variation in phonetic output, and even to a small extent in phonological output; in other words, people have to recognize a variety of accents, the different ways in which words are pronounced. Social conventionality has to have a measure of tolerance for different accents. Each person has their own individual voice, their 'idiolect'; but people's idiolects have to match closely for intelligible communication. Accents are therefore a concern for the phonologist.

The relationship between a word's meaning and its pronunciation is, generally speaking, quite arbitrary. If an English-speaking person, a German, a Welsh speaker and a Tera person from Nigeria all look at the very same object, and one calls it [dɒg], the next [hʊnt], the third [ki] and the fourth [jiɗa], it can be observed that there is no natural relationship between meaning and sound. The relationship is completely arbitrary. However, there is often a resemblance of a natural relationship when a word denotes a natural sound like a dog barking; English *bark* /bɑːk/ has the vowel with the greatest sonority and is preceded by a voiced plosive, which is relatively loud with a sudden start, and followed by a sharp closure with /k/; historically, /r/ would also have been sounded as a tap or even a trill, which would have added a degree of continuing roughness. The imitative power of Early English /bark/ has been reduced, but enough is retained to suggest a resemblance to the natural sound; such attempted imitation in phonological form is known as onomatopoeia ('name making'). A German person hearing the very same bark calls it *bellen* /ˈbɛlən/ or *kläffen* /ˈklɛfən/; a Welsh speaker calls it *cyfarth* /ˈkəvarθ/, and Tera person *bokhi* /boxi/. The same sound but interpreted differently, culturally and linguistically. Cultural and phonological divergences on replicating natural sounds – not only animal and human sounds, but also weather, the sound of physical movements, etc. – is a rich source of interesting study.

There is a further dimension to cultural associations with sounds, which is known as sound symbolism or 'secondary onomatopoeia'. This more symbolic, secondary onomatopoeia is an attempt to represent sensations rather than sounds; many English words with initial /sn-/ like *sneeze* have associations with actions related to the nose, e.g. *sniff, sneer, snarl, snigger, snot, snout*, not one of which is particularly pleasant, which leads to further associations of unpleasantness, e.g. *snaffle, snag, snake, snatch, sneak, snob*, etc. British people sense a link between words that rhyme with *jump*, e.g. *bump, thump, hump, lump, rump, dump, pump* that suggests some sort of projection, which might extend metaphorically, but negatively, to *chump, grump, frump*, etc.

Perhaps the most well-known example of vowel symbolism in English-speaking culture is the association between the close front vowels /iː, ɪ, ɪə/ and the qualities of smallness in size, movement, time, sound, light and sense (e.g. Tench 2014: 290–291, 293–294). Allied to this is the notion of euphony associated with girls' names in British culture and euphony in general, mentioned above in **1.1**. Sound symbolism and euphony are often referred to as *phonaesthetics* (or *phonaesthesia*); like primary onomatopoeia, they are language specific.

In all these cases, there is either a natural or a psychological relationship, which is determined by culture, which defies strict arbitrariness. Nevertheless, the arbitrary nature of the relationship between meaning and sound is overwhelmingly greater in the total lexicon.

Words come in all shapes and sizes, from single vowels: *I*, *eye*, *aye* /aɪ/, *owe* /əʊ/, *or*, *ore*, *oar*, *awe* in SESP /ɔː/, etc.; to long, polysyllabic words like the well-known *antidisestablishmentarianism*. The structure of words can be divided first of all into simple basic monomorphemic items and more complex, polymorphemic, items. The latter consist of a basic word or stem with accretions of affixes or, in the case of most compounds, an additional word or stem. All affixes have their own phonological form and often determine a change in the phonological form of the word or stem that they are attached to. The phonology of affixes is usually referred to as morphophonology; the phonology of compounds has its own patterns of compound stressing in SESP.

The phonological rank that corresponds to words is the foot in English, German and Welsh and to an equivalent mora-based unit in Tera. As we noted in **1.4** above, a foot consists of syllables, one of which functions as the 'nucleus' realized as primary stress; if there are other syllables in a foot, they carry either a lower degree of stress or no stress at all. The syllables themselves consist of phonemes, one of which functions as the nucleus, which is usually a vowel, but may also be a syllabic consonant; if there are other phonemes in a syllable, they constitute a margin, either initial (often called the 'onset') or final (often called the 'coda'); these are consonants, including the so-called 'semi-vowels'. In Tera, there is no foot, but a mora-based unit, which is characterized by sets of light and heavy syllables, which themselves consist of phonemes. The phonological ranks of words in the hierarchy inform us about what constitutes the complete phonology of words.

A full-scale description of the phonology of the words of a language therefore requires statements and descriptions about the foot (and its equivalent) and its range of prosodic shapes. It also requires statements and descriptions of the permissible number of syllables (syllable count) and their permissible structures, and the inventory of phonemes that are allowed to operate as their peaks and margins, the permissible combinations of phonemes (phonotactics) and the permissible range of allophonic variation.

The function of phonology, as we have already stated, is to provide a distinctive form for every item in the lexicogrammar. In other words, phonology provides an essential service to lexicogrammar. As a consequence, a functional view of phonology takes the relevant rank or ranks of the lexicogrammatical hierarchy as its starting point; hence the starting point of word phonology is the foot and its equivalent. It begins with the foot (and its equivalent) and its structures, through syllables, phonemes and even to the allophonic forms and distribution. A functional view of word phonology is a top-down scheme, unlike the descriptions of phonology in other traditions.

At each rank – foot, syllable, phoneme – there are choices of structures and units that a language uses ('permits'); for example, how many syllables a language allows in a foot, and what kinds of syllable, and what phonemes may operate in a syllable nucleus and also at its margins, what kinds of phoneme combinations are allowed, and what allophonic form those phonemes may take in different points in a syllable. These choices constitute systems. In Systemic Functional Linguistics, a system of options to choose from reflects the meaning potential of language, but in the case of word phonology, systems reflect merely the 'selection' of items that serve that meaning potential – apart from the possibilities of onomatopoeia and sound symbolism, which require their own separate systems.

Systems in systemic functional phonology are set out in the form of networks that respect structures of the hierarchy. These will be demonstrated in Chapter 2, where systems are displayed for the phonological features of basic, monomorphemic words, and in Chapter 3 for complex, polymorphemic words in English (SESP).

Accordingly, distinctive hallmarks of systemic phonology include system networks, a hierarchical arrangement of units and a specified function of phonology within the whole range of language. But there are others, which we will turn to, but first a historical perspective.

1.6 A Historical Perspective Towards Systemic Phonology

Towards the end of the nineteenth century, as modern linguistic description emerged from a preoccupation with comparative linguistics and historical change and development, linguists turned their minds to the description of contemporary languages. In the course of doing so, they established the notion of the phoneme, as we have seen, as a collection of related sounds that operate as a single unit of the pronunciation system of a language. Baudouin de Courtenay, a Polish linguist who worked in Russia, is acknowledged as the first to use this term (see Stankiewicz 1972). It proved crucial in the development of teaching materials for modern languages with its priorities in oral production. Henry Sweet also utilized this concept in his distinction between broad and narrow transcription: broad transcription employed what became known as phonemic symbols, whereas narrow transcription contained phonetic symbols that represented allophonic details. Interest in Europe led to the founding of the *International Phonetic Association* (IPA) through scholars like Paul Passy in France, Wilhelm Viëtor in Germany, Otto Jespersen in Denmark, Sweet himself in England. **Classical phoneme theory** was developed further by Daniel Jones, H.E. Palmer, Ida Ward, A.C. Gimson in Great Britain, and by Leonard Bloomfield, Ken Pike, Robert Hall, Zellig Harris and Charles Hockett in the USA, where it became incorporated within a structuralist theory of language.

The phoneme was, and is, generally regarded as the smallest unit in the phonological system of a language. It is sometimes referred to as a bundle of articulatory features that operates in a given language as a single unit; that unit may be thought as having a *primary realization* with the variations known as allophones: for instance, the English phoneme /l/ has a primary realization as a voiced alveolar lateral consonant, but with 'secondary' realizations in certain environments such as a 'dark' (velarized) variation as described above. Others follow Sapir (1933) and consider the phoneme rather as a *psychological reality* since native speakers are unaware of such variations. The principal function of the phoneme is to contrast one word with another as /l/ does in *light* in contrast with the /ɹ/ in *right* in English. The hallmarks of a phoneme are the complementary distribution of its allophones and their phonetic similarity.

There are occasional cases of free variation between phonemes, which do not establish a contrast in meaning. A well-known instance is that between /i:/ and /ɛ/ in certain English words like *economic* /i:kəˈnɒmɪk/ or /ɛkəˈnɒmɪk/, *paracetamol* /parəˈsi:təmɒl/ or /parəˈsɛtəmɒl/, etc. However, this only serves to emphasize the principal characteristics of phonemes: their contrastive function in the meanings of words, as well as phonetic similarity and complementary distribution of their allophones.

The phonemic principle of contrast applies not only to segments, but also to suprasegmentals: stress, pitch and length. Stress is contrastive in English words as in *protest* as a noun /ˈprəʊtɛst/ and as a verb /prəʊˈtɛst/; pitch is contrastive in the words of tone languages; and length is contrastive in the words of languages that employ mora distinctions of timing. Contrastive pitch and timing are illustrated in Tera, see Chapter 6. Pitch distinctions are also employed in the intonation systems of languages; Daniel Jones, H.E. Palmer, O'Connor and Arnold, Roger Kingdon all produced descriptions of English intonation in this tradition, and Bloch and Trager and Ken Pike did so in the USA.

The primary motivation of publications in classical phonemic phonology was not only the preparation of language teaching materials for modern languages, but also the development of spelling systems for languages that were without a written form; witness the subtitle of Pike (1947) *Phonemics: a technique for reducing languages to writing.* The emphases were on providing a transcription of the pronunciation of words and sentences for the benefit of teachers and learners of foreign languages and on providing a transcription as the basis for developing orthographies for unwritten languages. This required an inventory of phonemes that could be deployed in linear sequences representing words and sentences.

But these were not the emphases of other groups of linguists in the first half of the twentieth century. Ferdinand de Saussure, for instance was more interested in the essential nature of language and famously developed the theory of linguistic signs: *signes* are the words of the language that comprised not only a *signifié*, i.e. the meaning of a word, but also the *signifiant*, the acoustic image of the word, acknowledging both its phonological and phonetic properties (Saussure 1916).

Nikolai Trubetzkoy, of the renowned Prague School, led that group in phonological theory (Trubetzkoy 1958/1967). Phonology not only provided the contrasts that distinguished each word and sentence but often provided clues to their boundaries. This latter was known as the 'delimitative' function and was exemplified in words, for instance, by fixed word stress – word stress could therefore never operate contrastively – certain consonant sequences that could not appear word-initially, the glottal stop [ʔ] in the initial position of a morpheme before a vowel as in German, and vowel harmony.

However, he was most well-known for his interest in the nature of the contrasts between phonemes and developed sets of **distinctive oppositions**. Oppositions might be *eindimensional* ('bilateral') as for instance /t – d/, since there is only one factor that distinguishes them in German (and English and many other languages), whereas the distinction between /b – d/ is *mehrdimensional* ('multilateral') because what is common to them is shared by other phonemes too, e.g. /g/. Oppositions can, moreover, be 'proportional', i.e. their relationship is found elsewhere, e.g. the opposition between /t – d/

is found also between /p – b/ and /k – g/; on the other hand, an opposition may be *isoliert* ('isolated') because the relationship is not found elsewhere in the language, e.g. /l – r/ in German, English and some other languages (but not Welsh nor Tera). A third dimension of distinctive oppositions involves a classification of whether they are 'privative', 'gradual' or 'equipollent' ('of equal status'). Privative oppositions are those where the relationship can be described in terms of a feature that is either present or absent, e.g. voicing, nasalization, rounding, etc.; a gradual opposition exhibits a degree of a feature, e.g. tongue height among vowels, or pitch height in a tone language; equipollent oppositions cover all other relationships, e.g. /p – t/ or /f – k/ in German and many other languages.

The fourth dimension was the distinction between oppositions that were either *constant* or *aufhebbar* ('cancellable', hence 'neutralizable'). Constant contrasts are those that operate in all distributional environments as /ɛ – a/ do in English, or /p – t/ among the consonants. On the other hand, the contrast between /p – b/ is neutralized after word-initial /s/ as in *spin* in English; there are no cases of English words beginning */sb.../; what emerges in such a case is an 'archiphoneme', a substitute for the otherwise contrasting pair. Trubetzkoy described four types of such 'neutralizable' contrasts. First, the case where the archiphoneme is not identical to either of the pair, as in the case of /p – b/ in English; the archiphoneme is a voiceless unaspirated plosive, not identical to either the voiceless aspirated /p/ or the voiced unaspirated /b/. Secondly, the archiphoneme may be identical to one of the pair, as the case of /p – b/ in word-final position in German; e.g. *gelb* 'yellow' is pronounced /gɛlp/ [gɛlp^h]. The third type involves a contrastive pair where a marked phoneme, e.g. nasalized, gives way to its unmarked equivalent. The fourth type is where a contrastive pair is represented by one of the pair in one environment but by the other in another; in German, the contrast /s – z/ is realized word-medially, e.g. /raɪsən/ *reißen* 'to tear' and /raɪzən/ *reisen* 'to travel', but the contrast is neutralized in word-initial position where only /z/ may appear, and in word-final position where only /s/ may appear: *süß* 'sweet' is /zy:s/, but any reversal of the phonemes is prohibited, i.e. there can never be */sy:z/.

This general overview of opposition types will be seen to be relevant when system networks are introduced in the following chapters. Trubetzkoy presented all these kinds of oppositions in terms of articulatory features, although he also recognized that they all have 'psychological' reality through perception by the listener. On the other hand, Trubetzkoy's successor, Roman Jakobson, proposed a set of 12 phonological features that highlighted perceptual criteria, that were solely bilateral, or 'binary', i.e. either with or without the feature, and were valid universally. Phonemes were 'bundles' of those perceptual features that were distinctive for a given language; each phoneme in English, for instance, was identified by whether the 10 relevant distinctive features were present or not.

Noam Chomsky and Maurice Halle preserved the basic notion of distinctive features but reverted to mainly articulatory terms in *Sound Patterns of English* (1968). **Distinctive Feature Analysis** provides a comprehensive set of features for the phonemes of a language and a relatively simple procedure for displaying phonological processes like assimilation, elision and epenthesis. These processes became the source of rules that produce actual spoken forms.

Feature	Acoustic Description.	Articulatory Description.
[± Consonantal]	Low total energy.	Obstruction in vocal tract.
Example: all English consonants are [+ Consonantal].		
[± Vocalic]	Clearly defined formant structure.[12]	No obstruction in vocal tract.
Example all English consonants are [-Vocalic] except /l/ /ɹ/ /w/ and /j/.		
[± Compact]	Strong concentration of energy in central area of the spectrum.	Stricture in front of mouth is relatively larger.
Example: /ʃ/ /ʒ/ /tʃ/ /dʒ/ /k/ /g/ /ŋ/ and /ɑ/ are [+ Compact].		
[± Nasal]	Additional anti-formants which reduce formant intensity.	Soft palate raised.
Example: /m/ /n/ and /ŋ/ are [+nasal].		
[± Tense]	Higher energy with greater spread across the spectrum.	More strain and duration or a stronger airflow.
Example: /p/ /t/ /k/ /f/ /θ/ /s/ /ʃ/ /tʃ/ /iː/ /uː/ /ɑː/ /ɔː/ and /ɜː/ are [+ Tense].		
[± Voice]	Periodic low frequency excitation.	Vocal fold vibration.
Example all vowels plus /b/ /d/ g/ v/ /ð/ /z/ /ʒ/ /dʒ/ /m/ /n/ and /ŋ/ are [+ Voice].		
[± Continuant]	Interrupted sound.	Rapid opening and closing of Oral tract.
Example all vowels plus /f/ /v/ /θ/ /ð/ /s/ /z/ /ʃ/ /ʒ/ /l/ /ɹ/ /j/ and /w/ are [+ continuant].		
[± Strident}	High intensity noise.	Relatively complex stricture.
Example: /s/ /z/ /ʃ/ /ʒ/ /tʃ/ dʒ/ are [+ strident].		
[± Grave]	Energy concentrated in lower frequencies.	Articulated at peripheries of mouth.
Example: /uː/ /ʊ/ /ɔː/ /p/ /b/ /m/ /f/ /v/ /k/and /g/ are [+ Grave].		
[± Flat}	Weakening of upper frequencies.	Lip rounding or other forms of narrowed aperture.
Example: /uː/ /ʊ/ / /p/ /b/ and /w/ are [+ Flat].		

Figure 1.4 Jakobson's feature descriptions of English phonemes, courtesy of O'Grady, personal communication

Another quite distinct alternative to phonemic phonology in the first half of the twentieth century emerged, as we have noted, in the London School led by J.R. Firth, which can be viewed as a direct pre-cursor to Systemic Phonology. Firth and his colleagues were fascinated by the wide divergences between the salient characteristics of the phonology of different languages, principally the features that extended over sequences of sounds in syllables and words, such as vowel harmony, palatalization and velarization that affected not just single segments but also whole sequences of segments. These 'syntagmatic' features, known as 'prosodies', were not easily captured in the 'paradigmatic' format of phonemic phonology. The theory of phonology that emanated from the London School was known as **Prosodic Analysis.**

A succinct summary of the distinctives of the London School approach to phonology is found in Tench (1992: 8, with original italics):

> Prosodic Analysis is a *non-universalist* approach to the description of the phonology of a language that highlights the *syntagmatic* as well as the *paradigmatic* dimensions of the phonic material, in terms of *structures* and *systems* and is prepared to recognize *different systems* appropriate to different components of the language and to reflect *grammatical* categories wherever necessary, in such a way as to conform as fully, appropriately and elegantly as possible to a *general linguistic theory*.

It eschewed a universalist goal; each language has its own characteristic 'shape' of phonology without due reference to other languages or indeed to universal features. It was not primarily concerned with written transcription conventions or a strictly linear presentation of the phonic material; it sought to draw as much attention to sequential, 'syntagmatic', features of the sound of utterances as to the paradigmatic. Syntagmatic features, the 'prosodies', stretched beyond single segments, otherwise known as 'phonematic units'; in addition to the examples of 'prosodies' given above, other examples include nasalization and rounding through a whole or part of a syllable, lexical tone patterns, intonational tone over a whole clause/utterance. Systems, or paradigms, represent small sets of choices, e.g. all the strong vowels that appear in stressed syllables in English. But systems may vary according to position in a structure; so, for example, there is one system of consonants that operates at the onset of a syllable in English, but a different system that operates at its coda, i.e. there is a different set of choices in final position since /ŋ/ becomes available in final position but it is not available in initial position, but on the other hand, /h, j, w/ (and /ɹ/ in non-rhotic accents) are not available in final position, but are in initial position. This 'polysystemic principle' extends in delicacy to other possibilities at the onset: if the syllable has two initial consonants, then the first consonant belongs to a much smaller system and the second consonant likewise. (Note that in the English tri-consonantal onset, the obligatory /s/ does not form a system as there is no choice at that point of structure.) Similar, delicate, systems operate at the coda. There was also no strict division between phonological, grammatical and lexical units ('compartmentalization'), since phonological description was related to grammatical units like words, phrases and clauses. There might even be a separate phonology of nouns and pronouns in a language, for example, and separate phonologies for 'native' and 'loan' words.

Prosodic Analysis lay the foundations for what M.A.K. Halliday was to call **Systemic Phonology**. He developed the notion of a hierarchy of phonological units (Halliday 1961; Halliday et al. 1964: 25–27; Halliday 1967: 12–15). This structure-function relationship was not apparent in Prosodic Analysis, in which the units were simply domains in which prosodies operated. Each language would need to be described in terms of its own phonological hierarchy, which might not be parallel to that of English.

Halliday also developed the notion of system networks in phonology. System networks are graphic displays of the choices available in the phonology of a language, the conditions under which the choices are made and the degrees of delicacy of those choices. He produced whole, comprehensive, displays for all the intonation systems of English (Halliday 1967), and syllable finals of standard Chinese (Halliday 1992), as did Young for the consonant cluster systems of English (Young 1992).

It has to be conceded that within the tradition of Systemic Functional Linguistics (SFL) relatively little attention had been paid to the systemic phonology of words. The phonological hierarchy is presented in Berry (1975), but without much explication at the level of words; more appears in Butler (1985a), but fuller descriptions appear in Tench (1992) in a range of languages including English, Chinese, Welsh, Arabic, Telegu and the indigenous Australian language, Gooniyandi. Most attention until the present had been given to the level of intonation, principally because the *semantic* functional dimension is prominent, which has been the bedrock of SFL, and because as much attention is paid to spoken discourse as to written. Intonation systems appear regularly in all SFL descriptions of English, and intonation description and theory has been steadily advanced from Halliday (1967); see Tench (1990; 1996a; 1997; 2003a); Halliday and Greaves (2008). The Discourse Intonation approach of Brazil and others is basically an adaptation of Halliday's systemic-functional approach (Brazil 1975; 1978; 1985). Halliday's influence may also be seen in Wells's description of English intonation (Wells 2006).

Phonology is viewed as the formal aspect of the acoustic image of linguistic units; thus words and morphemes constitute *phonological* units as well as grammatical and semantic units. This is the case for other units as well: rhythm units are acoustic images of phrases/groups, and intonation provides systems at the levels of clauses/sentences and discourse.

In the whole applied linguistics enterprise, the primary role of the linguist is to present full and adequate accounts of the nature of language in general and of languages in particular (Halliday et al. 1964: xvi) in all their complexity. Descriptions of different languages allow comparison and contrast, which brings vital information to the attention of teachers, textbook writers and other language professionals, and also to others who are involved in related matters politically, administratively, academically, commercially, socially, therapeutically, forensically, technically, etc.

For example, the application of the polysystemic principle appears in a phonological 'interlanguage' study of English and Korean (Tench 2003b), which shows how Korean learners of English had consistently greater difficulty in producing intelligible renditions of final consonants than initial; Korean has a much simpler coda system than its onset system.

Even at the level of intonation, comparative descriptions also offer invaluable insights in applied linguistic work. Tone systems are perhaps the most obvious area for comparison: the number of primary and secondary tones and their corresponding functions. Tonicity too, especially whether a language has such a system or not. Comparison in tonality appears to be much rarer, but see, for example, Tench (1996b) for a comparison of tonality contrasts in English and German, mentioned earlier.

To conclude, we can adapt the summary of Prosodic Analysis to summarize the basic tenets of Systemic Phonology (Tench 1992: 15, with original italics, but with innovative terms bold):

> Systemic Phonology is a *non-universalist* approach to the description of the phonology of a language that highlights the *syntagmatic* as well as the *paradigmatic* dimensions of the phonic material, in terms of *structures* of ***hierarchically*** ranked units and *systems* displayed in ***networks*** and is prepared to recognize *different systems* appropriate to different components of the language and to reflect *grammatical* categories wherever necessary, in such a way as to conform as fully, appropriately and elegantly as possible to a *general linguistic theory.*

1.7 Systemic Phonology and Other Models

How does this approach differ from other recent approaches to the description of the phonology of languages?

The most obvious difference is that Systemic Phonology has a matching 'architecture' (Matthiessen 2021; Fawcett 2022) within Systemic Functional Linguistics. SFL is a model of language with the perspective of a resource for communicating messages, what Halliday (1975) calls its 'meaning potential'. The level of lexicogrammar is the resource of the mind for creating messages, consisting as it does of a hierarchy of units from the smallest – morphemes – through words, and ever larger units – groups and phrases, clauses and clause complexes and sentences, to paragraphs and beyond. At each rank within the hierarchy, there are systems of choices, the paradigmatic axis: choose declarative vs interrogative vs imperative; choose polar vs non-polar interrogative, etc.; choose interrogative word, etc., etc.

The level of phonology is the mental resource for sounding the lexicogrammar and, as we have seen, is organized similarly, as a hierarchy of units from the smallest – phonemes – through syllables, rhythmic units (e.g. feet), intonation units, paratones and beyond. At each rank within the phonological hierarchy, there are systems that represent the sounding potential for lexicogrammatical units: for the clause, a speaker must make tonality, tonicity and tone choices: choose neutral or marked tonality; choose tonicity placement for each intonation unit; and choose a tone. For groups/phrases and words, a speaker must choose appropriate wording with its representational sounding, and representational systems at the morpheme rank.

This is not to deny that other theories do not integrate phonology within their broad prospectuses of the components of language. Pike (1955) certainly did; witness his title: *language in relation to a unified theory of the structure of human behavior*. For instance, his concepts of 'particle', 'wave' and 'field', which correspond to unit, structure and system respectively, were inherent in his definitions of the 'tagmeme' in grammar, as well as the phoneme.

Transformational-Generative Grammar sought to deploy transformational rules to phonology as well as to syntax. However, on the other hand, the proponents of Metrical Phonology, Auto-Segmental Phonology and Optimality Theory provided explanatory rules for phonology without any explicit parallel matching to other components of language.

*

Secondly, phonology is understood as having a specific, distinct, function. It is not just a set of units based on phonetic properties at various levels of structures. It is more than an inventory of phonemes, syllable types, rhythmic units and intonation patterns; phonology has function. Its primary function is specifically to provide distinctive phonic shape for all lexicogrammatical units. The implication for linguistic descriptions is that phonology should not be regarded as an independent, unintegrated component of language.

There is a common representation of the components of language as layers on top of each other with phonetics and phonology at the base; rather, lexicogrammar should be taken as the base, with phonology (and orthography) as its representation, and semantics as its function. Phonology is not an independent component, but provides a service to lexicogrammar: it provides the distinctive forms of all lexicogrammatical items – without such forms, the lexicogrammar would be an amorphous mass. In fact, as we have already claimed (pp. 4, 10), there can be no lexicogrammar without phonology! But, equally, phonology would have no raison d'être without lexicogrammar.

*

Phonology serves all ranks of the lexicogrammatical hierarchy and discourse, from morphemes to paragraphs and whole discourses. It is not, therefore, restricted to the pronunciation of words, but there are processes and systems that operate at all ranks of the lexicogrammar and in discourse. It is true, however, that the main focus of phonology for SFL scholars has been the rank of intonation units; that was probably inevitable from the SFL focus on meaning potential and the engagement of analysis of actual language text. There is inevitably a deliberate intention to seek congruence of ranks between the lexicogrammatical and the phonological hierarchies. The starting point of word phonology is the word itself, not the phoneme; Systemic Phonology takes a top-down approach, from foot to phoneme and its allophonic features.

*

Fourthly, Systemic Phonology recognizes a hierarchy of ranks (levels, or strata) at which appropriate units operate. The relationship between higher and lower ranks is one of structure and function; units from an immediately lower rank have specific functions in the units in the rank immediately above; and units at one rank are composed of units from immediately below. At each rank, a range of systems operate as required by the language. These systems are not necessarily binary – a choice between two values; but as the language requires, choices may be multiple. A typical binary choice might be voiceless/voiced, but otherwise, choices might be multiple, such as degrees of aperture for vowels. In this respect, Systemic Phonology reflects the variety of oppositions that Trubetzkoy recognized. Binarity is not an essential quality, but an arbitrary, artificial device, which simply does not correspond to the rest of life!

*

Fifthly, Systemic Phonology does not envisage a single monolithic system for each of the ranks in the hierarchy for the whole of a language. For instance, there is no one single system of phonemes for all the words of a language, but different systems of vowels exist for stressed and for unstressed syllables in English; different systems of consonants in initial and final margins of syllables, etc. This will become apparent also in the description of word phonology in German (see Chapter 4), Welsh (Chapter 5) and Tera (Chapter 6). Furthermore, it becomes clear that there are different systems within a language between indigenous vocabulary and vocabulary borrowed from another language. Pike and Fries (1949, reprinted in Brend 1972) presented the methodology for exploring 'coexistent phonemic systems' in vernacular languages of Mexico, which Spanish as the prestige language has infiltrated. In a similar way, French has infiltrated German (Chapter 4), and English has infiltrated Welsh in Wales and Spanish in Argentina (Chapter 5). This polysystemic principle might extend elsewhere in a phonological description, e.g. to primary and secondary onomatopoeic systems, and to systems for different word classes.

*

Sixthly, just as SFL in general bases its descriptions on actual language text, the units and patterns of phonology are actual, and not hypothetical. There are no 'underlying' forms that are 'manufactured' in order to create a sequence of transformations from one form to another. Just as the intonation of spoken discourse is derived from actual spoken texts, word forms are accepted as they are without resorting to rules of transformations. As Coleman (2005: 4) admitted, 'From the perspective of spoken language processing, though, we might ask whether there is any point expending a great deal of effort writing rules to describe such unproductive derivations as *hymn* => *hymnal*, or *electric* => *electricity* (Halle and Mohanan 1985), when the output forms are easily (and arguably more plausibly) simply stored/memorized.' A person has to learn which words take *-al* as a suffix and which adjectives with final unstressed *-ic* take the nominal derivation *-icity* (since *basic*, for instance, does not) and which nouns with final *-icity* are derived from such adjectives (since *felicity*, for instance, does not), etc., etc. Such derivations have to be learnt; these processes are not phonological in terms of transformations from underlying forms, but lexical, although a knowledge of classical languages and their successors might well help (see Aitchison 2003: 126–136)!

This is not to deny that there are indeed a number of patterns of derivation discernible. Take, for instance, the pattern apparent in adjectives like *severe*, *austere*, *serene*, *obscene*, *extreme*, which 'transform' into noun derivations *severity*, *austerity*, *serenity*, *obscenity*, *extremity* with an identical pattern: long final stressed /iː/ is 'transformed' into short stressed /ɛ/ before the unstressed suffix /-ɪti/; however, although it is a frequent 'transformation', it is not regular. *Supreme* does not become **supremity* but takes a different suffix /-əsi/; *obese* keeps its long vowel in *obesity*; *pristine* likewise but takes *-ness*. In that last case, it could well be argued that *pristine* is spelled differently, but that is to call on orthographical criteria rather than phonological.

*

Seventhly, this leads to another feature of Systemic Phonology: the direct link between language competence in the mind and language performance in action, without intervening hypothetical underlying forms that rely on generative transformation rules. *Supreme* and *supremacy* are stored in the mind separately though closely together; likewise, *extreme* and *extremity*, *obese* and *obesity*, *pristine* and *pristineness*, etc. Our knowledge of words includes their derived forms, as well their pronunciation, inflections, range of meanings, collocations, colligations, connotations and other lexical relationships (Aitchison 2003). All these discrete features are acquired and, as Coleman put it, 'simply stored/memorized' (2005: 4).

The direct link between language competence and language performance leads to the consideration of phonology as a creative resource for 'sounding potential' (Matthiessen 2018), a notion based on Halliday's concept of language as meaning potential. On the one hand, the existing lexical stock of English does not exploit the full available stock of potential phonological forms; as Gimson (1989: 256) pointed out there are 'unused monosyllabic words' which 'conform to an already existing pattern' and gave the examples of /faʊd/, /saɪdʒ/, /mɒmp/, /bruːtʃ/, /pliːk/, /splʌk/, /strɛdʒ/. On the other, new words are for ever being coined, e.g. *Brexit* /brɛksɪt, brɛgzɪt/ and a plethora of scientific and medical terms with associated brand names. Therefore, the phonology of a language does not consist of a static set of forms but provides a resource to be exploited for the creation of new forms.

This resource allows users of a language a wide range of creative options: onomatopoeia, sound symbolism, poetic effects, paralanguage and the like. This creative potential is culturally determined and subject to the phonology of each language.

*

Finally, Systemic Phonology has no pretensions to universalism. SFL scholars have always maintained that the description of a language has to be made in terms of the language forms themselves. As each language has its own distinctive characteristics in lexis, syntax and discourse functions, that represent the meaning potential of its speakers, each language has to be described in terms of those characteristics. This is not to deny certain obvious universal characteristics, such as the existence of words representing things, qualities, actions and relationships, and syntax representing states and events ('happenings'), but the way such universals are construed in a language is unique to each language. This means that even the ranks within a hierarchy might differ from language to language, as well as the systems at each rank. This is true for phonology too. Apart from the most general universal features – each language, for instance, has sets of vowels and consonants – the actual inventories, ranks and systems differ noticeably.

*

Having identified eight features of Systemic Phonology, we are now in a position to briefly compare this approach with other recent approaches to the description of phonology.

Metrical Phonology focuses rather narrowly on stress placement in words and phrases. It was an attempt to predict cases of stress shift as in a phrase like *downstairs bathroom*. In citation form, *downstairs* has primary stress on the final syllable, with a secondary stress on the first: /ˌdaʊnˈstɛəz/; however, in the phrase *downstairs bathroom* its stress pattern is altered by switching the primary stress to the first syllable and the secondary to the final syllable: /ˈdaʊnˌstɛəz/. In other words, there is a rule in English that discourages two consecutive primary stresses. The rule also requires recognition of levels of phonological organization as a hierarchy: syllables were designated Strong or Weak in sequences; such sequences constituted a foot; a foot was designated Strong or Weak in sequences, which were basically construed in most cases as a phonological word; sequences of feet (or phonological words) constituted a phrase. Metrical grids displayed this hierarchy:

Phrase level			X	
Foot level	X		X	
Syllable level	X	x	X	x
	downstairs		bathroom	

In this way, Metrical Phonology from the 1970s sought to introduce a more sensitive set of transformational rules into Generative Phonology to account for stress phenomena in English (see Liberman 1979; Selkirk 1982; Hayes 1982). It had to be extended to account for stress shift in cases where in English primary stresses are not actually contiguous as in *continental breakfast*. In citation form *continental* is /ˌkɒntɪˈnɛntḷ/, xxXx; but with stress shift it becomes Xxxx.

```
Phrase level                      X
Foot level          X             X
Syllable level      X  x x x      X     x
                    continental breakfast
```

But a much more serious aspect was raising the hierarchy to include what was called 'intonation phrases' above the phrase level.

```
Intonation level                                X
Phrase level          X       X                 X
Foot level            X       X    X            X
Syllable level     x  Xx      X    X    xxx     X      x
                   We also serve continental breakfasts
```

Another attempt to enhance the descriptive power of Generative Phonology in the 1970s was **Autosegmental Phonology** (Goldsmith 1976; 1990; 1999) to account, initially, for lexical tone in tone languages. Lexical tone was clearly not a feature of segments but was realized on a separate level, or tier of phonology. Besides a tonal tier and the segmental tier, other tiers were required: the stress tier and timing tier. Other features of the phonological output were also conceived of as extending over more than one segment, rather like 'prosodies' of Firthian Prosodic Analysis; these 'melody levels', also required separate tiers such as vowel harmony, nasality, co-articulation effects like the spread of voiceless aspiration from a plosive to a following voiced segment, etc. The tiers did not form an organized hierarchy, but simply designated domains of phonological activity, again rather like Prosodic Analysis.

The segments were 'bundles' of distinctive features expressed in articulatory terms as in Generative Phonology. Co-articulation, or 'parametric' analysis, was known by the very appropriate metaphor of 'orchestration'. Melody levels were shown by association lines linking relevant features from segment to segment. Here is a simple example from Goldsmith (1999), which shows the segmental tier as bundles of distinctive features, and association lines for voiceless aspiration and nasality on different tiers.

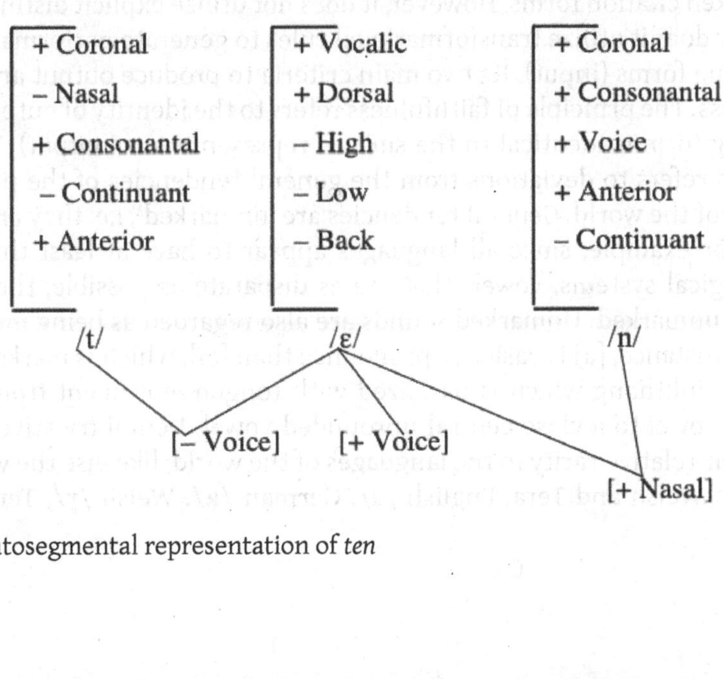

Figure 1.5 An autosegmental representation of *ten*

Metrical Phonology and Autosegmental Phonology were attempts to rectify inadequacies in Generative Phonology, with its reliance on binary features, its sets of rules to transform underlying forms into surface forms and its focus on words. Transformational-Generative Grammar focussed on syntactic form per se, and had originally regarded intonation as marginal for linguistic competence, and of little consequence apart from tokens of performance. That attitude gradually changed with the advent of Metrical Phonology and the addition of the **Tone and Break Index (ToBI)** to Autosegmental Phonology (Pierrehumbert 1980; Pierrehumbert and Hirschberg 1990; Ladd 1996/2008; Gussenhoven 2004). ToBI required a tonal tier and a break index tier in addition to a so-called lexical tier, which in fact was the orthographical representation of clauses and sentences. ToBI consisted of a series of binary choices between High and Low and combinations to denote contour tones, and four degrees of 'break' (called by others 'juncture'), two of which (3 and 4) indicated boundaries of intonation phrases. (An approximate guide to equivalences of intonation symbols can be found in Tench 2011: 133.) ToBI transcription might look like this:

Tonal tier	H		H*	L-H-		H	H*L-L%
Break index tier	1	1		1	3	1	4

Lexical tier We serve traditional breakfasts and continental
/|wi ˈsɜːv trə\/dɪʃn̩ ˈbɹɛkfəsts | əŋ ˌkɒntɪ\nɛntl̩||/

These three developments in phonological theory and description belong to the Generative tradition of linguistics but complement and extend the original proposal of SPE; they nevertheless adhere to some of its original hallmarks such as a focus on form, a reliance on binarity (e.g. Strong/Weak; High/Low), transformational rules from hypothetical underlying forms, distinctive features and token citation forms. These three developments do not appear to have emerged from the analysis of real, live, speech, recorded and transcribed, as Systemic-Functional Linguistics has.[2]

Similarly, **Optimality Theory (OT)** has emerged from the Generative Phonology tradition, with its underlying forms, now referred to as 'input'; a universalist target, and a reliance on token citation forms. However, it does not utilize explicit distinctive features as its base, nor does it utilize transformational rules to generate performance ('output') from underlying forms (input). Its two main criteria to produce output are faithfulness and markedness. The principle of faithfulness refers to the identity of output with input: the underlying form is identical to the surface representation (output). The principle of markedness refers to deviations from the general tendencies of the phonologies of the languages of the world. General tendencies are 'unmarked', i.e. they are statistically more likely; for example, since all languages appear to have at least three vowels in their phonological systems, vowels that are as disparate as possible, then the vowels [i, a, u] are all unmarked. Unmarked sounds are also regarded as being more natural to articulate; for instance, [a] is easier to pronounce than [ɔ̃ɪ̃], which is marked on account of its being a diphthong which is nasalized with tongue movement from a half-open back rounded vowel to a close central unrounded vowel. Dental fricatives are marked because of their relative rarity in the languages of the world; likewise the voiceless alveolar laterals of Welsh and Tera, English /ɹ/, German /ʀ/, Welsh /r̥/, Tera implosives, complex syllable-final clusters (English, German, Welsh), etc., etc. The phonological output of each language is the result of the relative ranking of markedness and faithfulness constraints.

What each language allows from marked features is subject to a set of 'constraints'; so, for instance, Welsh and Tera do not have a constraint on the voiceless alveolar lateral fricative [ɬ], but English and German do; furthermore, Tera has no constraint on a voiced alveolar lateral fricative [ɮ], but Welsh does, etc., etc. The phonology of each language consists of unmarked features and its own set of constraints on marked features.

Each language has its own underlying forms of words (input), and it is as if an input is 'fed' into a generator that evaluates various forms it might take (so-called 'candidates') against its own set of constraints and produces ('generates') the output. Each language also has its own underlying forms of clauses and sentences, which are subjected to a generator in the same way, producing an accompanying intonational form, but taking into account the speaker's pragmatic decision.

This recognition of speaker pragmatism is decidedly an improvement on Generative Phonology's primary focus on form – there are always many more ways of saying something according to different sets of circumstances. The intonation of a clause or sentence is not a fixed form. Also in its favour, OT does justice to the concept of markedness, which is a concept that is relevant to all the languages of the world. However, one problem with the way that OT works, its 'mechanism', is that the generator evaluates purely hypothetical 'candidates' in addition to the 'optimal' candidate; there is no evidence that the mind does this. In other words, this 'mechanism' is simply an artifice of the linguists' own making, in order to maintain a distinction between underlying forms and their output. Another criticism is that its 'mechanism' does not, in fact, cover all phonological cases; it does not achieve its target of universalism (see, for instance, O'Grady 2013: 99–100).

By contrast, Systemic Phonology makes no claim for universal generative power. It recognizes that each language has to be described in terms of its own characteristic features; this is true not only in its phonology, but also in its lexicogrammar and discourse features. Systemic Phonology has a matching architecture to the rest of the components of language and as such is fully integrated with them. It has a specific function – its sounding potential – of providing distinctive forms for all lexicogrammatical and discoursal items of the language. Those items are actual, verifiable items that occur in actual language. There are no hypothetical forms; there is no significant distinction between language competence and performance.

Systemic Phonology comprises a hierarchy of ranks (levels, or strata) with a structure of units composed of units from an immediately lower rank that have specific functions in an immediately higher rank. Each rank functions with sets of systems, which are not constrained by binarity; in many systems the options are multiple and extensive in delicacy. Systems operate polysystemically, i.e. different structures in the phonology may well have different systems.

Language is not only form, but also activity in communicating real time meaning. As language as a whole has meaning potential, phonology has sounding potential and therefore is suited for creative activity.

It is the case that the phonological aspect of Systemic Functional Linguistics has mainly focussed on intonation because of its meaning potential in discourse; again, the aim of this book is to show that the same features of system and function operate at the 'lower' rank of words also. Chapter 2 seeks to apply the principle of system networks for basic, monomorphemic, words in English; Chapter 3 seeks to extend the description to polymorphemic words in English; and Chapters 4 to 6 seek to present systemic descriptions of first, German, a language closely related to English; then Welsh, a Celtic language, within the Indo-European family; and finally to Tera, a Chadic language, unrelated to English either linguistically or geographically. Tench (2017) is an attempt at describing the word phonology of another African language, Etkwyan (Ichen), Nigeria; other attempts include Matthiessen (2021) on the syllable and phoneme networks of Akan, Ghana; and aspects of word phonology systems appear in Tench (1992) for Arabic, Telegu and Gooniyandi, Australia.

Chapter 2

Phonology of Basic Forms of Words in English

This chapter and those following are attempts to apply the features of a systemic-functional approach to phonology (**1.7**) to the description of basic, monomorphemic, forms of words in English in this chapter and to complex polymorphemic words in the next; and then to the phonology of words in German, Welsh and Tera.

In this particular chapter, which is based in part on Tench (2014; see also Tench 2017), we begin with one accent of English – Southern England Standard Pronunciation (SESP) – although the principles of description will apply to any accent. We will confine our attention to the phonology of monomorphemic words in citation form as an initial introduction to features of Systemic Phonology and to the basic design of system network displays.

System in word phonology is not like system in lexicogrammar or intonation, as sets of options from which a speaker chooses to create meaning; system at the rank of word (and also, largely, at the rank of groups/phrases) is rather the specifications of what the speakers of a language recognize as having been established in their language to represent its words.

Moreover, as we have maintained, the primary function in phonology is to serve lexicogrammar by providing each distinct unit with their uniquely distinctive shapes. However, as we have noted previously, we have to concede that in the historical development of the language, phonological shapes that were once distinctive and unique may no longer be so, and 'accidentally' become homophones; another example is English *right*, *write*, *rite*, *wright*, which were, in Early Modern English phonology, distinct: /rıçt/, /ʋritə/, /ritə/, /ʋrıçt/ (see e.g. Gimson 2014: 66–73); all eventually became SESP /raıt/ through various historical processes. Nevertheless, apart from such historical accidents, the primary function of phonology is to provide a distinctive shape to all the discrete units of the lexicogrammar.

Every word in citation form must be represented by one foot, apart from the few instances indicated in **1.4**. This is why in this presentation of Systemic Phonology the specifications of types of foot comes first, rather than the bottom-up approach from consonant and vowels segments.

As we stated in **1.5**, a full description of the phonology of words of any language would ideally include statements about the structures of the foot and its range of prosodic shapes, the permissible number of syllables ('syllabic count'), the permissible kinds of structure in a syllable, the inventory of phonemes at the nucleus of the syllable and at the margins, permissible combinations of phonemes and specific allophonic details.

2.1 The Foot and Syllable Count

The foot in English consists of at least one stressed syllable and may include a number of other syllables with a lower degree of stress. The degrees of stress that have contrastive function in English are: primary, secondary and no stress (unstressed). Most monomorphemic words in English have up to three syllables. There are a number of monomorphemic words with four syllables, most of them having an origin in another language. There are very few words with five or more syllables; examples include *abracadabra* (from Greek), *mulligatawny* (from Tamil) and *hippopotamus* – although it is a compound in Greek, it is not a compound in English. Other examples might include *onomatopoeia, Ecclesiastes, encyclopaedia,* but these can be analysed as being composed of two morphemes since there are also the forms *onomatopoeic, ecclesiastical, encyclopaedic*; the basic forms would then be construed as *onomatopoe+ia, Ecclesiast+es, encyclopaed+ia*; nevertheless, these stems consist of four or five syllables.

Four-syllabled words are also relatively rare and apart from the word *caterpillar* appear to be, like those mentioned above, obviously foreign in origin, e.g. *catamaran* (from Tamil), *hullabaloo* (possibly from Scottish Gaelic), *shenanigans* (apparently from Irish), *Hallelujah* (from Hebrew), and many names, e.g. *Abednego, Madagascar*. The largest number of four-syllabled words in fact derive from Greek, e.g. *apocalypse, apostrophe, catastrophe, cataclysm*; although classicists will point out that these words are in fact polymorphemic in Greek, they do not operate as such in English. Most English speakers will not readily be able to deconstruct the composition of such words as they might words like their derived forms *apocalyptic, catastrophic, cataclysmic,* or other sets of words like *befriend, friendship, friendly, unfriendly, unfriendliness* and *comprehend, apprehend, comprehension, apprehension* (Aitchison 2003). These latter words are not included in this chapter because they are all polymorphemic; English morphophonology will be considered in Chapter 3.

Most words that are native to English consist of just one, two or three syllables. A monosyllabic word spoken in isolation must be a stressed syllable and contain a strong vowel. (The distinction between strong and weak vowels was presented in **1.3**.) Even if a monosyllabic word is normally unstressed in context, such as grammatical items like determiner, preposition, etc., it will contain a strong vowel when stressed, and in citation form. *Of* is /ˈɒv/ in citation form; *a* is /ˈa/ or /ˈeɪ/, *an* is /ˈan/, etc.

Disyllabic words have one syllable stressed as primary (containing a strong vowel) and the other must either be less so (secondary, but still containing a strong vowel) or unstressed (containing a weak vowel).

There are four possible patterns: s represents a stressed syllable (ˈ), w a weak unstressed and s^2 a secondarily stressed syllable (ˌ):

s . w
w. s
s . s^2
s^2 . s

A secondarily stressed syllable contains a strong vowel, but the syllable itself is less stressed than the other. The difference between primary, secondary and no stress can be illustrated with the words:

s . w	*river*	/ˈrɪvə/
w. s	*revere*	/rəˈvɪə/
s . s^2	*romance*	/ˈrəʊˌmans/
s^2 . s	*robust*	/ˌrəʊˈbʌst/

The range of three-syllabled stress patterns is naturally much greater, but a number of potential patterns are unattested (indicated by *; see Guierre 1970: 13, which still seems valid).

s . w . w	*energy*	/ˈɛnədʒi/
*s . s^2 . w		
s . w . s^2	*envelope*	/ˈɛnvəˌləʊp/
*s . s^2 . s^2		
s^2 . s . w	*embellish*	/ˌɛmˈbɛlɪʃ/
s^2 . s . s^2	*embargo*	/ˌɛmˈbɑːgəʊ/
s^2 . w . s	*entertain*	/ˌɛntəˈteɪn/
*s^2 . s^2 . s		
w . s . w	*eleven*	/ɪˈlɛvən/
w . s . s^2	*inferno*	/ɪnˈfɜːˌnəʊ/
* w . w . s		
* s . s^2 . s		

The potential range of stress patterns in four- and five-syllabled words would be enormous if it were not for the observation already made that they are relatively rare; in the system network below, we simply present the range of attested stress patterns. If a system consists of but two choices, i.e. binary, it would be drawn as:

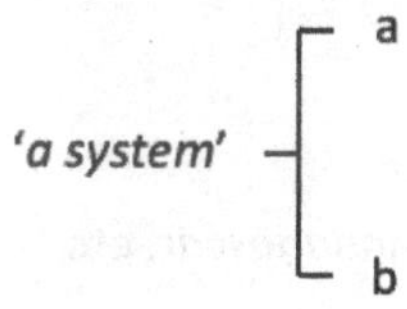

Figure 2.1 A system

However, Systemic Phonology is not restricted to binary options, but allows multiple options as the language specifies. Hence a multiple-choice system would be drawn as:

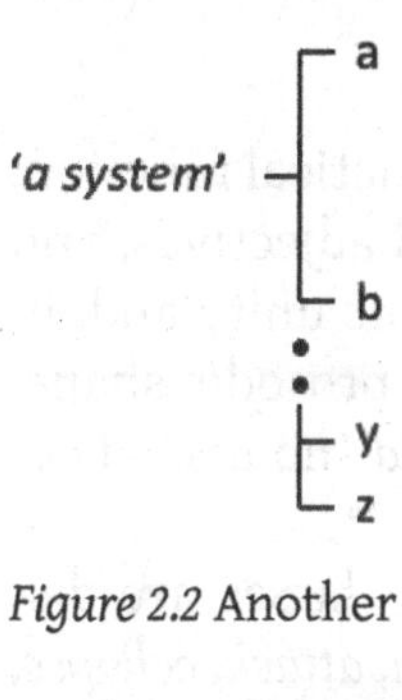

Figure 2.2 Another system

If an option allows for greater delicacy in further options, e.g. if 'a' is specified, then either 'c' or 'd' must also be specified; the network would be drawn as follows:

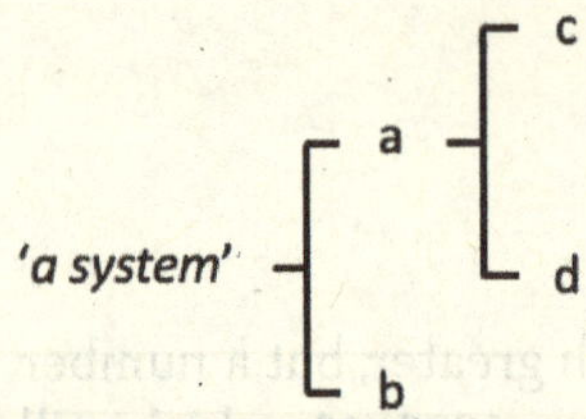

Figure 2.3 A more delicate system

A system network for the foot in English recognizes structures that contain a syllable count from 1 to 5; structures with more than a single syllable each have their own specifications. The foot system then might look like this:

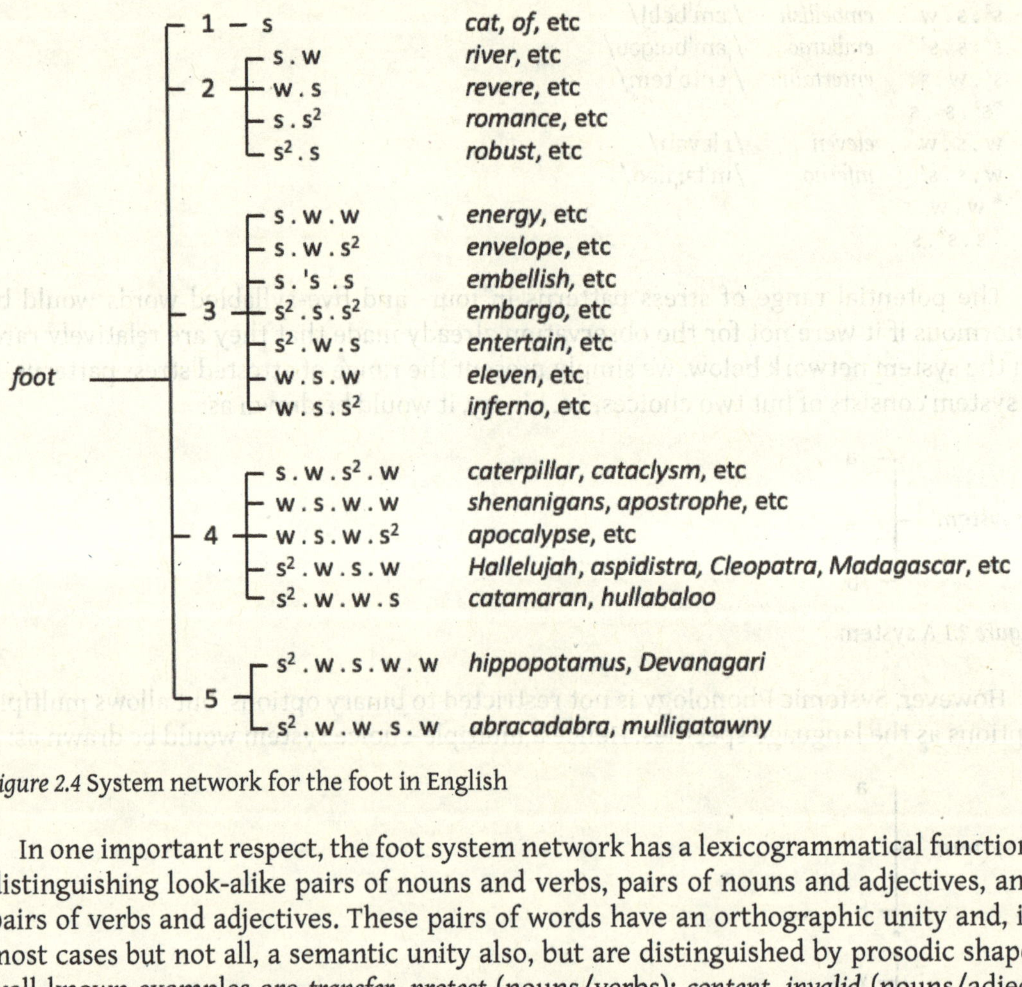

Figure 2.4 System network for the foot in English

In one important respect, the foot system network has a lexicogrammatical function: distinguishing look-alike pairs of nouns and verbs, pairs of nouns and adjectives, and pairs of verbs and adjectives. These pairs of words have an orthographic unity and, in most cases but not all, a semantic unity also, but are distinguished by prosodic shape; well-known examples are *transfer*, *protest* (nouns/verbs); *content*, *invalid* (nouns/adjectives); and *perfect*, *present* (verbs/adjectives).

However, it should be noted that not all similar pairs across word classes are distinguished phonologically; these others remain homonymous: *approach*, *attack*, *collapse*, *command*, etc,, remain identical as both nouns and verbs; *complete*, *correct*, etc., remain identical as both adjectives and verbs; *present*, *second*, *suspect* remain identical as noun/adjective pairs, although they change as verbs. In all cases of change, the noun has initial stress, the verb final, and the adjective varies according to the word class it partners: initial stress when contrasting with verbs, but non-initial stress when contrasting with nouns. This mini-system might be presented as:

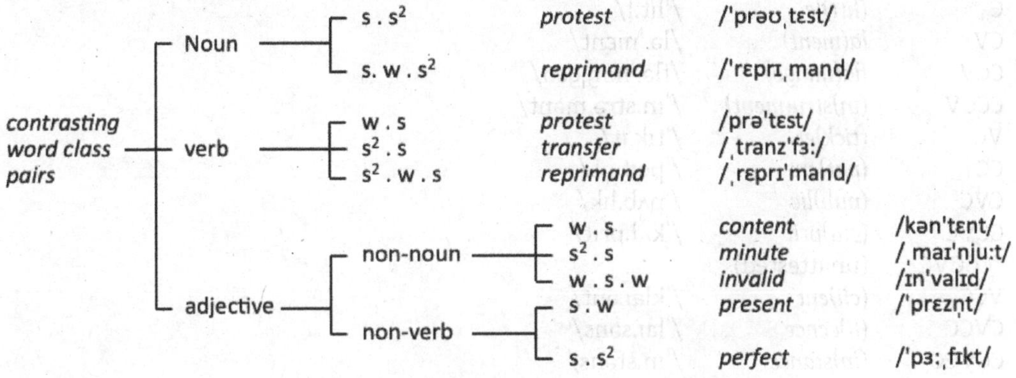

Figure 2.5 Mini-system network for feet in contrasting word class pairs

2.2 Syllable Structure

The phonology of English words also specifies the permissible structures of syllables. Some languages have a very limited range of structures, e.g. V and CV. English has open syllables like these, with no final margin, and it also permits 'extended' structures, i.e. closed syllables (or 'checked syllables') with a final margin. Furthermore, English permits up to three consonants in initial position in stressed syllables and also up to three consonants in final position. (It even permits a sequence of four consonants in polymorphemic inflected forms, e.g. *glimpsed* /glɪmpst/; see Chapter 3.) In unstressed syllables, English permits up to two consonants in initial position as a rule, but rare cases of three consonants do exist; in final position, up to two consonants. In addition, the consonants /l̩, n̩, m̩/ can function syllabically, i.e. without a vowel, as the nucleus of a weak syllable.

There are thus the following possible patterns in stressed syllables:

V	*awe*	/ɔ:/
CV	*law*	/lɔ:/
CCV	*flaw*	/flɔ:/
CCCV	*straw*	/strɔ:/
VC	*it*	/ɪt/
CVC	*sit*	/sɪt/
CCVC	*slit*	/slɪt/
CCCVC	*split*	/splɪt/
VCC	*ask*	/ɑ:sk/
CVCC	*task*	/tɑ:sk/
CCVCC	*flask*	/flɑ:sk/
CCCVCC	*splint*	/splɪnt/
VCCC	*oomps*	/ʊmps/ (but otherwise unattested)
CVCCC	*waltz*	/wɒlts/
CCVCCC	*glimpse*	/glɪmps/
CCCVCCC	(unattested, but not impossible, e.g. **sprinx*[1])	

In unstressed syllables, the possible patterns, following the syllable divisions in Wells (1990) are:

V	*a(long)*	/ə.ˈlɒŋ/
C	*(litt)le*	/ˈlɪt.l̩/
CV	*la(ment)*	/lə.ˈmɛnt/
CCV	*fla(mingo)*	/flə.ˈmɪŋˌɡəʊ/
CCCV	*(in)stru(ment)*	/ˈɪn.strə.mənt/
VC	*(tick)et*	/ˈtɪk.ɪt/
CC	*(pat)ent*	/ˈpeɪt.n̩t/
CVC	*(pub)lic*	/ˈpʌb.lɪk/
CCVC	*(cul)prit*	/ˈkʌl.prɪt/
*CCCVC	(unattested)	
VCC	*(cli)ent*	/ˈklaɪ.ənt/
CVCC	*(li)cence*	/ˈlaɪ.səns/
CCVCC	*(in)stance*	/ˈɪn.stəns/
*CCCVCC	(unattested)	

A system network for the rank of syllable in terms of its structure in English might then look like this:

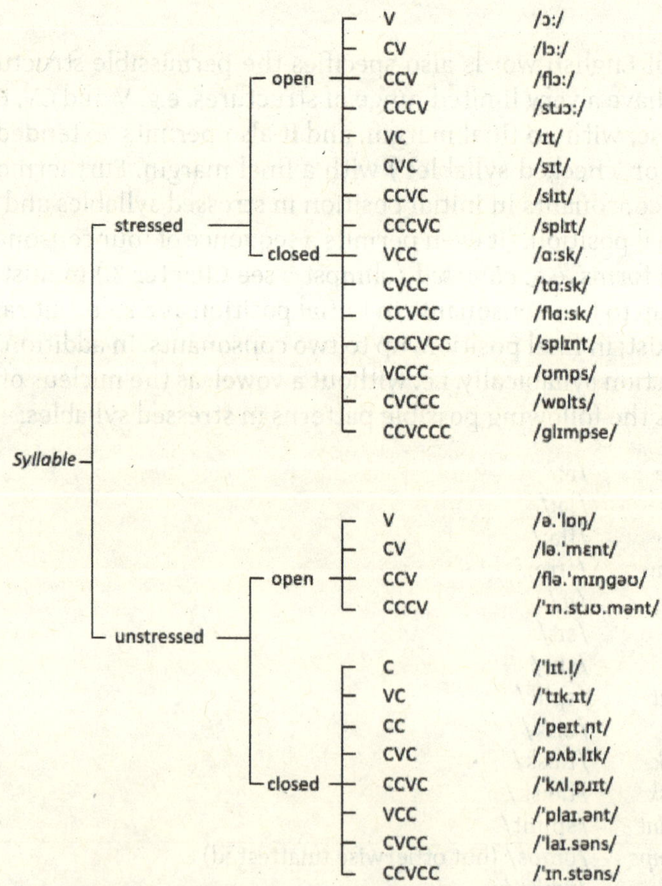

Figure 2.6 A system network for the rank of syllable in terms of its structure in English

2.3 Syllable Nucleus Systems

Vowels and syllabic consonants from the rank below Syllable function as the nucleus of an English syllable. The nucleus of a stressed syllable is a strong vowel. There is an inventory of vowel articulations that only occur in syllables with primary or secondary stresses, hence the term 'strong vowel'. There is also a very much smaller inventory of vowel and consonant articulations that can only occur in unstressed syllables, and they are referred to as either a 'weak vowel' or 'syllabic consonant'. Word phonology specifies what a language has engaged in these respects. The two separate systems demonstrate the polysystemic principle in Systemic Phonology; there is no one single system of vowels in English, but two, and each operates in different environments. On the other hand, there is no distinction between relatively stable long ('monophthongal') vowels and diphthongs; they belong to the same system. This latter point is borne out across accents where diphthongs in SESP are realized as monophthongs, and vice versa.

There are two vowel articulations that occur in both stressed and unstressed syllables: /ɪ, ʊ/; in unstressed syllables they may only be followed by a single consonant, but there is no restriction in the number of consonants that follow them in stressed syllables (apart from the permissible number in the syllable structure network).

Strong vowels are classified by whether they may function in closed syllables only, or also in open syllables. The so called 'short vowels' are restricted to closed syllables, i.e. they must be followed by a consonant; the 'long vowels', on the other hand, function in both closed and open syllables, i.e. they need not be followed by a consonant. The short vowels of SESP are: /ɪ, ɛ, a, ɒ, ʊ, ʌ/; and the long vowels are: /iː, ɑː, ɔː, uː, ɜː, eɪ, aɪ, ɔɪ, aʊ, əʊ, ɪə, ɛə, ʊə/. (The vowel /ʊə/ does not feature in all SESP speakers' speech; see Gimson 2014: 155–156.)

The weak vowels /ɪ, ʊ/ only function in closed syllables; there are two weak vowels that only function in open syllables: /i, u/ and there is one weak vowel that functions in both: /ə/. True 'syllabic consonants' are confined to a set of resonant consonants that are articulated homorganically with the final consonant of the preceding syllable with no intervening vowel articulation; in the case of /l̩, n̩/, they occur in both open and closed syllables, as in *little* /ˈlɪtl̩/, *basalt* /ˈbazl̩t/, *sudden* /ˈsʌdn̩/, *patent* /ˈpeɪtn̩t/, *tunnel* /ˈtʌnl̩/, *Arnold* /ˈɑːnl̩d/; /m̩/ occasionally occurs in the words *happen* /ˈhapm̩/ and *open* /ˈəʊpm̩/. These three consonants are often cited as 'syllabic consonants' in other contexts, but where the contexts do not fulfil these precise requirements, such as *apple* /ˈapəl/, *quarrel* /ˈkwɒɹəl/, *kitchen* /ˈkɪʧən/, *autumn* /ˈɔːtəm/. (The /ə/ is often transcribed as an open transition: /ˈapᵊl/, /ˈkwɒrᵊl/, /ˈkɪʧᵊn/, /ˈɔːtᵊm/.)

In the system network for syllable peaks below, there is first the distinction between strong and weak vowels, and in both cases, there is a more delicate distinction between open and closed syllable systems. In order to show a 'deeper' delicacy, that strong short vowels can only occur in closed syllables, but that strong long vowels can occur in both open and closed syllables, the network must be read as follows: if you take 'strong' and then 'open syllables', you can only have long vowels; but if you take 'strong' and then 'closed syllables', you can then take either long vowels or short.

Moreover, if you take 'weak', then you can take either open or closed syllables; if you take 'open syllables' you can take either of two options: /i, u, m̩/ or /ə, l̩, n̩/; but if you take 'closed syllables', you can also take either of two options: /ə, l̩, n̩/ (which is common to open and closed syllables), or /ɪ, ʊ/.

The network design

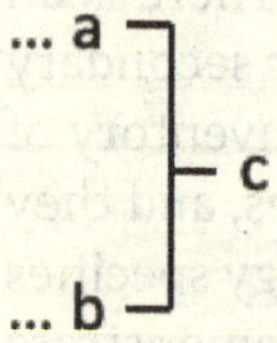

Figure 2.7 Network design

indicates that the more delicate system *c* is common to the two preceding systems, *a* and *b*.

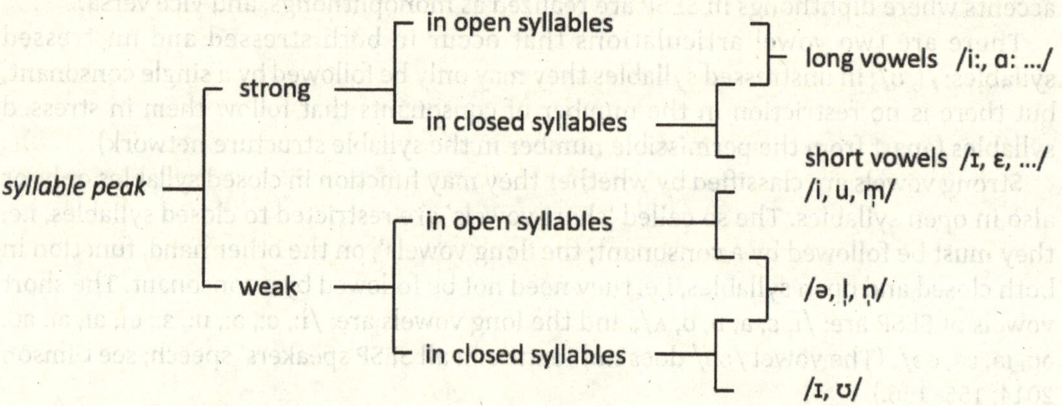

Figure 2.8 A system network for syllable peaks in English

2.4 Syllable Margin Systems

Consonants function at syllable margins that occur either at the beginning of a syllable (syllable-initial, often termed the 'onset') or, in the case of closed syllables, after the nucleus (syllable-final, often termed the 'coda').[2] Word phonology in English specifies what the two systems are, which are both a good deal more complex than those of many other languages on account of the permissible syllable structures. The syllable structure network specifies in general terms what the size of the syllable-initial and -final margins may be; the syllable margin networks specify what consonants actually figure in the two systems. Here is another demonstration of the polysystemic principle in Systemic Phonology.

2.4.1 Syllable-initial Margin Systems

The syllable-initial margin system allows for single consonants and clusters of two and three consonants. Single consonants may be one of the following: the obstruents /p, t, k, b, d, g, f, v, θ, ð, s, z, ʃ, ʧ, ʤ/ (and in a very limited number of cases /ʒ/, e.g. *genre*, (*force ma*)*jeure*), and resonants /m, n, ŋ, l, r, j, w/.

The system for double-consonant clusters is complicated by the fact that if the second of the two consonants is /j/ then the vowel following is limited to /u:, ʊ, ʊə, u/. It seems appropriate therefore to separate that cluster potential from the others where there is no restriction on following vowels; the latter is known as the primary syllable-initial margin system, and the former, with /j/, as the secondary.

The regular pattern of consonants in the primary syllable-initial margin consists of an initial obstruent consonant followed by a resonant consonant; this sequence follows the pattern of least sonorous to greater sonority (see **1.3**). There are three exceptions to the general rule: /ts/, /sf/ and /sv/, sequences of two obstruents. /ts/, which incidentally, does follow the sonority rule, is limited to a few loan words, each of which has a regular alternative pronunciation in SESP (*tsetse* as /ˈtɛtsi/ and *tsunami* as /sʊˈnɑ:mi/); as a result, it has not reached the status of an acceptable cluster. /sf/, which is counter to the sonority rule, is limited to a small number of words from Greek (e.g. *sphere*) and Italian (e.g. *sforzando*), and because there is no alternative pronunciation in SESP, it is accepted as a permissible cluster; whereas /sv/ has a regular alternative as /sf/, e.g. *svelte* as /sfɛlt/. The full list of permissible double consonant clusters is therefore:

/pl/	*ply*	
/pr/	*pry*	
/pw/	*pois*	(rare, confined to a few loan words from French and Spanish)
/bl/	*blight*	
/br/	*bright*	
/bw/	*bwana*	(rare, confined to a few loan words from Swahili, French and Spanish)
/tr/	*try*	
/tw/	*twin*	
/dr/	*dry*	
/dw/	*dwindle*	
/kl/	*climb*	
/kr/	*crime*	
/kw/	*quite*	
/gl/	*glide*	
/gr/	*grime*	
/gw/	*(lan)guish*	
/fl/	*fly*	
/fr/	*fry*	
/fw/	*fois*	(rare, confined to a few loan words from French and Spanish)
/vw/	*(reser)voir*	(rare, confined to a few loan words from French)
/θr/	*thrive*	
/θw/	*thwart*	
/sp/	*spy*	
/st/	*sty*	
/sk/	*sky*	
/sf/	*sphere*	(rare, confined to words of Greek origin and loan words from Italian)
/sm/	*smile*	
/sn/	*snide*	
/sl/	*sly*	

/sw/	*swipe*	
/ʃm/	*shmuck*	(rare, confined to a few loan words from German and Yiddish)
/ʃn/	*schnapps*	(rare, confined to a few loan words from German and Yiddish)
/ʃl/	*schlock*	(rare, confined to a few loan words from German and Yiddish)
/ʃr/	*shrine*	
/ʃw/	*schwa*	(rare, confined to a few loan words from German and Dutch)

The regular pattern of consonants in the secondary syllable-initial margin consists of an obstruent or nasal consonant followed by /j/; the only possible exception is that for some speakers, the initial consonant system may include /l/, e.g. *allure*, /ə.ˈljʊə/. The regular secondary system, which also follows the sonority rule, is as follows:

/pj/	*pew*	
/bj/	*beauty*	
/tj/	*tune*	
/dj/	*due, dew*	
/kj/	*cue*	
/gj/	*gules*	(rare)
/fj/	*few*	
/vj/	*view*	
/θj/	*(en)thuse*	
/sj/	*(as)sume*	
/zj/	*(pre)sume*	
/hj/	*hue, hew, Hugh, Huw*	
/mj/	*mute*	
/nj/	*new*	

The pattern of consonants in both primary and secondary triple-consonant clusters must consist exclusively of initial /s/ followed by a selection of permissible double consonant clusters. Since there is no choice of initial consonant, there is actually no system at that point. The triple primary system, which also observes the sonority rule, consists of the following clusters:

/spl/	*splint*	
/spr/	*sprint*	
/stɹ/	*stray*	
/skl/	*sclera*	(rare, confined to a few words of Greek origin)
/skr/	*scream*	
/skw/	*squint*	
/sfr/	*sphragistics*	(rare, confined to a few words of Greek origin)

and the secondary:

/spj/	*spew*	
/stj/	*stew*	
/skj/	*skewer*	
/smj/	*smew*	(rare)

The system network for syllable-initial margins might be presented as follows:

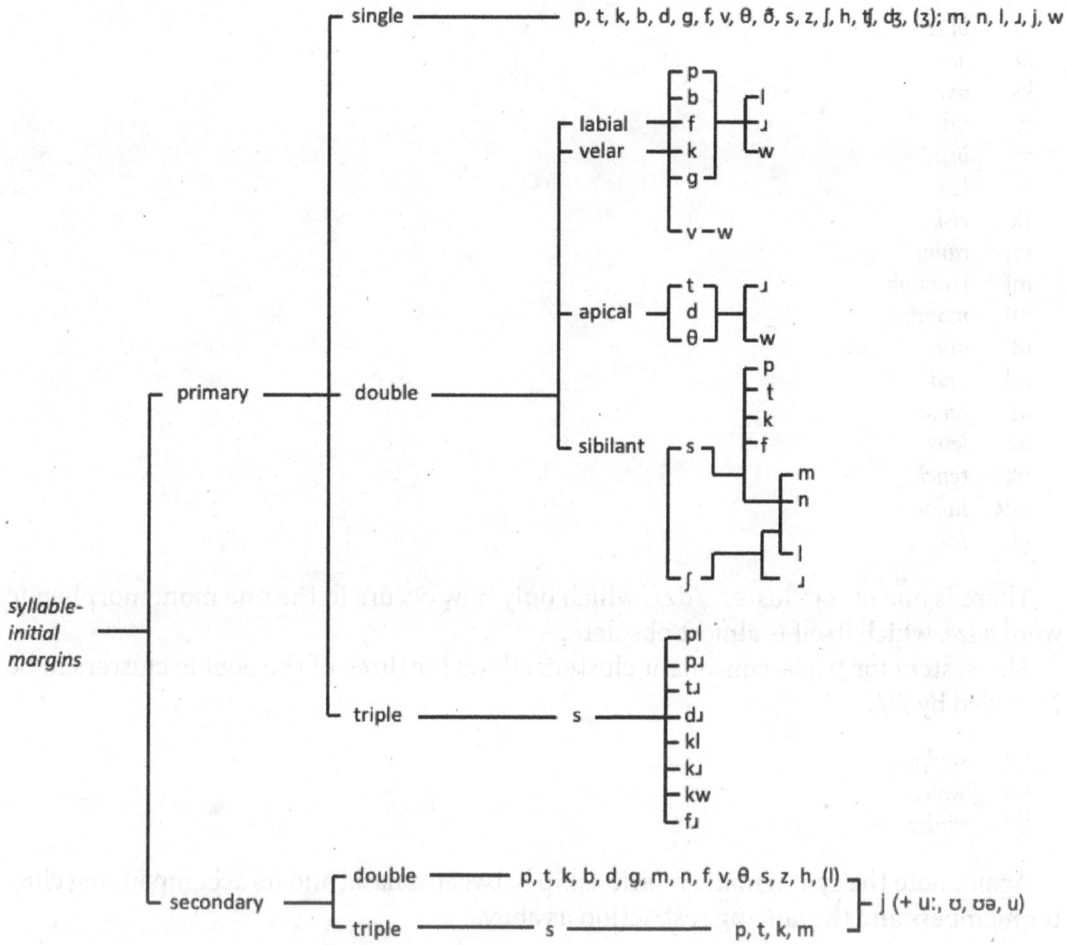

Figure 2.9 A system network for syllable-initial margins in English

2.4.2 Syllable-final Margin Systems

The syllable-final margin system allows for single consonants and clusters of two and three consonants. Single consonants may be one of the following: /p, t, k, b, d, g, m, n, ŋ, f, v, θ, ð, s, z, ʃ, ʒ, ʧ, ʤ, l/. This syllable-final inventory differs from the syllable-initial by excluding /h, j, w/ and /ɹ/ (in non-rhotic SESP) and by including /ŋ/.

The system for double-consonant final clusters allows any of the final singletons to be preceded by /l/, except /g, ð, z, ʒ, ŋ/; it also allows the following sequences of voiceless obstruents, and nasals to be followed by an obstruent, keeping the English phonological sonority rule (see **1.3**) in reverse; note that once voicelessness enters the cluster, it persists, whereas when a cluster begins with /l/ or a nasal, a selection in voicing is still permissible. Note too, the syntagmatic relationship between a nasal and its following cluster member: bilabial with labials; alveolar with apicals; and velar with /k, g/.

pt *apt*
ps *apse*

ts *blitz*
kt *act*
ks *axe*
ft *lift*
sp *lisp*
st *list*
sk *risk*
mp *ramp*
mf *triumph*
nθ *month*
nt *ant*
nd *and*
ns *tense*
nz *lens*
ntʃ *tench*
ndʒ *hinge*
ŋk *ink*

There is one other cluster: /dz/, which only now occurs in the one monomorphemic word *adze*, which itself is almost obsolete.

The system for triple-consonant clusters allows for three of the double clusters to be preceded by /l/.

lpt *sculpt*
lts *waltz*
lkt *mulct*

Again, note the syntagmatic relationship between a nasal and its accompanying cluster members and the voicing restriction as above:

mpt *tempt*
mps *glimpse*
ŋkt *instinct*
ŋks *lynx*

and one combination of /k/ and /st/:

kst *text*

It is debatable whether also to include /-lst, -dst, -ŋst/ as in *whilst*, *midst*, *amidst* and *amongst*, because although the /-st/ is clearly an addition to a monomorphemic word, it is an 'unproductive' inflexion, whereas the very same /-st/ in *next* /nɛkst/ can not be separated – at least, not in modern English. However, in the permissible triple clusters above, there is a pattern of maintaining the voice selection of the first plosive, but that is not the case in *(a)midst*. It is thus perhaps more appropriate to treat those four words as bimorphemic words and so exclude them from this present (monomorphemic) network.

The system network for syllable-final margins might be presented as follows:

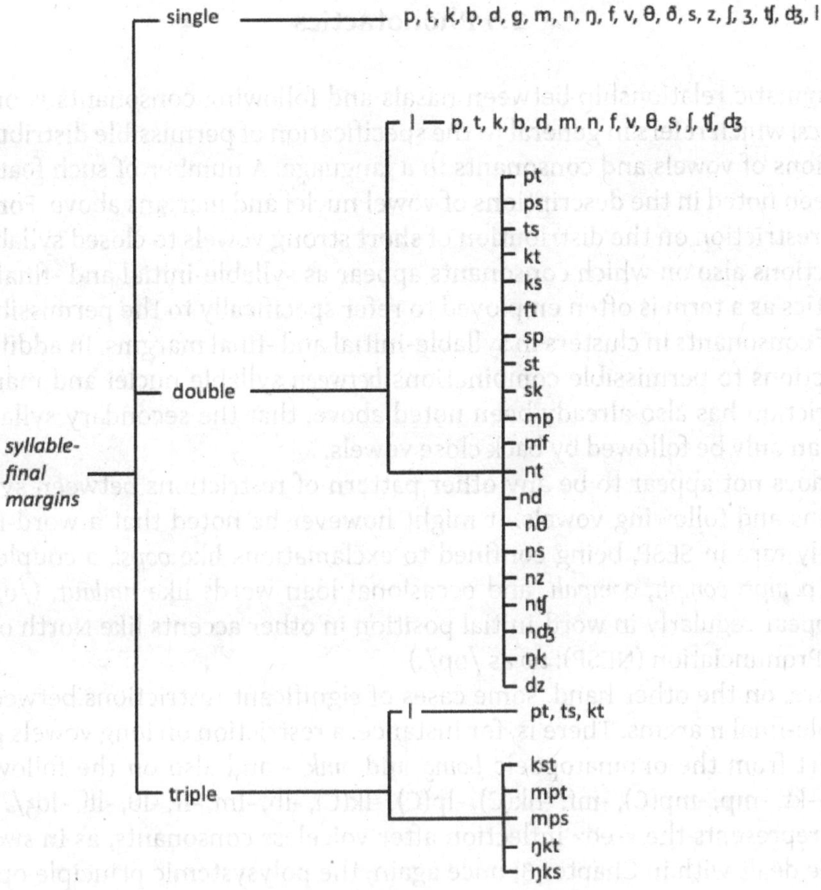

Figure 2.10 A system network for syllable-final margins in English

The syntagmatic relationship between nasals and following segments can be shown in an alternative network specific to this relationship, employing the notion of archiphoneme (see **1.6**). Syllable-final margin nasal-led clusters can be 'codified' as /-N_#/; *N* represents all the nasals in the English system, and # represents a word boundary. (Articulatory details are further discussed in **2.7** below.) This mini system will then look like this:

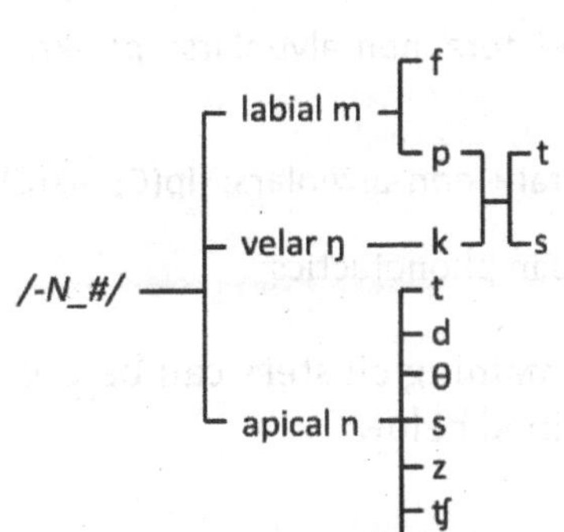

Figure 2.11 Mini-system for nasal-led syllable-final margins in English

2.5 Phonotactics

The syntagmatic relationship between nasals and following consonants is one case of *Phonotactics*, which refers in general to the specification of permissible distributions and combinations of vowels and consonants in a language. A number of such features have already been noted in the descriptions of vowel nuclei and margins above. For instance, there is a restriction on the distribution of short strong vowels to closed syllables; there are restrictions also on which consonants appear as syllable-initial and -final margins. Phonotactics as a term is often employed to refer specifically to the permissible combinations of consonants in clusters in syllable-initial and -final margins. In addition, there are restrictions to permissible combinations *between* syllable nuclei and margins; one such restriction has also already been noted above: that the secondary syllable initial margins can only be followed by back close vowels.

There does not appear to be any other pattern of restrictions between syllable initial margins and following vowels. It might however be noted that a word-initial /ʊ/ is relatively rare in SESP, being confined to exclamations like *oops!*, a couple of colloquialisms *oomps*, *oomph*, *oompah*, and occasional loan words like *umlaut*. (/ʊ/ does, of course, appear regularly in word-initial position in other accents like North of England Standard Pronunciation (NESP): *up* as /ʊp/.)

There are, on the other hand, some cases of significant restrictions between vowels and syllable-final margins. There is, for instance, a restriction on long vowels preceding /ŋ/ – apart from the onomatopoeic *boing* and *oink* – and also on the following clusters: /-pt, -kt, -mp, -mp(C), -mf, -ŋk(C), -lp(C), -lk(C), -lb, -lm, -lf, -lθ, -lʧ, -lʤ/. (Final /t/ regularly represents the <-ed> inflection after voiceless consonants, as in *swooped*, but this will be dealt with in Chapter 3; once again, the polysystemic principle operates, as there is one system for monomorphemic words and a separate, extended, system for inflected words. However, it is noticeable how often a word with a long vowel before /p/ changes to a short vowel, as *sweep* becomes *swept*, conforming to the observation made above.) This phonotactic restriction can be captured in a 'regressive' system, whereby a following segment or cluster of segments determines a preceding segment. This regressive system excludes any alveolar segment or cluster with an initial alveolar consonant, apart from /l/; even clusters with /l/ have no alveolar consonant following. This system is limited to non-alveolars apart from /l/.

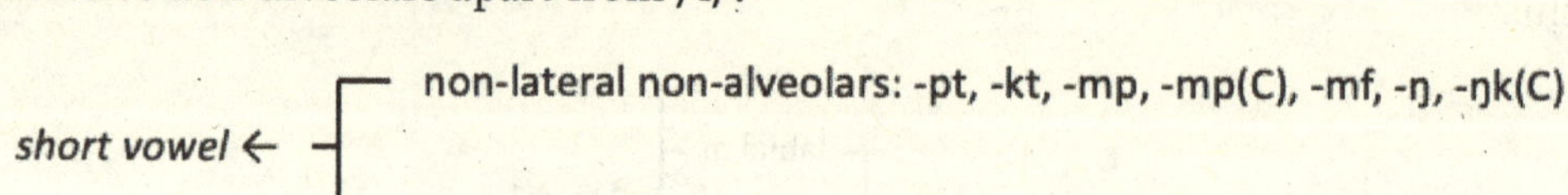

Figure 2.12 Mini-system networks in phonotactics

On the other hand, the remaining clusters can be preceded by either short or long vowels; the latter are exemplified below:

-ps	*traipse*	/treɪps/
-ft	*draft*	/drɑːft/
-ts	*quartz*	/kwɔːts/

-ks	*coax*	/kəʊks/
-sp	*clasp*	/klɑ:sp/
-st	*feast*	/fi:st/
-sk	*ask*	/ɑ:sk/
-nt	*flaunt*	/flɔ:nt/
-nd	*fiend*	/fi:nd/
-ns	*ounce*	/aʊns/
-nz	*Heinz*	/haɪnz/
-ntʃ	*launch*	/lɔ:ntʃ/
-ndʒ	*range*	/reɪndʒ/
-lt	*colt*	/kəʊlt/
-ld	*cold*	/kəʊld/
-ls	*false*	/fɔ:ls/
-lʃ	*Walsh*	/wɔ:lʃ/
-lv	*solve*	/səʊlv/
-lts	*waltz*	/wɔ:lts/

There is, obviously no need to create a system network for regular occurrences between long/short vowels and these consonant clusters, because they conform to the system network for the rank of syllable (**2.2** above). However, it should be noted that the above examples with the vowels /ɑ:, ɔ:, əʊ/ with a voiceless segment in the following cluster have common alternative pronunciations with short vowels /a, ɒ/. *Draft*, for example, has the alternative /draft/. When /ɔ:, əʊ/ are followed by /l/, they may become /ɒ/: *colt* /kɒlt/, *false* /fɒls/, *Walsh* /wɒlʃ/, *waltz* /wɒlts/; but also *solve* has the alternative /sɒlv/, even though there is no voiceless element.

Full phonotactic charts appeared in Gimson (1989: 241–256), but it should be noted that they include inflected forms of words and hence not strictly monomorphemic. We noted in Chapter 1 (1.7, p. 27) that Gimson pointed out that not all possible combinations that conform to general patterns are utilized. This under-utilization of all possible combinations is not, it should be noted, subject to specifications in English word phonology, but rather to the specifications of the lexicon itself. More new words with permissible phonotactics may well yet enter the lexicon, i.e. English word phonology as a resource with creative potential.

2.6 Phoneme Inventories

Having described the units in English word phonology at the ranks of foot and syllable, we now turn to the rank of phoneme.

The inventory of vowels has already been given under **2.3 Syllable Nucleus Systems.** The polysystemic principle was invoked because there are two systems in English: strong vowels for stressed syllables and weak vowels for unstressed syllables. Word phonology specifies their classification criteria for a given language. The criteria for the strong vowels of SESP are well known and may be presented in a system network as follows. Brace ('curly') brackets mean that all options have to be taken: the vowel system of English requires that both 'quality' and 'quantity' are taken; that 'quality' requires that both tongue and backness are taken; but that 'quantity' requires a choice between 'short' and 'long'. The horizontal and vertical lines show realizations.

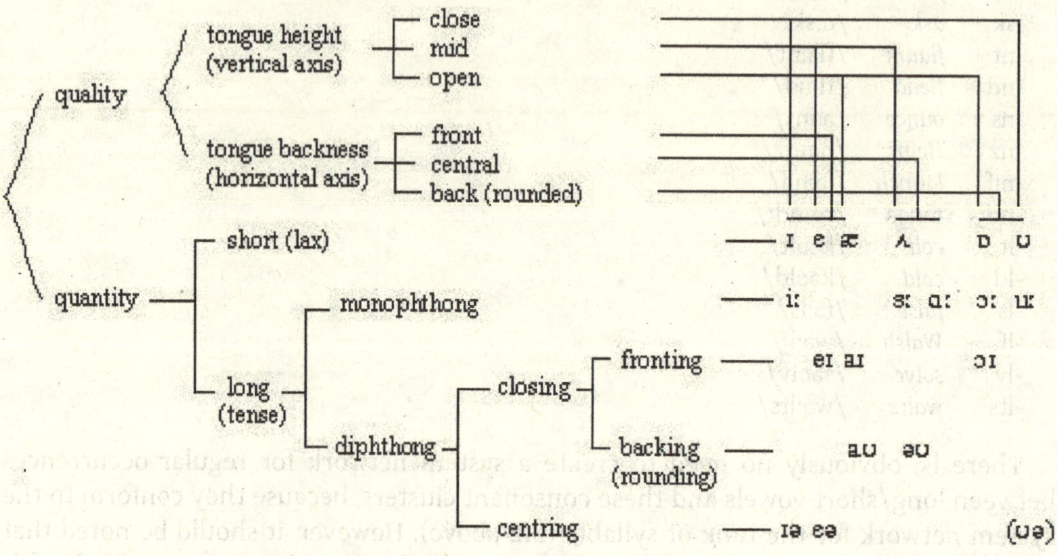

Figure 2.13 System network of the strong vowels of Southern England Standard Pronunciation

The incidental advantage of this display is that it not only separates the two systems, strong and weak, but also separates within the strong vowel system short vowels from long vowels with their particular phonological constraint in distribution. Also, the display integrates diphthongs with long monophthongs into one single strong vowel system. The brackets around /ʊə/ are intended to indicate that not all SESP speakers have this vowel in their speech, it being replaced either by /ɔː/, as in *poor* /pɔː/, or by /uːə/, as in *dour* /ˈduːə/.

The network for weak vowels is very much simpler: that for closed syllables is shown below left, and that for open syllables below right:

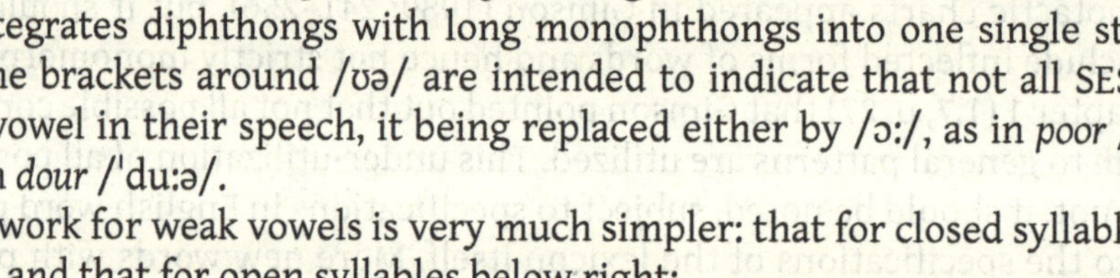

Figure 2.14 System network of the weak vowels in SESP closed syllables (left) and open (right)

The inventory of consonants has already been introduced under **2.4 Syllable Margin Systems.** The classification criteria, again well known, may be presented in a system network for syllable-initial consonants as below; that for syllable-final consonants would require the addition of /ŋ/ 'nasal velar flat' and the deletion of /h/ and the 'articulator' row 'glottal', and also the 'manner' row 'approximant'.

Brace ('curly') brackets again show the consonant system requires that both 'manner' and 'articulator' must be taken; and that 'obstruent' requires that both 'voice' and 'stricture' must be taken.

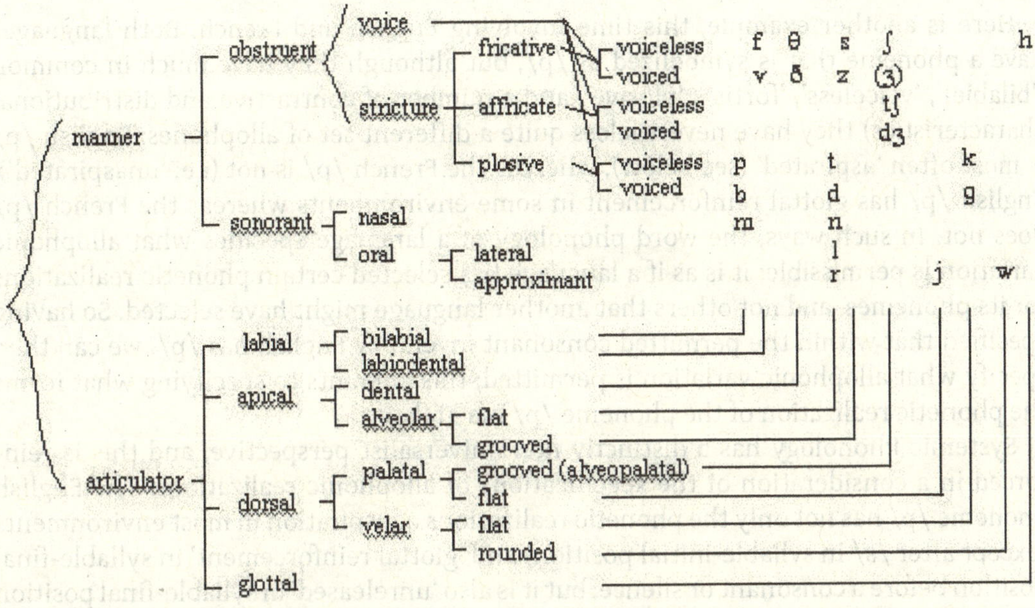

Figure 2.15 System network of the syllable-initial consonants of SESP

The incidental advantages of this display over traditional consonant charts include the close link between affricates and both fricatives and plosives; the close link between nasals and plosives (in points of articulation) on the one hand, and approximants (as 'fellow' resonants) on the other; the labelling of grooved articulations and the close links between them, and the avoidance of redundant 'cells' for voicelessness for sonorants. (There is, however, a redundant voiced 'cell' accompanying /h/.) The brackets around /ʒ/ indicate its marginal status in the syllable-initial system; brackets would not be required in the network for the syllable-final system.

2.7 Allophonic Realizations

It is frequently maintained that *allophonic variation* does not belong to phonology as such, but rather to phonetics. However, allophonic features of phonemes vary according to the specifications of a given language, as we noted in **1.3**. For instance, English, German, Welsh and Tera all have a phoneme symbolized as /l/; but English has an allophonic variation that is peculiar to itself, as we have seen (**1.3**): a clear [l] that occurs before vowels at the beginning of words and syllables and before /j/, a dark [ɫ] that occurs before other consonants and at the end of words and syllables, and other variations in particular environments. The difference between clear and dark /l/ helps, incidentally, in determining syllable boundaries in English, since the clear [l] precedes vowels; e.g. *follow* has clear [l] and so the syllable boundary must be: /ˈfɒ.ləʊ/. German and Tera, on the other hand, do not have this kind of variation, but 'select' the clear [l] in all positions. Welsh has both varieties but does not employ them phonologically, but sociolinguistically, according to accents; in brief: the clear [l] occurs in all positions in South Walian Welsh, the dark [ɫ] in all positions in North Walian Welsh (see Chapter 5).

Here is another example, this time involving English and French. Both languages have a phoneme that is symbolized as /p/, but although they have much in common ('bilabial', 'voiceless', 'fortis',[3] 'plosive', and a number of contrastive and distributional characteristics) they have nevertheless quite a different set of allophones: English /p/ is most often 'aspirated' (see below), whereas the French /p/ is not (i.e. 'unaspirated'); English /p/ has glottal reinforcement in some environments whereas the French /p/ does not. In such ways, the word phonology of a language specifies what allophonic variation is permissible; it is as if a language has selected certain phonetic realizations for its phonemes, and not others that another language might have selected. So having specified that within the permitted consonant inventory English has /p/, we can then specify what allophonic variation is permitted; this amounts to specifying what forms the phonetic realization of the phoneme /p/ may take.

Systemic Phonology has a distinctly non-universalist perspective, and this is reinforced in a consideration of the specifications of allophonic realizations. The English phoneme /p/ has not only the phonetic realizations of aspiration in most environments (except after /s/ in syllable-initial position) and 'glottal reinforcement' in syllable-final position before a consonant or silence, but it is also 'unreleased' in syllable-final position before a consonant; and there is regular assimilation to following labiodental fricatives. Its system network might be presented as follows, with square brackets indicating an allophonic transcription, where → means 'realized as'; . = syllable boundary; _ the 'slot' occupied by the phoneme; # = word boundary/silence; [ʰ] aspiration, and [ʰ] weaker degree of aspiration as in unstressed syllables.

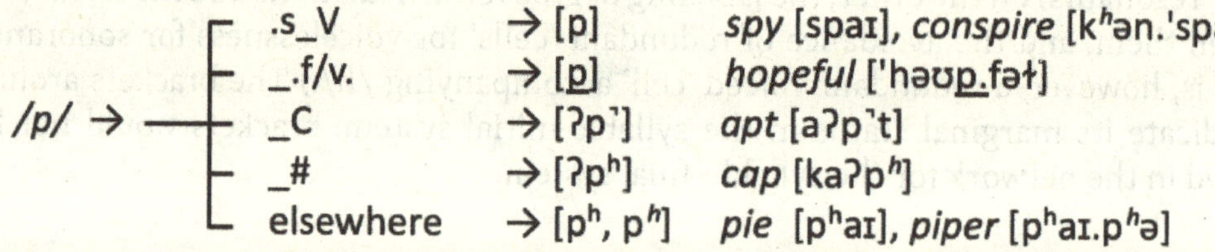

Figure 2.16 A system network of allophonic variations of the phoneme /p/ in English

Similarly, English /b/: it has the following phonetic realizations. It is fully voiced in most environments, but 'devoiced' before a voiceless consonant or silence; there is also regular assimilation to following labiodental fricatives. (It is also, like /p/, 'unreleased' in syllable-final position before a consonant, but in the case of /b/ the following consonant must be an affix; since that constitutes more than a 'monomorphemic' word, it will feature in Chapter 3.) The system network for /b/ in basic, monomorphemic, words might simply be presented as:

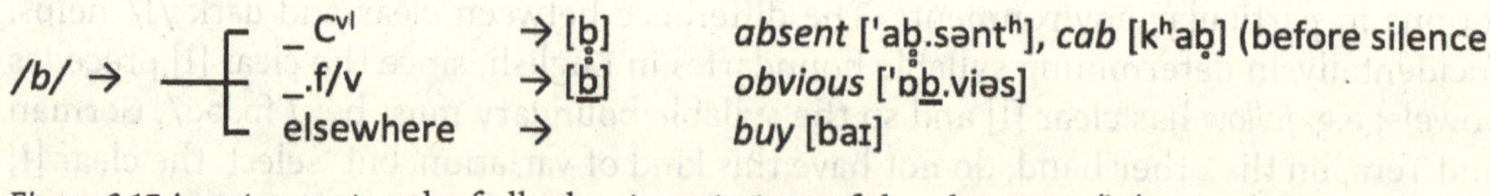

Figure 2.17 A system network of allophonic variations of the phoneme /b/ in English

It would then be possible to present such networks for each consonant and vowel phoneme of English as part of a full presentation of English word phonology; see Tench (2011: 66–72) for a comprehensive summary of consonant and vowel allophony in English. However, simply listing allophonic variation phoneme by phoneme would miss general tendencies in English allophony. As can be seen from the above two examples, there are a number of features that are common to /p/ and /b/ as well as those that are distinct; such shared features are part of the phonology of the word in English.

Shared allophonic features indicate patterns in the specifications of allophony, and in most cases, they are syntagmatic in nature, affecting more than a single segment in sequence. These syntagmatic features are similar to what Firth called 'prosodies' in Prosodic Analysis; they may affect whole syllables and words, or only parts of syllables. The direction of the effect is either forwards ('progressive') or backwards ('regressive'); this is shown by the position of the diacritic either after or before the relevant phonemic symbol. Here is a list of syntagmatic features.

- *Aspiration* is a progressive feature that refers to the release of a plosive in English that delays the onset of voicing of an immediately following voiced segment, whether it is a vowel or a voiced consonant; it occurs with all voiceless plosives, except when preceded by /s/; e.g. *coo* /ku:/ [kʰu:], *clue* /klu:/ [kʰlu:], *crew* /kɹu:/ [kʰɹu:], *acute* /əˈkju:t/ [əˈkʰju·ʔt*ʰ*]. (NB, [ʰ] can also be rendered by subscript [̥] below the devoiced segment, or by a distinct symbol: [kᵾu:], [kˡ̥u:], [kɹ̥u:], [əˈkçju·ʔt*ʰ*].[4]) But *school* /sku:l/ [sku:ɫ]. Aspiration in unstressed syllables is weaker; token /ˈtəʊkən/ [ˈtʰəʊ.k*ʰ*ən], where italicized [*ʰ*] is used to indicate a lesser degree of aspiration.
- *Devoicing* is a regressive feature that affects all voiced obstruents when they occur immediately before voiceless consonants and silence; e.g. *obstruct* /ɒbˈstɹʌkt/ [ɒb̥ˈstɹʌʔk̚tʰ]. (NB [b̥] could also be rendered as [bᵖ], etc.)
- *Place assimilation* is a regressive feature that affects all plosives and nasals before adjacent obstruents with a similar, approximate, point of articulation, including also /k, g/ before front and back open vowels; e.g. *month* /mʌnθ/ [mʌ̃n̪θ], *true* /tɹu:/ [t̠ʰɹu:], *key* /ki:/ [k̟ʰi:], *goose* /gu:s/ [g̠u·s].
- *Epenthesis* is a regressive feature caused by a voiceless fricative after a nasal. It requires very careful synchronization to move from a nasal with its voicing and complete closure in the mouth, to an oral articulation with voicelessness and partial, fricative, closure, without any intervening articulatory transition (epenthesis). Very frequently, a transitional element is produced and heard. *Month* /mʌnθ/ is therefore more accurately transcribed in this case as [mʌ̃n̪t̪θ]. In the case of *prince*, a transitional articulation takes place that is identical to English /t/: it shares the complete closure and 'flat' apical articulation of /n/ and the voicelessness and oral articulation of /s/: /pɹɪnts/, which makes it identical to *prints*. If required, the transitional nature of /t/ can be symbolized by a raised symbol, [ᵗ]: /pɹɪnᵗs/; [mʌnᵗθ]. A parallel example is found in *hamster* after /m/: /hamstə/, /hamᵖstə/. Other examples involve suffixes as in *warmth*, *length*, *youngster*, *Simpson*, etc.; see Chapter 3, **3.3**.

- *Breaking* is a regressive feature that affects long close and closing vowels (/iː, eɪ, aɪ, ɔɪ/) before dark [ɫ]; it is similar to epenthesis in that the tongue adjustment to the velarization of [ɫ] resembles the vowel /ə/. It is usually transcribed as a raised symbol: *eel* /iːᵊl/, *ale* /eɪᵊl/, *isle, aisle* /aɪᵊl/, *oil* /ɔɪᵊl/ (see Wells 1990).
- *Rounding* is a regressive feature that affects any consonant before /w/ or rounded vowels; *quite* /kwaɪt/ [ʷkʰwaɪ̆ʔtʰ], *coot* /kuːt/ [ʷkʰuˑʔtʰ], *acute* /əˈkjuːt/ [əˈʷkᶣ̊juˑʔtʰ] (introducing the voiceless (rounded) labial-palatal [ᶣ̊] equivalent to [ᶜ̧]).
- *Clipping* (reduction in vowel length) is a regressive feature that affects all vowels before voiceless consonants in the same syllable; it is symbolized as [ˑ], one dot instead of the two dots of a colon, with long vowels, and as [˘] with short vowels; compare *seed* /siːd/ [siːd], *seat* /siːt/ [siˑʔtʰ] and *sight/site/cite* /saɪt/ [saɪ̆ʔtʰ]; also *save* /seɪv/ [seɪv] and *safe* /seɪf/ [seɪ̆f].
- *Nasalization* is both a progressive and a regressive feature that affects vowels adjacent to nasal consonants; e.g. *my* /maɪ/ [mãi] (progressive), *line* /laɪn/ [laɪ̃n] (regressive), *mine* /maɪn/ [mãɪ̃n] (progressive and regressive). The regressive form is identical to the place matching noted above for consonant clusters in syllable-final margins that are led by nasals (**2.4**, p. 45); this place matching, however, occurs over syllable boundaries as well, as in *bumble*, *bundle*, *bungle*: /ˈbʌm.bəl/, /ˈbʌn.dl̩/, /ˈbʌŋ.gəl/.

Allophonic syntagmatic features are summarized as follows:

syntagmatic feature	direction of effect	symbol
aspiration	→	[Cʰ] (strong) [Cʰ] (weak)
devoicing	←	[C̥]
place assimilation	←	[C̠, ɱ] (retracted) [̪] (dentalized) [C̟} (advanced
epenthesis	←	[ᵖC, ᵗC ᵏC]
Breaking	←	[ᵊɫ]
rounding	←	[ʷC]
clipping	←	[vˑ], [v̆]
nasalization	←/→	[ṽ]

Figure 2.18 Allophonic syntagmatic features in English word phonology

On the other hand, glottal reinforcement [ʔ] is not regarded as a syntagmatic feature because it is an essential part of a voiceless plosive in syllable-final position before a consonant or silence; it certainly contributes to clipping, but no more so than voiceless fricatives in that context.

2.8 Conclusion

We have now concluded a comprehensive description of the phonology of basic, monomorphemic, words in English from a systemic-functional perspective, illustrating the **primary function** of phonology as supplying unique forms for every unit of the lexicogrammar, with the exceptions of homonyms as the accidents of history. But we have illustrated other dimensions of a systemic-functional approach. We have described the functions and structures of units in the ranks of the phonological **hierarchy** for English, taking a top-down approach from foot to syllable to phoneme and even to the specifically English phonetic realizations of its phonemes.

We have also explained and illustrated the design of **system networks** at each rank and illustrated the **polysystemic principle** where multiple systems are required: strong and weak vowels systems; syllable-initial and syllable-final systems of consonants; primary and secondary systems in the syllable-initial margin. We have also made reference to **syntagmatic features** in phonotactics and allophonic realizations. We drew particular attention to the **non-universalist** dimension of those allophonic realizations.

We have not had to engage in hypothetical constructions such as 'underlying forms', although this will be more relevant in the description of polymorphemic words in the following chapter. We have not only covered **actual forms** but also touched on the **potential** for new words; *Covax* is a neologism but it conforms to all the phonological structures and systems of English: a single extended foot, which happens to have 'selected' two syllables, the first happens to be an open syllable with primary stress, the second a closed syllable with secondary stress, both containing a strong vowel as required, both happen to have 'selected' a single consonant in their initial margins and the second happens to have selected a double consonant cluster in its final margin.

Covax
Foot: prosodic shape: s . ˌs
Syllable: 1: CV; 2: CVCC
Phoneme: 1: /kəʊ/ [kʰ]; 2: /vaks/ [ʔk˺]

The description represents Southern England Standard Pronunciation (SESP) with occasional references to alternative realizations in other accents. The networks can simply be adapted to other accents. It may well be that the networks for **the foot** and **syllable** do not change appreciably for other accents, but they could do. However, the networks for **syllable nuclei** and **syllable margins** do so and in some cases considerably so. There may be 'systemic' differences in the phonemic inventory of accents; this means simply that either fewer choices (e.g. omission of /ʌ/) or more (e.g. the addition of /eː, oː/ appear in the networks. A second phonological dimension to accents is 'distributional'; in rhotic accents like General American, /r/ will appear in the syllable-final margin network; in many accents the secondary syllable-initial margin system either may not exist (e.g. instances of *beautiful* with no /j/) or may be severely reduced (e.g. *news* as /nu:z/, but *fuse* as /fju:z/). Thirdly, but in respect of phonetic realization, networks will again differ for accents; e.g. Welsh accents do not distinguish between clear and dark /l/; many accents in the North of England, Scotland, etc. render certain diphthongs as long monophthongs, e.g. /eɪ/ as [e:], /əʊ/ as [o:], etc. On the other hand, instances of 'incidential' lexical variation do not affect the networks; the alternatives of /ɛ/ or /i:/ in *economic* exist in the peak system already; General American *harass* has a different syllable pattern /həˈræs/ from SESP /ˈharəs/, but both patterns already exist in the network. Incidential lexical options fit into existing stress pattern networks.

This presentation of the phonology of the basic, monomorphemic, form of words in English goes very much further than previous attempts within Systemic Functional Grammar (Halliday 1961; Hudson 1974; Berry 1977; Butler 1985b; Tench 2014, 2017). The next chapter examines the phonological networks required for multi-morphemic words, with inflections, derivations and compounding.

Chapter 3

Phonology of Complex Words in English

In this chapter we extend our presentation of the phonology of English words from free, basic, monomorphemic words to a consideration of words with complex structures, i.e. with affixes and compound elements. Linguists in the SFL tradition have been preoccupied with the grammar of the clause and have not shown a great deal of interest in morphology; it barely gets a mention beyond an acknowledgement that morphemes exist as the very smallest unit in the grammatical hierarchy (see Halliday et al. 1964: 51; Berry 1975: 91; Young 1980: 13–14; Halliday 1985: 20; Thompson 1996: 20; Downing and Locke 2004: 10, 13; Halliday and Matthiessen 2004: 9; Fontaine 2013: 35). For this reason, we must seek support from elsewhere, from other traditions including psycholinguists such as Aitchison (2003). We will show how the principal features of Systemic Phonology apply to complex, polymorphemic words as well as simple, free forms.

Affixes, i.e. bound morphemes, provide specifications of details of a grammatical nature to the meanings of the words and stems that they are attached to. Likewise, compound elements provide a more specific focus of the meaning of the words and stems they are attached to.

Just as the primary function of phonology is to provide a (more or less) unique spoken form of all the units that make up a language's lexicogrammar, this applies to affixes and compound structures too. We noted that typically words in citation form are represented in phonology as feet, which display a prosodic shape and a structure of syllables, which themselves have a structure of phonemes. In the case of compound words in citation form, there are two elements, each represented by a foot, but one subordinate to the other as an 'extension'; however, in a small number of cases the second element is simply an unstressed syllable. In the case of affixes, the matching phonology is the syllable and phoneme.

We will deal with the bound morphemes of affixes first, where, traditionally, a division has been established between affixes that designate either inflections or derivations. Inflections indicate the addition of a grammatical category to a word that does not alter their word class designation, whereas derivations indicate a change of word class or an additional category of meaning. We consider inflections first, and then derivations, with a brief interlude on numerals that share some features of both. And then, finally, compounds.

3.1 Inflections

In English, there is only a fairly limited range of grammatical categories that are marked by an additional affix. These affixes themselves are bound, i.e. they cannot occur independently, and they are bound in final position only, i.e. they are exclusively suffixes. They consist either of single consonants or of unstressed syllables. As such, the phonology of English inflections is relatively simple. The phonology of derived forms is a good deal more complicated as we shall see, requiring extra systems for prefixing and for stress.

We will also look, briefly in passing, at the phonology of contractions, because in one conspicuous case, its rules follow exactly the rules of inflections. However, strictly speaking, contractions do not belong to word phonology, but to the phonology of groups and clauses; and in the case of contractions rhythm is the significant phonological factor, not the phonemic and prosodic factors of word phonology.

The grammatical categories involved in inflections are number and possessives in nouns, tense and participle markers in verbs, and comparative and superlative forms of adjectives and adverbs.

But before we can proceed with outlining this simple phonology, there is an important theoretical question to consider. This relates to the matter of irregular forms marking these categories. Whereas we can uncontroversially identify the phonological marking of number in the word *horses*, how do we do so in the word *oxen*? It is not as if all nouns ending in <x> /ks/ add /-ən/, since *fox* and *lynx* do not. The /-ən/ is added only to certain lexical items that exhibit a different form from that of 'regular' nouns.

Similarly, we can identify the phonological marking of past tense in the word *baked*, how do we cope with the form *made*? Again, it is not as if all verbs that rhyme with *make* change their final consonant to /d/, since *bake*, *take*, *shake*, *break*, etc., do not. And whereas *baked* keeps its form as past tense and past participle, *take* does neither. The vast majority of verbs follow the patterns of *bake*, but certain verbs exhibit quite different patterns; hence their designation as 'irregular verbs'.

Finally, we can identify the phonological marking of comparative and superlative forms in the adjective/adverb *faster* and *fastest*; but what about the adjective *good* and the adverb *well* with their common comparative form *better*, and superlative form *best*?

These irregular forms do not exhibit the regular phonological patterns that are found in the vast majority of nouns, verbs, adjectives and adverbs. They have to be treated separately as additional lexical forms that do not enter into the phonological network for inflections. From our personal experiences, we know that children have to acquire them separately and individually as they gain competence in their mother tongue; they are corrected from saying **buyed*, **sheeps*, **badder*, etc. Likewise, learners of the language make the same kind of mistakes and have to learn them as 'exceptions to the rule'. In this way, they are eventually stored in the mind of the child and of the learner as separate items and they learn that regular phonological rules do not apply to either the mono- or the polymorphemic form of such words. Irregular forms of words do not enter the phonological system as such, although a branch in the relevant network might refer to them. They have to be listed separately as belonging to the system of lexicogrammatical items.

Just as speakers learn to establish in their minds separate word forms for these irregular cases, they also have to recognize that certain single forms are 'polygrammatical', or 'grammatical synonyms'. For instance, the form *sheep* /ʃi:p/ is the form for both singular and plural number; similarly, *fish* /fɪʃ/, *deer* /dɪə/, *series* /ˈsɪəɹi:z/, etc. Also, there is group of monosyllabic verbs ending with /-t, -d/ that keep a single form for their base form, past tense and past participle, e.g. *cut*, *hit*, *hurt*, *let*, *put*, *set*, *shed*, *spread*, etc. There are also lexical forms that function as both adjective and adverb like *fast*, *hard* and *well*. All these 'grammatical synonyms' have also to be listed separately as belonging to the system of lexicogrammatical items.

Incidentally, the child's and learner's attempts at forming the morphemes of irregular words show that they have begun to acquire the phonological patterns. These patterns are therefore being established in their mental phonology alongside their mental lexicon and grammar. Aitchison (2003: 126–130) points out that there is sufficient evidence of a psycholinguistic nature that regular forms of inflections are stored as a kind of 'lexical tool-kit' separately from what she calls the 'mental lexicon proper', but irregular forms are stored alongside basic forms in the lexicon proper. The implication of the psycholinguistic evidence is that regular inflections are added by a speaker in the course of speech and are not stored as part of the mental lexicon.

We turn now to that phonological system of inflections in English.

3.1.1 Number

The category *singular* is the default form of free, basic, monomorphemic nouns. The phonological marker for *plural* in regular nouns has a 'full' suffix form as an unstressed syllable, /-əz/ (or /-ɪz/) and non-syllabic variations, voiced and voiceless, /-z/ and /-s/, syntagmatically maintaining the voicing feature of the final phoneme of the item that it is affixed to. The 'full' form is affixed to an item with a final sibilant; e.g. *buses* /ˈbʌsəz/, *lenses* /ˈlɛnzəz/, *dishes* /ˈdɪʃəz/, *mirages* /mɪˈɹɑːʒəz/, *crutches* /ˈkɹʌʧəz/, *bridges* /ˈbɹɪʤəz/. The form /-ɪz/ is a characteristic, generally speaking, of the older generations of speakers of SESP, whereas younger generations, again generally speaking, use /-əz/; this latter form is being taken here as the default token.

The non-syllabic forms maintain the voicing feature of the final (non-sibilant) phoneme: either voiced, e.g. *bees* /biːz/, *boys* /bɔɪz/, *ladders* /ˈladəz/, *robes* /ɹəʊbz/, *bells* /bɛlz/, etc.; or voiceless, e.g. *ropes* /ɹəʊps/, *rocks* /ɹɒks/, *cuffs* /kʌfs/, etc.

The system network needs to show first the selection between items that flout phonological norms (irregular instances) and those that conform; the latter requires the distinction between the forms of affixes attached to final sibilants and to final non-sibilants, which must also be distinguished by voice; the network can be presented as follows, with # marking the end of the basic form of a word:

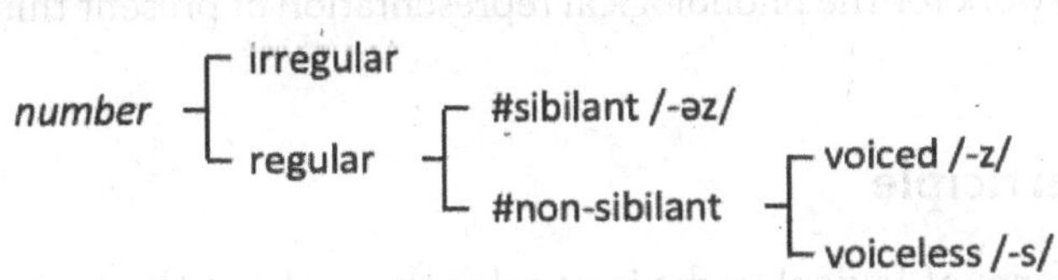

Figure 3.1 System network for the phonological representation of grammatical number

3.1.2 Possessives

The possessive (or 'genitive') morpheme is identical to that of the regular phonological marker of number. This is regular right throughout the lexicon, except perhaps for one notable exception: the traditional possessive form of *Jesus* is /ˈʤiːʒuz/, although a common modern variant is the regular /ˈʤiːzəsəz/, matching, by analogy, *James'* /ˈʤeɪmzəz/. However, there is another form, *Jesu*, a relic of a Latin vocative case; we could therefore rationalize the two forms and conclude that they conform to the regular pattern of possessives: /ˈʤiːzəs/ → /ˈʤiːzəsəz/, and /ˈʤiːʒu/ → /ˈʤiːʒuz/; in this way we can despatch this apparent anomaly.

Despite the difference in the orthographical position of apostrophes, the distinction between singular and plural is lost in the possessive; *boy's* and *boys'* are both /bɔɪz/. However, the number distinction is revealed in the case of irregular plural forms, e.g. *child's* and *children's*, except in the case of 'grammatical synonymy': *sheep's clothing* is ambiguous in pronunciation as it is in spelling.

The system network is simply:

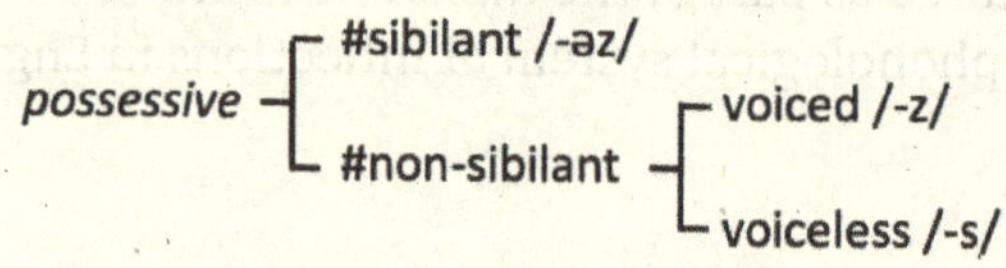

Figure 3.2 System network for the phonological representation of grammatical possession

3.1.3 Present Third Person Singular

The so-called *s*-form of lexical verbs is regular throughout the lexicon apart from the forms of *be*, *have* and *do*, as lexical verbs, and *say*. *Be* becomes *is* /ɪz/, *have* changes to *has* /haz/, *do* to *does* /dʌz/ and *say* to *says* /sɛz/. *Be*, *have* and *do* as 'operators' ('auxiliary' verbs) have weak forms that do actually conform to the regular pattern of the *s*-form phonology, but that, strictly speaking, belongs to the phonology of groups and clauses.

Modal verbs do not have the *s*-form; *needs* and *dares* act as lexical verbs.

Again, the system network for Present third person singular in lexical verbs is simply:

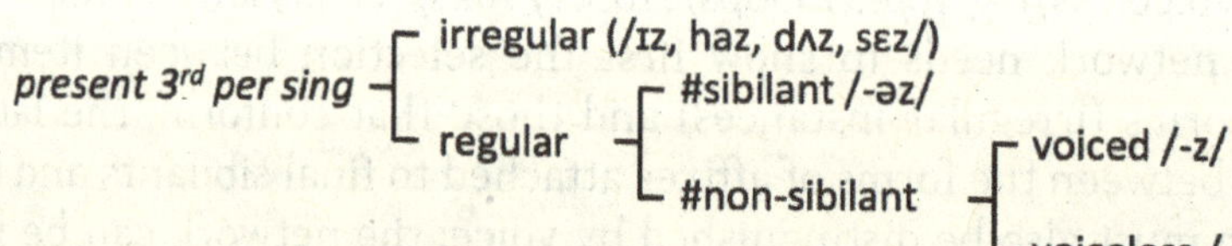

Figure 3.3 System network for the phonological representation of present third person singular in lexical verbs

3.1.4 Present Participle

The so called *ing*-form of lexical verbs is regular throughout the lexicon; there is therefore no phonological network of selections. Modal verbs do not have the *ing*-form; *willing* is the *ing*-form of the lexical verb *to will*, and, separately, an adjective.

3.1.5 Past Tense/Participle

The so called *ed*-form has both regular and irregular forms of lexical verbs. The irregular forms are very varied, including the 'grammatical synonymy' of many monosyllabic verbs ending in /-t, -d/, e.g. *cut, hit, hurt, let, put, set, shut, split, spread, shed.* As we noted above, irregular forms have to be learnt separately and individually to be established in the mental lexicon, and as such do not 'submit' to phonological marking.

The regular *ed*-form takes three forms: a 'full' suffix form as an unstressed syllable, /-əd/ or /-ɪd/ and non-syllabic variations, voiced and voiceless, /-d/ and /-t/, syntagmatically maintaining the voicing feature of the final phoneme of the item that it is affixed to. The 'full' form is affixed to an item with a final alveolar plosive, /t, d/: *hated* /ˈheɪtəd/, *aided* /ˈeɪdəd/. The /-ɪd/ form, like the /-ɪz/ form noted above, is more characteristic of older generations; we are taking /-əd/ as the default token.

The non-syllabic forms maintain the voicing feature of the final phoneme (other than an alveolar plosive): either voiced, e.g. *rowed* /ɹəʊd, raʊd/, *barred* /bɑ:d/, *shivered* /ˈʃɪvəd/, *robbed* /ɹɒbd/, *loved* /lʌvd/, *gained* /geɪnd/, etc.; or voiceless, e.g. *stopped* /stɒpt/, *baked* /beɪkt/, *laughed* /laft, lɑ:ft/.

The system network can be presented as

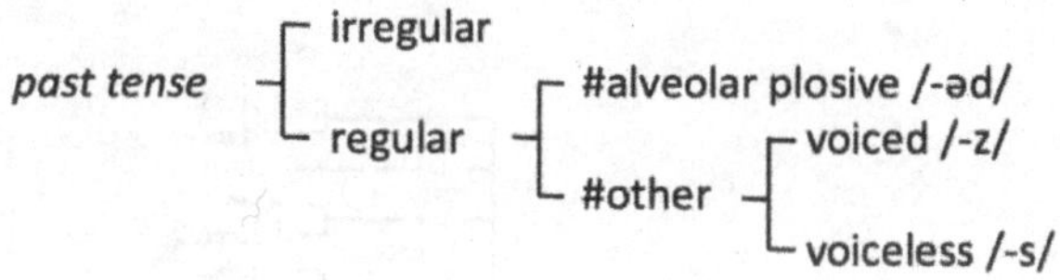

Figure 3.4 System network for the phonological representation of past tense/participle

3.1.6 Comparative and Superlative

There are two main indications of comparative and superlative forms in adjectives and adverbs: one is phrasal with the words *more* and *most*, the other is inflectional with suffixes of *-er* and *-est.* The inflectional options are mostly confined to single syllable adjectives and adverbs and some common disyllabic ones. The regular phonological markers are /-ə/ and /-əst/ (or /-ɪst/, which like /-ɪz/ and /-ɪd/ are the traditional forms preferred by the older generations). Examples include *faster, fastest, harder, hardest, smaller, smallest, tinier, tiniest, narrower, narrowest.*

There are a few irregular forms: *better, best, worse, worst, farther, farthest* (or *further, furthest*); *old* has both a regular pattern and an irregular one that is usually restricted to denoting relative age within families: *elder, eldest.* Most adverbs with the *-ly* derivational suffix take the phrasal pattern, e.g. *more quickly, most quickly.*[1]

The system network for the phonology of the inflectional suffix is fairly straightforward:

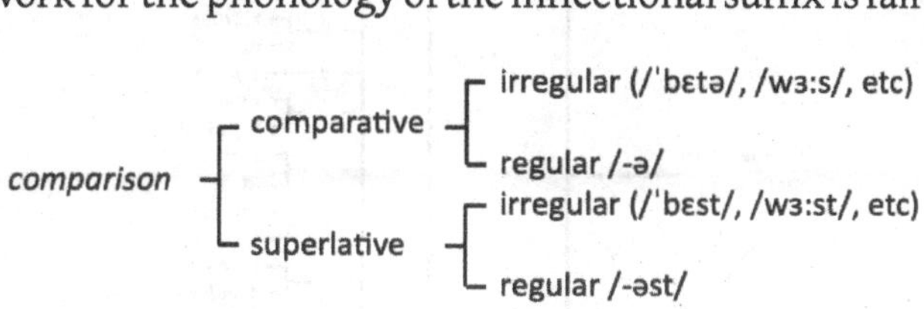

Figure 3.5 System network for the phonological representation of comparative and superlative

Putting all these systems together would produce a total system network of inflections in English.

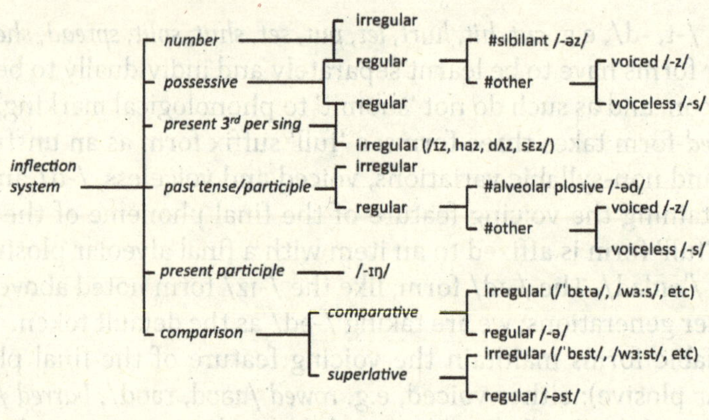

Figure 3.6 System network of inflections in English

The inflection system of single consonants adds to the complexity of word final clusters (**2.4.2**).

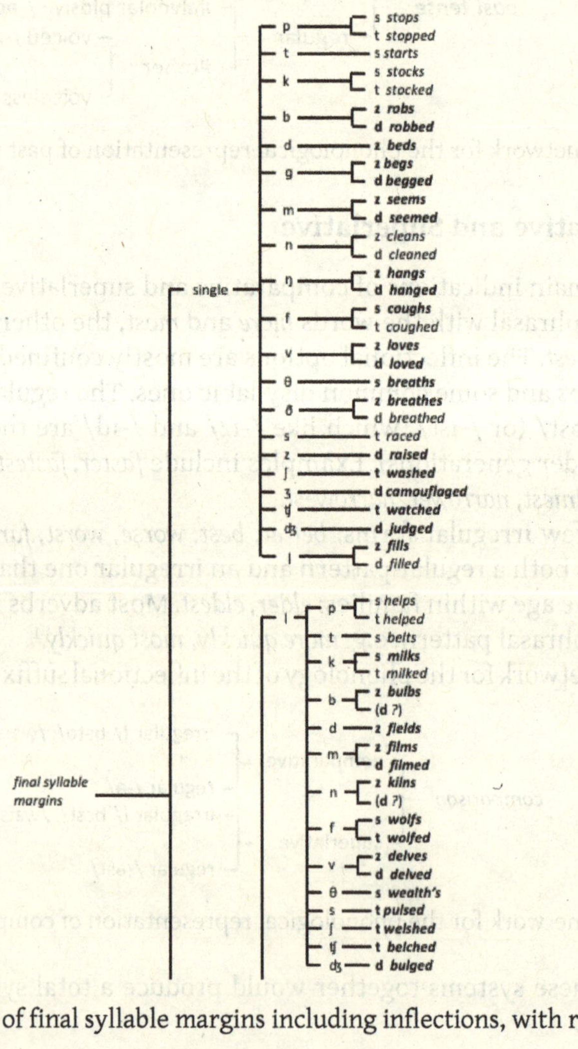

Figure 3.7 Explicit network of final syllable margins including inflections, with realizations; new margins marked in **bold**

3.2 Contractions

Contractions are not inflections, but they act as suffixes, like inflections. Contractions really belong to the phonology of groups and clauses, but as we know, the contractions involving *is* and *has* follow exactly the pattern of the present third person singular of lexical verbs. A short note at this point deals with other cases.

Operators/auxiliary verbs

Besides the forms for *is* and *has, am* is contracted to *-m* and is attached to *I; are* is contracted to *-re* /-ə/ and is attached to *we, you* and *they; have* is contracted to *-ve; had* to *-d.*

Modal verbs

Shall and *will* contract to *-ll*, either non-syllabic /l/ as in *I'll* (homophonous with *isle, aisle*), or as a syllable /-əl/ as in *it'll* /ɪt əl/, *Jan'll go* (rhyming with *channel*), etc. *Should* and *would* contract to *-d*, again as either (non-syllabic) /d/ as in *I'd* (homophonous with *ide*) or as a syllable /-əd/, as in it'd /ɪt əd/, *Jan would do it* /ˈdʒan əd ˈdu: ɪt/, etc.

Negative

The negative contraction *n't* is attached to operators ('auxiliary' verbs) and modal verbs either as a final margin /-nt/ or as an unstressed syllable /-n̩t/. In the case of the operators, the contraction is attached to a strong form: *aren't, isn't, wasn't, weren't; haven't, hasn't, hadn't; don't, doesn't, didn't.* With some modal verbs also, *n't* is attached to the strong forms of *could, should, would, might, must, ought* and *need* as /-n̩t/ and as /-nt/ with *dare.* This might then be called the regular pattern. An irregular pattern has a non-syllabic *n't* attached to a changed form of a modal verb: *can't* /kɑ:nt/, *shan't* /ʃɑ:nt/ and *won't* /wəʊnt/. The form *mayn't* is no longer common, nor is the form *usedn't; n't* in both cases has been replaced by the full form *not* /nɒt/ with either primary or secondary stress, or by the regular pattern in the case of *didn't use.*

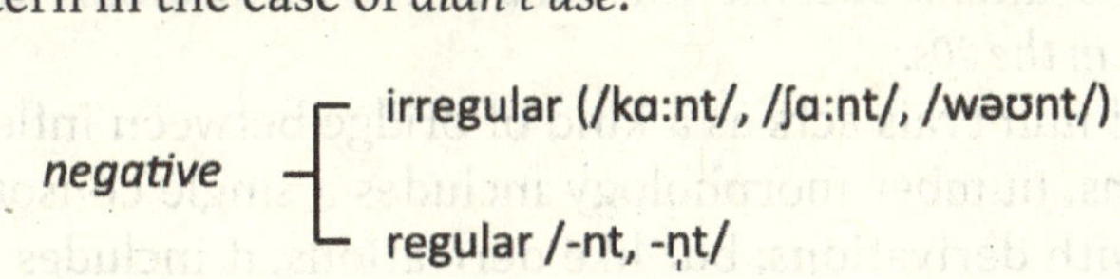

Figure 3.8 System network for reduced negative

3.3 Numerals

Before we turn to the vastly more complicated cases of derivation, we will consider English numerals separately because there is a difference in word class function between cardinals (*one, two, three, four ...*) and ordinals (*first, second, third, fourth ...*), which might suggest a case of derivation. However, the formation of the ordinals from the base form of the cardinals, mainly by the suffix *-th*, suggests a case of inflection. Ordinals function as pronouns and determiners: e.g. *he was fifth/he was the fifth person*; cardinals function as nouns as well as pronouns and determiners: e.g. *she had a ten on her shirt* (noun); *there are ten in her group* (pronoun); *there are ten girls in her group* (determiner).

Both cardinals and ordinals can take plural forms: *in ones and twos, two threes are six, at sixes and sevens, tens, hundreds*, etc.; *firsts, seconds, thirds, three fifths*, etc. This latter case is unique within English with two inflections in one word form.

If we take cardinal numbers as the base form, then the general rule is that the single consonant /-θ/ is suffixed for the ordinals, e.g. *fourth, hundredth, millionth*, etc. Examples include *six* /sɪks/, *sixes* /ˈsɪksəz, ˈsɪksɪz/, *sixth* /sɪksθ/, *sixths* /sɪksθs/; *thousands* /ˈθaʊzəndz/, *thousandths* /ˈθaʊzəndθs/. The ordinal *nth* is /ɛnθ/. However, there are irregular forms: *first, second, third, fifth* and *twelfth*; again, this underlines the sixth feature of Systemic Phonology, noted in **1.7**, that we disregard the notion of hypothetical underlying forms.

The phonological network for numerals can now be displayed, as follows, together with the plural option, that is identical to the number system above:

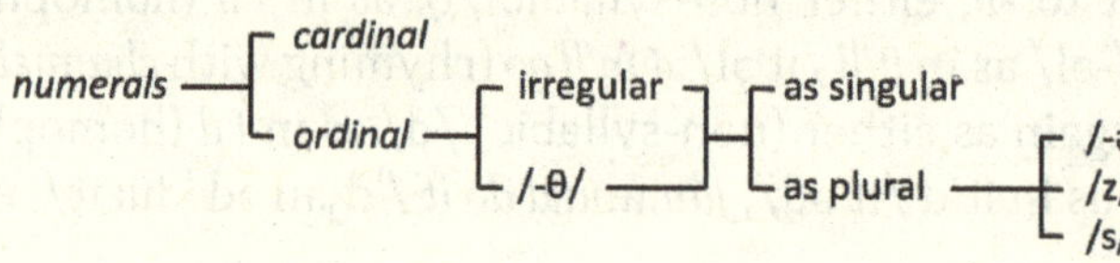

Figure 3.9 System network for numerals

Numerals also take *-teen* and *-ty* suffixes. The *-teen* suffix provides the forms of the 'teen' ordinals, 13 to 19, by being added to respective base forms, apart from *three* and *five* taking the forms /θɜ:-, fɪf-/. This suffix normally takes a secondary stress as in /ˈθɜ:ˌti:n/, although it is subject to stress shift in certain cases in groups – another instance of group phonology (see **1.7** under **Metrical Phonology**).

The *-ty* suffix provides the forms of the 'decile' ('ten') ordinals, 20, 30, etc. It is unstressed and is added to base forms, apart from *two, three* and *five*, which take the forms /twɛn-, θɜ:-, fɪf-/.

The *-teen* and *-ty* ordinals become the root forms for ordinals and plurals of both: *twentieth, twentieths, in the 20s.*

The phonology of numerals acts as a kind of bridge between inflections and derivations. Like inflections, number morphology includes a single consonant suffix, a form that rarely occurs with derivations; but like derivations, it includes stress as a feature, which is a significant feature throughout derivational morphophonology.

The inflection system of numerals adds further to the complexity of word final clusters: /-fθ, -fθs/ (*fifth, fifths*); /-ksθ, -ksθs/ (*sixth, sixths*); /-tθ, -tθs/ (*eighth, eighths*); /-lfθ, -lfθs/ (*twelfth, twelfths*); /-dθ, -dθs/ (*hundredth, hundredths*); and /-ndθ, -ndθs/ (*thousandth, thousandths*).

It will be simply a convenience at this point to refer to one case of derivational suffix, ahead of our main discussion. It concerns the suffix *-th* that turns a limited number of adjectives into nouns: *warmth, depth, width, breadth, length, strength*; and less transparent cases like *filth* (from *foul*), *health* (from *hale*), *wealth* (from *weal/well*) and, from a verb, *stealth* (from *steal* 'to pass unnoticed'). This suffix is no longer productive; no new words are formed with it. The convenience is simply that we can include the additional clusters /-mθ, -pθ, -ŋθ/ into one final consonant cluster network, without having to repeat it later. An observation on epenthesis is relevant at this point (see **2.7**), since a nasal followed by a voiceless fricative usually attracts an intervening transitional element; the transition involved in /-mθ/ is very likely to be expressed by epenthetic /-p-/; similarly, /-ŋθ/ with epenthetic /-k-/.

The inclusion of the morpheme /θ/ adds to the complexity of the syllable-final consonant cluster system; likewise, the inclusion of the non-productive *-st* suffix of *whilst, midst, amidst, amongst*, the residue of the inventory of final margins of the syllables of basic, monomorphemic words. English specifies 101 forms in all.

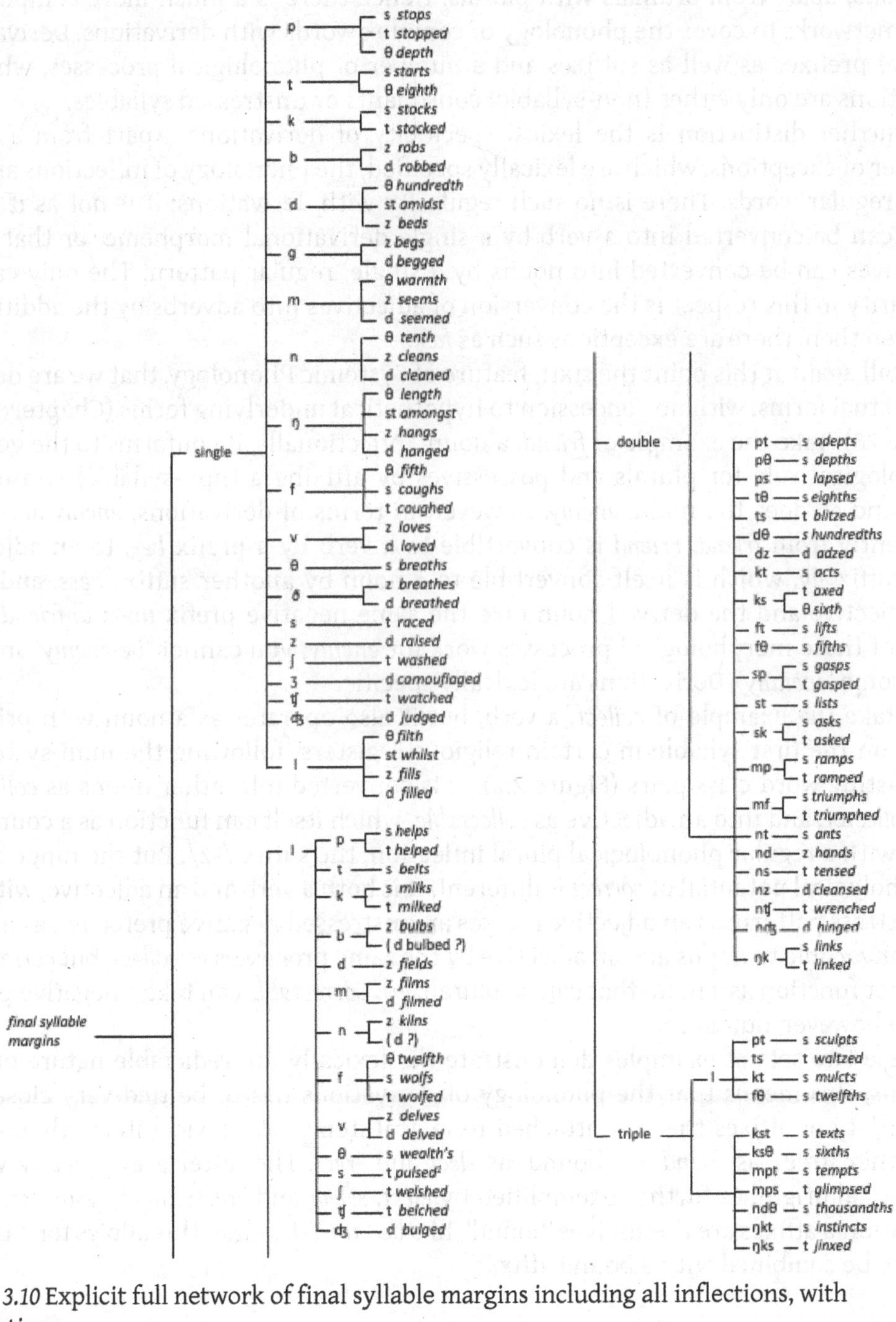

Figure 3.10 Explicit full network of final syllable margins including all inflections, with realizations

3.4 Derivations

There is a far greater number of affixes and phonological processes involved in derivations than there are in inflections. Derivations are used for changing word classes and for adding extra dimensions of meaning. Furthermore, a complex word might incorporate a number of derivational elements, whereas inflections are confined to single additions, apart from ordinals with plurals. Hence there is a much more complicated set of networks to cover the phonology of complex words with derivations. Derivations involve prefixes as well as suffixes and a number of phonological processes, whereas inflections are only either (non-syllabic) consonants or unstressed syllables.

A further distinction is the lexical specificity of derivations. Apart from a small number of exceptions, which are lexically specified, the phonology of inflections applies to all regular words. There is no such regularity with derivations; it is not as if every noun can be converted into a verb by a single derivational morpheme, or that most adjectives can be converted into nouns by a single, regular pattern. The only case of regularity in this respect is the conversion of adjectives into adverbs by the addition of *-ly*; even then, there are exceptions such as *fast.*

Recall again at this point the sixth feature of Systemic Phonology, that we are dealing with actual forms, with no concession to hypothetical underlying forms (Chapter 1, **1.7**, pp. 27–28). Take the example of *friend*, a noun. Inflectionally, it conforms to the general phonological rule for plurals and possessives by affixing a (non-syllabic) consonant, /-z/. And so does the noun, *enemy.* However, in terms of derivations, *enemy* acts very differently from *friend. Friend* is convertible to a verb by a prefix *be-*, to an adjective by a suffix *-ly*, which is itself convertible to a noun by another suffix *-ness*, and both the adjective and the derived noun take the same negative prefix *un-* : *unfriendliness.* None of these morphological processes work for *enemy*; you cannot '*be-enemy*' anyone, or become '*enemily*'. Derivations are lexically specific.

Or take the example of *collect*, a verb, but it also operates as a noun with primary stress on the first syllable in certain religious registers, following the mini-system of contrasting word class pairs (Figure 2.2). It is converted into other nouns as *collection* and *collector*, and into an adjective as *collectable*, which itself can function as a countable noun with a regular phonological plural inflection, the suffix /-z/. But the range of the morphological potential of *correct* is different. It is both a verb and an adjective, with the same stress pattern; as an adjective it takes an unstressed negative prefix, *in-*; as a verb, it is convertible to nouns and an adjective by the same processes as *collect*, but *correctable* does not function as a noun that can be pluralized. *Correctable* can take a negative prefix: not *in-* however, but *un-*.

These two sets of examples demonstrate the lexically unpredictable nature of derivations; this means that the phonology of derivations has to be tied very closely to the variety of affixes that get attached to lexical items. The lexical items themselves are either 'free', as *friend*, or 'bound' as *-lect* and *-rect*. The latter are typically words of classical origin, as further exemplified by *elect, select* and *erect, direct, resurrect*. Most derivational affixes are themselves 'bound', like *be-, un-, -ly, -ness*; this allows for a bound stem to be combined with a bound affix.

Another consideration that needs to be taken into account is that some derivational affixes operate with a variety of word classes. For example, *un-* operates not only with adjectives as in *uncorrectable*, but also with verbs as in *untie*, with nouns as in *unbelief*, and in adverbs as in *unwisely*; possibly also as in the prepositions *until* and *unto*, but these might simply be historical 'accidents'. Likewise, *in-* operates not only with a negative meaning in adjectives, but also with a 'locative' meaning in nouns, verbs and adverbs as in *income, input, inhale, inland, inside.*

Perhaps the most important factor is the functional potential of derivational affixes, either grammatical or lexical. Consider the prefixes *for-* and *fore-* as in *forbid, forgive, forgo, forsake* on the one hand and *forearm, forebode, forecast, forehead, foreleg, foretell, forewarn* on the other. It is possible to discern a meaning in the latter set such as 'ahead in time or place'; but no meaning is now discernible in the former.

Functional potential is often also referred to as being 'productive'. Consider the prefix *pro-* in three contexts: firstly, in noun-verb pairs, e.g. *produce*: /ˈprɒdju:s/ as a noun, and /prəˈdju:s/ as a verb (Chapter 2); secondly, a strong form option: /ˈprəʊ-/ as in *programme*, etc.; thirdly, a semantic function in words like *pro-active, pro-Africa*, etc., adding the sense of 'in favour of' and taking the form of a prefix with secondary stress: /ˌprəʊˈaktɪv/, /ˌprəʊˈafrɪkə/. This kind of 'semantic' or productive prefix is very similar to compound words like *far-seeing, blue-eyed*, etc., where each element contributes a separate semantic value; we will treat them further under *Compound Words* below. It should be noted that the *pro-* prefix in the other examples above, *produce* (as a noun), *produce* (as a verb) and *programme* has no consistency of function or meaning and can therefore simply be regarded as a relic from borrowing from another language, and now non-productive, or, as Aitchison (2003: 132) puts it, the prefix is simply 'glued to their stem' and is stored as a single lexical item.

It is worth noting certain other bound prefixes that have a similar semantic function as that of *pro-*. They are *a-* (/eɪ-/ 'no', 'without'), *ante-* ('in front'), *anti-* ('against'), *co-* ('together with'), *de-* ('away from'), *ex-* ('former'), *extra-* ('outside'), *inter-* ('between'), *intra-* ('within'), *non-* ('not'), *pre-* ('before'), *post-* ('after'), sub- ('below'), super-/supra- ('above'), *trans-* ('across') and *re-* ('again'). So, besides *pro-war*, we have *anti-war, pre-war, post-war, inter-war*; also *amoral, co-operate, de-ice, ex-marine, extramural, intramural, non-stop, transatlantic* and *re-cover.* This last item is to be distinguished from *recover* /ɹɪˈkʌvə/, as it has the meaning to 'cover again/anew': /ˌɹi:ˈkʌvə/. *In-* has two meanings, as noted already, indicating either a location, *in*^{1}-, or a negative, *in*^{2}-; the first works like these 'semantic' prefixes, e.g. *in-house, inland* with secondary stress, while the latter is normally unstressed, e.g. *inactive, incorrect.*

Another relevant feature to consider is the phonological forms themselves of derivational affixes. They occasionally appear as non-syllabic consonants, as we have already seen in the previous section, as /-θ/ in *warmth*; but also as /-t/ in *weight*; and as fricative voicing in a series of words like *grief/grieve* and *use/use*, /ju:s, ju:z/. More commonly, they appear as syllables with different degrees of stress. Primary stresses typically occur, for example, with certain suffixes like *-ette* and *-ese*, as in *kitchenette* and *Chinese.* Secondary stresses occur with both prefixes and suffixes, e.g. *trans-, mal-, -ize/-ise*: as in /ˌtɹansˈleɪt/, /ˌmalˈfɔ:md/, /ˈɹɪəˌlaɪz/. Some unstressed suffixes like *-ic, -ical, -ics* generally impose primary stress on the preceding syllable, e.g. *electric, electrical, electrics*;

others impose primary stress on the preceding syllable but one, like *-fy*, e.g. *electrify, liquefy.* Yet others, like *-al*, impose primary stress on a preceding syllable if it contains a strong vowel, e.g. *trial, refusal*, but if the preceding syllable contains a weak vowel, primary stress is imposed on the syllable preceding that one: *burial, cereal, serial.* So while some suffixes are stress-imposing, others are not.

To sum up, derivations are lexically specific, involve both prefixes and suffixes, constitute both free and bound morphemes, are attached to both free and bound forms, are to be distinguished from lookalike compound semantic items and take a variety of phonological forms at the rank of syllable. It seems best to cover this complexity by presenting two networks to cover prefixes and suffixes respectively; then indicate phonological forms in each network; and finally, list the affixes, both free and bound, according to those phonological forms, without particular reference to grammatical or semantic functions.

3.4.1 Derivational Prefixes

Derivational prefixes are either unstressed syllables or syllables that take secondary or primary stress. Derivational prefixes can therefore be classified as two groups, as follows.

Group 1: Unstressed derivational prefixes
a- /ə-/ changes words from one class to either adjectives or adverbs: *ablaze, aglow, alive, along, awake, away*, etc.
be- /bɪ-/ changes nouns into verbs, but historically also produced conjunctions and adverbs: *befriend, behave, bequeath; because, before; behind, below, beneath*, etc.
with- /wɪð-/ added the notion of 'against': *withdraw, withhold, withstand*
and also *in²-* (and its allomorphs, *im-, il-, ir-*) adds the notion of negative: *inactive, incorrect; impossible, imperfect; illicit, illogical; irrational, irregular*, etc.

In addition, the prefix *en¹-* that contains a sense of 'in' and that belongs to the prefixes that are variable according to word class (see Chapter 2) must be distinguished from *en²-* that converts adjectives and nouns into verbs and remains unstressed. Both forms have allomorphs with /m, ŋ/:

en²- /ɛn-, ɪn-/ *enlarge, enrich, embody, empower, encourage, engross.*

These prefixes are largely unproductive in modern English.

Group 2: Prefixes that take secondary stress
This is a larger group consisting of three types: those that consist of locative adverbs of Anglo-Saxon origin; those that consist of locative elements of a classical origin; and those that express a negative element. As nouns, they tend to take a foot structure with initial primary stress:

s . w ; s . w . w ; etc.

as verbs and adverbs, they take a late stress:

w . s ; s² . s ; etc.

In this respect they follow the foot pattern of contrasting word class pairs as we saw in Figure 2.2, and as we shall see later in this chapter the foot patterns of compound words. It is not easy to distinguish these prefixed words from true compounds, but the main clue is that these prefixes do not consist of lexical items.

The first sub-group with locative adverbs of Anglo-Saxon origin are illustrated as follows:

back- s . s^2 *backlog, backup*
s^2 . s *backdate, backfire;* s^2 . s . w *backpedal*

Prefixed words like these should be distinguished from true compounds like *backache, backbone*, where *back-* is a lexical item.

fore- s . s^2 *forearm, forethought*
s^2 . s *foresee, foretell*

Other illustrations could be cited with *cross-, down-, off-, over-, out-, under-, up-.*

The second sub-group with locatives of a classical origin act slightly differently from those with an Anglo-Saxon origin as they do not all cross word classes; they can be illustrated as follows:

co- ('together with') s . s^2 *Co-op;* s . s^2 . w *co-pilot, co-worker*
s^2 . s *co-opt;* s^2 . s . w. s^2 *co-operate*
de- ('away from') s^2 . s *de-ice, demist*
extra- ('outside') s . w . s^2 *extravert, extradite*
s^2 . w . s *extrapose;* s^2 . w . s . w *extramural*

Extraordinary used to have, presumably, a foot structure of s^2 . w . s . w . w ; the collapse of the unstressed syllable before the primary stress illustrates the rapid articulation of syllables before the nucleus of the foot (see **1.3**).

Other illustrations could be cited with *ante-, anti-, ex-, in*[1]*-, inter-, intra-, post-, pre-, pro-, re-, trans-*. Special note might be made of a number of contrasting word class pairs with re-: *rebound, rebuild, recall, recount, refill, refit, refund, rehash, remake, replay, reprint, rerun, retake, retread, rewrite; research* seems to be following by analogy.

The third sub-group indicating a negative meaning can be illustrated as follows:

a-/eɪ-/ s . w . w *atheist*
s^2 . s . w *amoral*
mal- s . w . s^2 *malcontent*
s^2 . s *maltreat, malformed;* s^2 . s . w *malfunction,*
mis- s . s^2 *miscount, misfit, mismatch* (nouns)
s^2 . s *miscount, mismatch, mislay, mislead, misspell, mistake* (verbs); etc.
non- s . w *nonsense*
s^2 . s *nondrip, nonplus, non-stick, nonstop, non-U*
s^2 . s . w *non-smoker, nonfiction, non-profit, nonstarter;* etc.
un- s^2 . s *undo, unearth, unmute, untrue, unzip*
s^2 . s . w *uncommon, undaunted, unfasten, unwitting, unwritten,* etc.;
s^2 . w . s *unbelief, unconcern, uninspired,* etc.

The network of phonological systems for derivational prefixes takes this form:

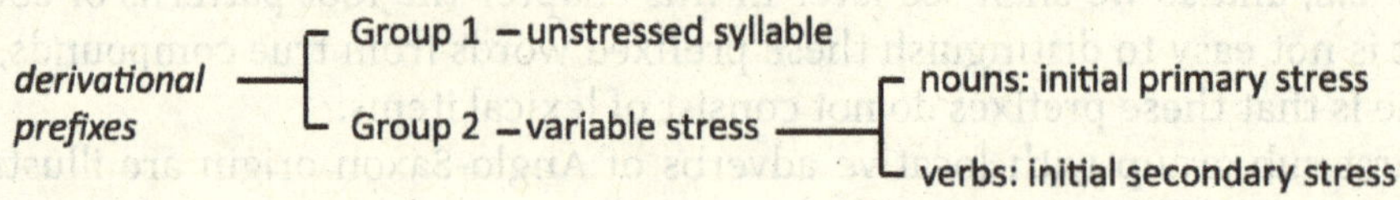

Figure 3.11 Foot system network of derivational prefixes

3.4.2 Derivational Suffixes

Derivational suffixes also have a range of phonological forms, which include non-syllabic and syllabic consonants, unstressed syllables that may either impose a stress placement in the root they are attached to, or not, and secondary and primary stresses. Derivational suffixes can therefore be grouped together on phonological grounds as follows.

Group 1: Non-syllabic consonants.
These have been dealt with already; they include
-th /-θ/ *warmth, depth, fourth, tenth*
-t /-t/ *weight, height* (possibly also historical cases like *see* → *sight*)
and voicing of final voiceless fricatives
/-v, -ð, -z/ *grieve, teethe, use* (verb: /ju:z/)

Group 2: Unstressed suffixes that do not impose a stress placement.
Suffixes that are unstressed syllables that do not impose a stress placement on the free form that they are attached to. They fulfil a number of functions. They change

i) nouns into adjectives:
-ful /-fəl/ *useful, hopeful*
-ish /-ɪʃ/ *foolish, selfish*
-less /-lɪs, -ləs/ *hopeless, useless*
-ly /-li/ *manly, earthly, daily, lovely*
-some /-səm/ *handsome, quarrelsome*
-y /-i/ *hasty, weighty*

ii) nouns into other nouns:
-dom /-dəm/ *kingdom, officialdom*
-ful /-fʊl/ *spoonful, eyeful, cupful*
-hood /-hʊd/ *childhood, manhood*
-let /-lət, -lɪt/ *piglet, booklet, hamlet, singlet, cutlet*
-ling /-lɪŋ/ *duckling, gosling, hireling, inkling, dumpling*
-ship /-ʃɪp/ *friendship, worship, companionship*
-ster /-stə/ *hipster, prankster, gangster, youngster*

iii) verbs into nouns:
-age /-ɪdʒ/ *stoppage, wreckage, wastage, marriage* (NB: also *percentage*)
-er -or /-ə/ *driver, winner, actor, advisor*
-ing /-ɪŋ/ *banking, camping, feelings, earnings*
-ment /-mənt/ *government, movement*
-y /-i/ *delivery, battery* ('assault')

iv) adjectives into nouns:
-ness /-nɪs, -nəs/ *happiness, sadness*
-ty /-ti/ *loyalty, honesty*
(also /-θ/, as we have already seen, as in *warmth, depth*, etc.)

v) adjectives into verbs:
-en /-ən, -n̩/ *quicken, deepen*; and with /-n̩/, *sweeten, soften*

vi) adjectives in adverbs by a regular pattern:
-ly /-li/ *happily, sadly* (NB: *absolutely* as an intensifier is often stressed as: /ˌabsəˈluːtli/)

vii) simple numerals to decile ordinals, as we have already noted:
-ty /-ti/ *forty, ninety*
Group 2 suffixes also include *-ism* and *-ist* that are attached to either free or bound forms ('stems').
-ism /-ɪzəm/ (free) *socialism, alcoholism, Buddhism* (NB different stress pattern of *Catholicism*)
(bound) *deism, communism*
-ist /-ɪst/ (free) *socialist, Buddhist, rapist*
(bound) *Trappist, oculist, therapist*

The forms *seeing (that)* and *providing (that)* are not treated as verb + derivation, but rather as verb + inflection functioning as subordinating conjunctions, in similar fashion to *given (that)* and *provided (that)*; likewise, *according (to)* as a preposition.

Group 3: Unstressed suffixes that do not impose stress placement on free forms, but do so on bound forms.

Certain unstressed suffixes impose a stress placement on the bound root they are attached to, but do not do so on free forms, in which case the stress pattern of the free form is retained. For instance, the suffix, *-able* occurs with free forms like *rely, value, distinguish, interpret* without requiring a change of stress placement, while with bound forms like *prob-, aff-, ami-*, it imposes stress placement. This difference becomes very noticeable with a modern tendency to 'regularize' the stress pattern of certain free forms like *admire, compare, lament.*

-able /-əbəl/ (free forms) *reliable, valuable, distinguishable, interpretable*
(modern tendency) *admirable, comparable, lamentable*
(bound forms) *probable, affable, amiable, delectable*
(traditional) *admirable* /'admɪrəbəl/, *comparable* /'kɒmprəbəl/, *lamentable* /'laməntəbəl/
-ible /-ɪbəl/ (free forms) *convertible, discernible*
(bound forms) *possible, visible, gullible*
-uble /-jʊbəl/ (bound forms) *soluble, voluble*

Group 4: Unstressed suffixes that regularly impose stress placement on preceding syllable. These suffixes regularly impose primary stress placement on both free and bound forms on the immediately preceding syllable. This is illustrated in the following case:
-ic, -ical, -ics /-ɪk, -ɪkəl, -ɪks/ *electric, electrical, electrics; comic, comical; acidic, chronic, athletic*

However, in the case of certain lexically specified items, primary stress is placed on the preceding syllable but one, with the suffixes *-ic* and *-ics*:

Arabic, arithmetic, arsenic, Catholic, choleric, heretic, lunatic, politics, rhetoric

but with the suffix *-ical*, the regular pattern is maintained

arithmetical, heretical, political, rhetorical

Other suffixes that regularly impose primary stress on the immediately preceding syllable are

-icle /-ɪkəl/ *chronicle, particle, testicle*
-ish /-ɪʃ/ *abolish, admonish, astonish, distinguish, finish, impoverish* /ɪm'pɒvrɪʃ/
-ity /-ɪti/ *ability, electricity, laity, enmity*
-ety /-əti/ *society, variety, sobriety*
-tion, -ssion, -xion /-ʃən/ *nation, completion, condition, notion, solution, mission, crucifixion*
-sion /-ʒən/ *vision, fusion, invasion*
-gion /-dʒən/ *region, religion, contagion*

Group 5: Unstressed suffixes that impose primary stress on the nearest preceding strong syllable.
These suffixes impose primary stress on the nearest preceding strong vowel, which may either immediately precede the suffix as in *appraisal* /ə'preɪzəl/, or precede it with an intervening weak vowel as in *annual* /'anjuəl/. The stems may be either free or bound. In the following list, examples are given with a strong vowel immediately preceding and with a weak vowel immediately preceding. Examples with * allow alternative pronunciations.

-al /-əl/ (strong) *appraisal, denial, trial, universal, torrential,*
(weak) *annual, burial, cereal, individual, architectural*
-an /-ən/ (strong) *ocean, urban, Sri Lankan, European*
(weak) *Indian, American, comedian, guardian, gargantuan*

Likewise with following suffixes: *-ant, -ance, -ancy* /-ənt, -əns, -ənsi/; *-ar* /-ə/; *-ary* /-(ə)ri/; *-ative* /-ətɪv/; *-ature* /-əl/; *-ent, -ence, -ency* /- ənt, -əns, -ənsi/; *-ery* /-(ə)ɹi/; *-i* /-i/; *-id* /-ɪd/; *-ine* /-ɪn/; *-is* /-ɪs/; *-ive* /-ɪv/; *-on* /-ən/; *-or* /-ə/; *-ory* /-(ə)ɹi/; *-our* /-ə/; *-ous* /-əs/; *-ry* /-ri/; *-um/us* /-əm, -əs/; *-ure* /-ə/ (but *architecture* has an intervening secondary stress: /'ɑːkɪˌtɛktʃə/).

Group 6: Suffixes with secondary stress that impose primary stress on the nearest preceding strong syllable. In this list also, examples are given with a strong vowel immediately preceding and with a weak vowel immediately preceding.

-ide /-ˌaɪd/ (strong) *monoxide, sulphide*
(weak) *fluoride, thalidomide*
-ile /-ˌaɪl/ (strong) *exile, hostile, mobile, prehensile, projectile*
(weak) *crocodile, domicile, infantile, mercantile, versatile*
(It should be noted that General American treats this suffix as /-l̩/: e.g. /'hɒstl̩/, etc.)
-ine /-ˌaɪn, -ˌiːn/ (strong) *morphine, internecine*
(weak) *alkaline, crystalline*

-oid /-ˌɔɪd/ (strong) *thyroid, vocoid, cylindroid*
(weak) *adenoid, alkaloid, hominoid, polaroid*

-on /-ˌɒn/ (strong) *proton, electron, neon, nylon*
(American pronunciation of *Pentagon* follows the weak pattern: /ˈpɛntəˌgɑn/

Group 7: Suffixes with primary stress in disyllables, but secondary stress in polysyllables. A number of suffixes take primary stress in disyllabic words but secondary stress in polysyllabic words.

-age /-ˈɑːʒ/ (disyllabic) *mirage, barrage*
/-ˌɑːʒ/ (polysyllabic) *camouflage, entourage, espionage*
(NB: *collage, montage* are now often pronounced as /ˈkɒlˌɑːʒ; ˈmɒntˌɑːʒ/ and SESP *garage* is variously pronounced with permutations of stress placement, vowel strength and consonant choice, e.g. /ˈgaˌɹɑːʒ; gəˈɹɑːʒ; ˈgaˌɹɑːdʒ; ˈgaɹɪdʒ/, etc.)

-fy /-ˈfaɪ/ (disyllabic) *defy*
/-ˌfaɪ/ (polysyllabic) *electrify, liquefy, rectify, satisfy*

-ise, -ize /-aɪz/ (disyllabic) *advise, baptize, capsize, chastise*
(polysyllabic) *advertise, circumcise, realize, exercise, recognize, westernize*

-ite /-ˈaɪt/ (disyllabic verbs) *excite, incite, recite, unite, ignite* (also *indict* /ɪnˈdaɪt/)
/-ˌaɪt/ (disyllabic nouns and adjectives) *graphite, nitrite, contrite, finite, Hittite*
(polysyllabic) *anthracite, expedite, parasite, stalactite*

-ose /-ˈəʊs/ (disyllabic) *verbose, morose, jocose* (but not: *glucose* /ˈgluːˌkəʊs, -z/)
/-ˌəʊs, -z/ (polysyllabic) *bellicose, cellulose, comatose, diagnose, metamorphose*

-ute /-ˈjuːt/ (disyllabic) *refute, salute, dilute, pollute, acute*
/-juːt/ (disyllabic nouns) *statute, tribute*
(polysyllabic) *absolute, resolute, execute, attribute, contribute, distribute*

A notable variation within Group 7 is the suffix *-ate*, which in SESP performs with the above patterns but has an additional unstressed form for a number of nouns and adjectives.

-ate /-ˈeɪt/ (disyllabic) *donate, abate, create, migrate* (But General American treats these verbs as Group 6.)

-ate /-ˌeɪt/ (polysyllabic) *candidate, magistrate* (but also disyllabic: *cognate, magnate, primate, innate, irate*)

Contrasting noun/verb pairs with *-ate* like *dictate, mandate* follow the relevant foot mini-system (Chapter 2). Something similar happens with another set of word class pairs, but not at foot rank, but at syllable rank; *associate* as a verb takes secondary stress in the final syllable: /əˈsəʊsiˌeit/, but as a noun or adjective has an unstressed syllable: /əˈsəʊsiət/. Other such examples include *delegate, separate, alternate, consummate*, etc. A mini-system can be established with the function of discriminating between verb/non-verb pairs with final *-ate*.

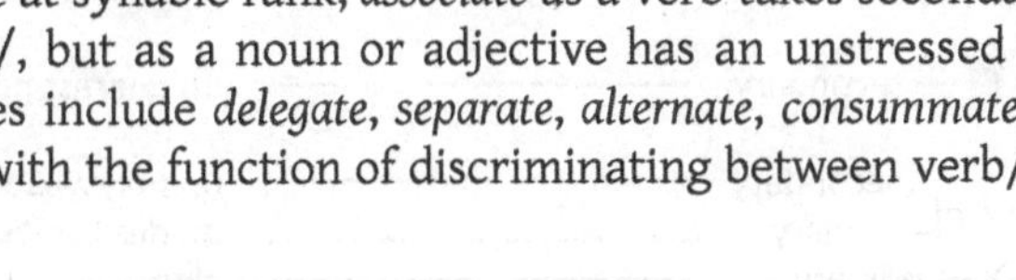

Figure 3.12 Mini-system network for syllables in contrasting word class pairs

(Words such as *climate*, *pomegranate* happen to have a final unstressed syllable /-ət/ spelled *-ate*, but are not suffixes.)

Group 8: Suffixes with primary stress
Suffixes with primary stress are attached to both free and bound forms, and it is noticeable that a good number of them originate from French, which normally places primary stress on final syllables with a strong vowel.

-ade /-ˈeɪd/ *blockade, lemonade, masquerade* (but not: *accolade, marmalade*)
-ade /-ˈɑːd/ *roulade, promenade*
-aire /-ˈɛə/ *millionaire, questionnaire, doctrinaire, solitaire*
-aise /-ˈeɪz/ *liaise, malaise, mayonnaise*

Likewise the following suffixes: *-ee* /-ˈiː/; *-eer* /-ˈɪə/; *-esce* /-ˈɛs/; *-ese* /-ˈiːz/; *-esque* /-ˈɛsk/; *-ess* /-ˈɛs/ (but not *actress, waitress*); *-esse* /-ˈɛs/; *-et* /-ˈɛt/; *-ette* /-ˈɛt/ (but not *etiquette*); *-eur* /-ˈɜː/ (but not *grandeur*); *-ier* /-ˈɪə/; *-ine* /-ˈiːn/ (but not *vaccine*); *-ique* /-ˈiːk/; *-ise* /-ˈiːz/; *-oon* /-ˈuːn/; *-stan* /-ˈstan, -ˈstɑːn/ *-teen* /-ˈtiːn/.

It is also noticeable that many words with final *-een* /-ˈiːn/ and *-oo* /-ˈuː/ follow the pattern of *-ee* /-ˈiː/ and *-oon* /-ˈuːn/ above, even though they are not actually identified as suffixes:

canteen, smithereens
bamboo, kangaroo, shampoo, taboo, hullabaloo (also: *canoe, lasso*)
(but not: *cuckoo, igloo*)

The system network for derivational suffixes identifies the 8 groups: Group 1 takes non-syllabic consonants only; Groups 2 to 5 take unstressed syllables only, but Groups 3 to 5 have a selection option between imposing stress on words/stems, or not; Group 6 takes secondary stress and imposes primary stress on nearest preceding strong syllable; Group 7 takes primary stress on disyllables, but secondary stress on polysyllables, but with one deviation that distinguishes polysyllabic verbs from nouns and adjectives; and Group 8 only takes primary syllables.

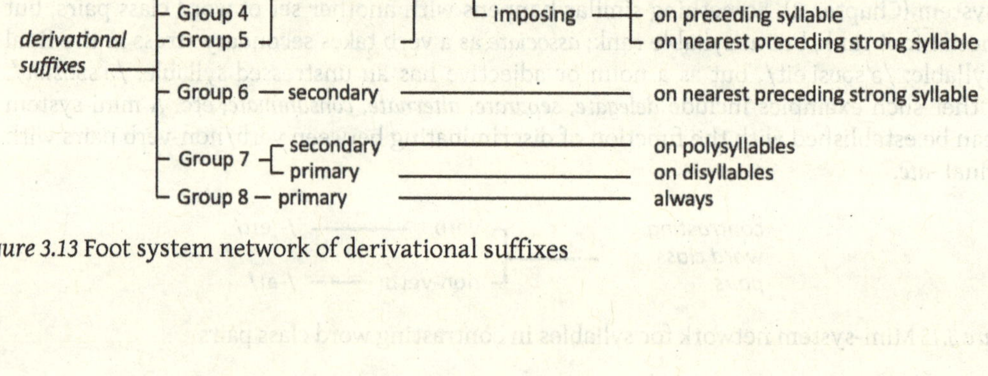

Figure 3.13 Foot system network of derivational suffixes

3.5 Compound Words

A compound word is a word constructed from two lexicogrammatical forms constituting a single lexical item. We distinguished compound words from prefixed words on the grounds that the prefixes exhibited grammatical meaning.

The nominal group *a black bird* contains two separate lexical items, whereas *blackbird* is a single lexical item, namely a particular species of bird. The item *black* in the group is subject to the inflections *-er* and *-est*: *a blacker/blackest bird*; furthermore, it can be separated from *bird* by an intervening word: *a black little bird*. In addition, each lexical item retains its own primary stress, in separate feet. None of these features apply to a compound; nothing can intervene between the two parts – it is single lexical item, with a single primary stress. The compound element with the primary stress can be said to constitute the main foot; the other compound element is either a subordinate foot with a secondary stress, or an 'extension' of the main foot if it is unstressed. This arrangement will be illustrated in the presentations below.

It should also be noted, however, that there is no single, consistent, orthographical representation of compounding in English; they are spelled either as a single word as *blackbird*, or as two words as *black spot*, or as hyphenated as *black-tie*.

Compound words comprise nouns, verbs, adjectives and adverbs, but nouns are by far the most common class. From a structural perspective, there are three types of compounds: a combination of two free forms, a combination of a bound form with a free form, and a combination of two bound forms. We will look at the phonological characteristics of the three in turn (see also Gimson 2014: 248–252; Sanchez-Stockhammer 2018: 145–153).

3.5.1 Compounds of Two Free Forms

There are three different stress patterns: primary + secondary (main + subordinate foot); primary + unstressed (one single foot); and secondary + primary (subordinate + main foot). This latter is often difficult to distinguish from a sequence of two primary stresses in running speech, but it is possible to do so in citation form, which is what we are dealing with in the present context. We can illustrate all three patterns with compounds with *back-* as their first element, but excluding where it acts as a prefix and signifies movement of some kind. The vast majority belong to the primary + secondary pattern, and indeed the vast majority of them are nouns (data is taken from the *Longman Pronunciation Dictionary*; Wells 1990):

backache
backblocks
backboard
backbone
backbreaking
backcloth

and about another 30 nouns.

There are two instances of the primary + unstressed pattern, namely the adjective and adverb:

backward
backwards

and there are a number of cases of the secondary + primary pattern for adjectives and adverbs:

backhanded
backlit
backstage
backstairs

It should be noted that a compound with the structure of secondary + primary stress is subject to stress shift if the compound is followed immediately by another stress in running speech. So, for instance a *back-handed compliment* becomes /ə ˈbakˌhandəd ˈkɒmplɪmənt/ and *backstage workers* becomes /ˈbakˌsteɪdʒ ˈwɜːkəz/, etc. This is another instance of a feature of group phonology.

In addition, a compound noun might become a single element in a further compound, e.g. *backroom boys* /ˈbakˌɹuːm ˌbɔɪz/, *background information* /ˈbakˌɡɹaʊnd ɪnfəˌmeɪʃən/, etc.

Primary + secondary pattern

This is by far the commonest type. It is claimed that 90% of compounds are nouns and that 75% of them take this form; they are simply too numerous to list, from *action man* to *zoo-keeper*.

Adjectives that indicate a quality in respect of something take this pattern; e.g.

in respect of air, tight: *airtight*;
in respect of love, sick: *lovesick*;
in respect of children, like: *childlike*;

and words with *-fold*: *twofold*, i.e. two in respect of number of parts, *threefold*, *manifold*, etc.

Other examples: *bloodthirsty*, *carefree*, *headstrong*, *seasick*, *seaworthy*, *trustworthy*, *waterproof*, *workshy*. Also, adjectives that comprise a 'passive' participle with an agent, e.g. pecked by a 'hen': *hen-pecked*; other examples include *moth-eaten*, *snowbound*, *time-honoured*, *weather-beaten* and also *bedridden*.

Certain compound verbs follow this pattern from corresponding compound nouns, e.g. *blackmail*, *floodlight*, *jack-knife*, *muckrake*, *sidestep*, *steamroller*. Others with no corresponding noun: *babysit*, *browbeat*, *headhunt*, *ring-fence*. These seem to be exceptions to the expectation that compound verbs would follow the example of contrasting word class pairs (Figure 2.2) and verbs with prefixes with secondary stress (**3.4.1**).

A few compound adverbs take this pattern: *clockwise*, *French-style*, *piecemeal*. And compound pronouns with *any-*, *every-*, *no-*, *some-* attached to *-body*, *-one*, *-thing*, *-where*.

Primary + unstressed pattern

There are a few second elements that normally take no stress like *backward/s* above. Examples include *-land*, e.g. *England, Ireland, Scotland*, etc.; *-man/-men*, e.g. *gentleman/-men, Welshman/-men, postman/-men*, etc.; *-mas*, e.g. *Christmas, Michaelmas*. Also *-lace* in *necklace.*

Secondary + primary pattern

There are sets of compound nouns that take this pattern. For instance, one set that indicates a value, e.g. *pound coin*. Commonly recognized sets include indications of

value	*pound coin, dollar bill, ton weight, three wheeler*
material	*cotton shirt, rubber duck, paper bag, iron rod*
ingredient	*orange squash, apple pie, ham sandwich* (except with *cake, juice, water*: *ˈfruit cake, ˈorange juice, ˈbarley water*)
status	*prince regent, major general, queen bee, master mariner, town council, vice president, local government, fellow-feeling, self-service, great grandmother*
name	*Julius Caesar, Buckingham Palace, North Island, Trafalgar Square, Oxford Circus, Oxford Road* (but: *ˈOxford Street, ˈLowgates*)

Compound adjectives that take this pattern include those that indicate the extent of a quality, e.g. not just *cold*, but cold as stone: *stone cold*; those that are formed with a present participle, e.g. *fast-moving*; and those that are formed with a quasi past participle, like *black-eyed.*

Here are some more examples of the first kind:

bloodred, skyblue, knee high, knee deep, dirt cheap

and of the second kind:

easy-going, far-seeing, free-thinking, good-looking, two-timing, English-speaking

and of the third:

absent-minded, broad-shouldered, nicely-spoken, tender-hearted, two-faced, well known

Compound adverbs with this pattern include the following, as well as *backstage*:

downstream, indoors, offhand, outside, overseas, head on, head first, halfway, upside down.

3.5.2 Compounds of a Bound Form Before a Free Form

Nouns usually take the sequence primary + secondary stress (main + subordinate foot), e.g. the bound form *amphi-* has primary stress before the secondary stress of *theatre.* There are plenty of examples of this pattern. Adjectives and adverbs, on the other hand, fall into line with the requirements of suffixes. Here are a few examples:

amphi- *amphitheatre*
ante- *antechamber* *anteroom*
anti- *antibody* *antifreeze* (but: *anti-climax, anticyclone*; *antinuclear* follows the pattern of the *-ar* suffix; *anticlockwise* is an adverb).
auto- *automobile* *autopilot* (but *automatic* follows the pattern of the -ic suffix).

Other examples of bound first elements include: *bi-*, *bio-*, *demi-*, *di-*, *dia-*, *epi-*, *equi-* (but: *e'quivocal*), *hetero-*, *homo-*, *hydro-*, *hyper-*, *infra-*, *macro-*, *meta-*, *micro-*, *milli-*, *multi-*, *nano-*, *neo-*, *omni-*, *para-*, *pseudo-*, *psycho-*, *quadr-*, *quasi-*, *retro-*, *semi-*, *tele-* (NB: both *'teleˌvision* and *ˌtele'vision*), *tri-*, *ultra-*.

3.5.3 Compounds of Two Bound Forms

Compound nouns of two bound forms tend to follow a rule according to the structure of lexicogrammatical items:

Structure 1: when the second element of the compound is monosyllabic, the word stress pattern is usually primary + secondary (main + subordinate foot), e.g. *'alloˌphone*

Structure 2: when the second element is polysyllabic, the word stress pattern is secondary + primary (subordinate + main foot), e.g. *ˌall'ophony.* The following 'second elements' impose primary stress on the preceding syllable: *-chrony*, *-cracy*, *-graphy*, *-logy*, *-nomy*, *-nymy*, *-pathy*, *-phony*, *-scopy*, *-sophy*, *-tomy.* Derived nouns, adjectives and adverbs with suffixes follow the suffix rule concerned, e.g. *ˌanthro'pologist*, *ˌallo'phonic*, *ˌam'biguously.* A few examples follow:

Structure 1 main + subordinate	Structure 2 subordinate + main
allophone	*allophony*
ambiance	*ambiguity*
amphibrach	*amphibian*
anthropoid	*anthropology*
antonym	*antonymy*
archive	*archaeology*
autocrat	*autocracy*

Other examples that follow this dual structure pattern include bound first elements included in the preceding list (**3.5.2**): *bi-*, *bio-*, *cata-*, *cent-*, *circum-*, *deca-*, *deci-*, *demo-*, *dia-*, *dys-*, *endo-*, *epi-*, *equi-*, *hemi-*, *hetero-*, *holo-*, *homo-*, *hydro-*, *hypo-*, *idio-*, *iso-*, *kilo-* (NB: both *'kiloˌmetre* and *ˌki'lometre*); *macro-*, *mega-*, *meso-*, *meta-*, *micro-*, *milli-*, *mono-*, *multi-*, *neo-*, *omni-*, *ortho-*, *para-*, *peri-* (NB: also *pe'rimeter*), *phil-*, *photo-*, *physi-*, *poly-*, *proto-*, *pseudo-*, *psycho-*, *quadr-*, *retro-*, *semi-*, *syn-*, *sym-* (but: *'symmetry*), *tele-*, *the-*, *thermo-*, *tri-*.

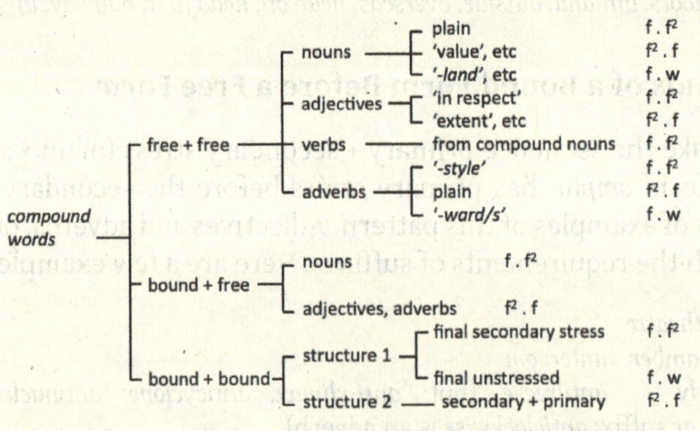

Figure 3.14 System network of the element structure of compound words in English

It should also be noted that in a few cases, the second element in Structure 1 is in fact unstressed, e.g. *hydrogen* /ˈhaɪdɹədʒən/; *multiple*, *quadruple* with final /-pəl/. Taking this note into account, it is now possible to show the complete network of phonological forms with all compound words. Apart from those with a final unstressed syllable, they comprise two feet: a foot with primary stress (symbol = f) and a subordinate foot: f².

We have now considered all the factors that constitute complex words in English. If we put together all the networks of the inflections, including numerals, and those of derivations and compound words, we obtain an amalgamated display of networks of the phonology of complex words in English.

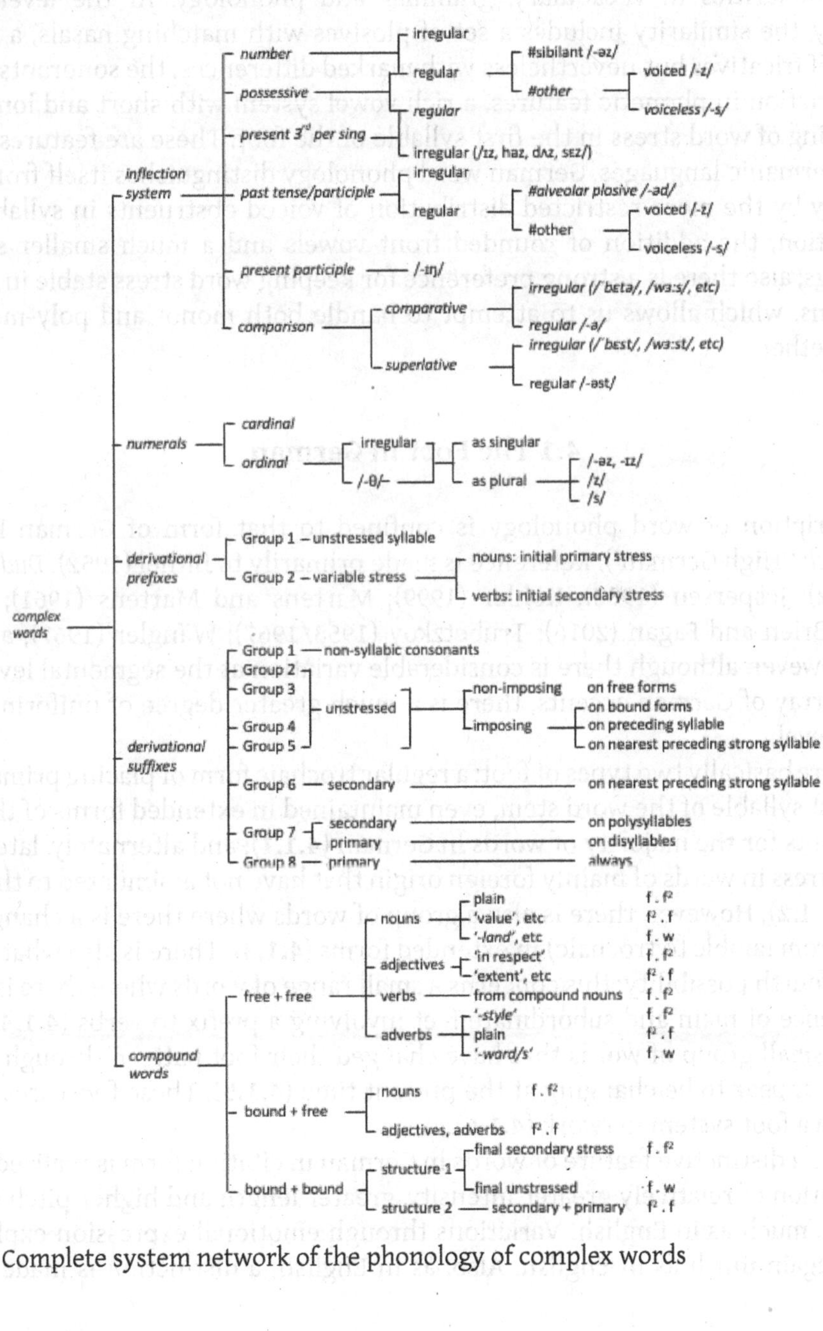

Figure 3.15 Complete system network of the phonology of complex words

Chapter 4

Word Phonology in German

German is a cousin of English in the family of Germanic languages; hence the many notable similarities in vocabulary, grammar and phonology. At the level of word phonology, the similarity includes a set of plosives with matching nasals, a relatively large set of fricatives but nevertheless with marked differences, the sonorants /l, r/ but with a variation in phonetic features, a rich vowel system with short and long vowels, and marking of word stress in the first syllable of the foot. These are features common to most Germanic languages. German word phonology distinguishes itself from English principally by the more restricted distribution of voiced obstruents in syllable/word-final position, the addition of rounded front vowels and a much smaller system of diphthongs; also there is a strong preference for keeping word stress stable in extended word forms, which allows us to attempt to handle both mono- and poly-morphemic words together.

4.1 The Foot in German

This description of word phonology is confined to that form of German known as *Hochdeutsch* ('High German'). Reference is made primarily to Bithel (1952); *Duden* (2015); Hall (1992); Jespersen (1932); Kohler (1999); Martens and Martens (1961); Moulton (1962); O'Brien and Fagan (2016); Trubetzkoy (1958/1967); Wängler (1967); and Wiese (2000). However, although there is considerable variation at the segmental level among the vast array of German accents, there is a much greater degree of uniformity at the prosodic level.

There are basically two types of foot: a regular trochaic form of placing primary stress on the first syllable of the word stem, even maintained in extended forms of the word – this accounts for the majority of words in German (**4.1.1**); and alternately, late (iambic) primary stress in words of mainly foreign origin that have not assimilated to the regular pattern (**4.1.2**). However, there is also a group of words where there is a change of foot pattern (from iambic to trochaic) in extended forms (**4.1.3**). There is also what might be termed a fourth possibility; this concerns a small range of words where there is contrastive sequence of main and subordinate feet involving a prefix to verbs (**4.1.4**). Finally, there is a small group of words that have changed their foot pattern through time and some that appear to be changing at the present time (**4.1.5**). These five cases are summarized in a foot system network (**4.1.6**).

Stress as a distinctive feature of words in German in citation form is realized through a combination of relatively greater intensity, greater length and higher pitch (Wängler 1967: 175), much as in English. Variations through emotional expression exploit these features, again much as in English. Also, as in English, a distinction is made between primary and secondary stress, as well as no stress, yet the distribution of stressed syllables is noticeably different from English.

4.1.1 Regular Initial Primary Stress

The 'regular' trochaic foot relates to the stem of a word, i.e. the monomorphemic base form that in German usually consists of one or two syllables; see, for instance, Wiese (2000: 56f). A monosyllabic stem of a lexical item or stressed grammatical item must contain either a short vowel with a final consonant margin or a long vowel that may or may not have a final margin. A disyllabic stem has primary stress on its initial syllable; hence, we usually refer to *Regular Initial Primary Stress.* Some examples:

Sicht	/zɪxt/[1]	'sight'
seh!	/zeː/	'see!'
Auge	/ˈaʊgə/	'eye'
munter	/ˈmʊntəʀ/	'lively'

Occasionally, the stem might consist of three or more syllables, but it is difficult to find examples without resorting to loanwords from another language, e.g.

Risiko	/ˈʀiːziko/	'risk'
Paprika	/ˈpapʀika/	'paprika'

Such words maintain initial primary stress, but extend the foot structure to two unstressed syllables. Such an additional unstressed syllable to what is otherwise a regular foot is sometimes called 'extrametricality' (Wiese 2000: 276).

There is a single example of a four syllable stem of native German origin (Wiese 2000: 286), but it is stressed as if a compound word:

Abenteuer /ˈaːbənˌtɔʏəʀ/ 'adventure'

The location of primary stress remains fixed whatever inflections and derivations are suffixed to the stem, e.g.

sichten	/ˈzɪxtən/	'to sight, examine'
sichtbar	/ˈzɪxtbaʀ/	'visible'
Sichtbarkeit	/ˈzɪxtbaʀkaɪt/	'visibility'
etc.		
sehen	/ˈzeːən/	'to see'
Sehlehre	/ˈzeːˌleːʀə/	'optics'
sehenswürdig	/ˈzeːənsˌvʏʀdɪx/	'worth seeing'
Sehenswürdigkeiten	/ˈzeːənsˌvʏʀdɪxkaɪtən/	'(the) sights'
etc.		
Augen	/ˈaʊgən/	'eyes'
äugeln	/ˈɔʏgəln/	'to eye, make eyes (at)'
Augenarzt	/ˈaʊgənˌaʀtst/	'oculist'
Augenärzte	/ˈaʊgənˌɛʀtstə/	'oculists'
Augenärztinnen	/ˈaʊgənˌɛʀtstɪnən/	'female oculists'

Augenblick	/ˈaʊgən,blɪk/	'moment'
Augenblickserfolg	/ˈaʊgən,blɪksɛʀ,fɔlk/	'momentary success'
etc.		
munterer	/ˈmʊntəʀəʀ/	'livelier'
munterest	/ˈmʊntəʀəst/	'liveliest'
Munterkeit	/ˈmʊntəʀkaɪt/	'liveliness'
Abenteuerin	/ˈa:bən,tɔʏʀɪn/	'woman adventurer'
abenteuerlich	/ˈa:bən,tɔʏʀlɪx/	'adventurous'
Abenteuerlichkeit	/ˈa:bən,tɔʏʀlɪxkaɪt/	'adventurousness'

It should be noted that all syllabic inflexional suffixes contain the weak unstressed vowel /ə/: *-e, -en, -em, -er, -est, -er* and so do not affect the principle of *Regular Initial Primary Stress*, even though they add an extra unstressed syllable. Derivational suffixes also maintain the principle even when they contain strong vowels, including those forming nouns, *-heit, -keit, -ung,* and *-chen, -er, -in, -lein, -ling, -schaft, -sal, -tum*, those forming adjectives, *-bar, -haft, -ig, -isch, -lich, -los, -mässig, -sam*, and those forming certain adverbs, *-falls, -seits, -wärt.*[2]

A word stem that constitutes the second element of a compound takes secondary stress, as shown in a number of examples above. This is also notably the case when a recognized set of stressed prefixes precede the word stem. Taking *Sicht* and *sehen* (as an infinitive) as examples:

Absicht	/ˈap,zɪxt/	'intention'	absehen	/ˈap,ze:ən/	'to perceive'
Ansicht	/ˈan,zɪxt/	'view'	ansehen	/ˈan,ze:ən/	'to look at'
Aufsicht	/ˈaʊf,zɪxt/	'inspection'	aufsehen	/ˈaʊf,ze:ən/	'to look up'
Aussicht	/ˈaʊs,zɪxt/	'outlook'	aussehen	/ˈaʊs,ze:ən/	'to look out, appear'
Einsicht	/ˈaɪn,zɪxt/	'examination'	einsehen	/ˈaɪn,ze:ən/	'to look into'
			hersehen	/ˈhɛʀ,ze:ən/	'to look'
Hinsicht	/ˈhɪn,zɪxt/	'respect'	hinsehen	/ˈhɪn,ze:ən/	'to have a look'
Nachsicht	/ˈnax,zɪxt/	'forbearance'	nachsehen	/ˈnax,ze:ən/	'to look after'
Vorsicht	/ˈfɔʀ,zɪxt/	'foresight'			
			wegsehen	/ˈve:k,ze:ən/	'to look away'
			zusehen	/ˈtsu:,ze:ən/	'to watch'

The recognized set of stressed prefixes also includes:

Antwort	/ˈant,vɔʀt/	'answer'	antworten	/ˈant,vɔʀtən/	'to reply'
Beilage	/ˈbaɪ,la:gə/	'supplement'	beilegen	/ˈbaɪ,le:gən/	'to supplement'
Fortschritt	/ˈfɔʀt,ʃʀɪt/	'progress'	fortschreiten	/ˈfɔʀt,ʃʀaɪtən/	'to progress'
Gegenstand	/ˈge:gən,ʃtant/	'object'	gegenstehen	/ˈge:gən,ʃte:ən/	'to face'
Loskauf	/ˈlo:s,kaʊf/	'ransoming'	loskaufen	/ˈlo:s,kaʊfən/	'to ransom'
Mitarbeit	/ˈmɪt,a:ʀbaɪt/	'co-operation'	mitarbeiten	/ˈmɪt,a:ʀbaɪtən/	'to co-operate'
Urteil	/ˈu:ʀ,taɪl/	'judgement'	urteilen	/ˈu:ʀ,taɪlən/	'to judge'
Zwischenzeit	/ˈtsvɪʃən,tsaɪt/	'interval'			

It is also to be noted here that there is also a recognized set of prefixes that *never* take primary stress; they act as an anacrusis to the foot of the word stem. Whereas the above set of prefixes constitute, in effect, the first element of a compound, this unstressed set does not:

Beruf	/bə'ʀu:f/	'vocation'	berufen	/bə'ʀu:fən/	'to appoint'
Empfang	/ɛmp'faŋ/	'receipt'	empfangen	/ɛmp'faŋən/	'to receive'
Entschluß	/ɛnt'ʃlʊs/	'decision'	entschließen	/ɛnt'ʃli:sen/	'to decide'
Erfolg	/ɛʀ'fɔlk/	'success'	erfolgen	/ɛʀ'fɔlgən/	'to succeed'
Gesicht	/gə'zɪxt/	'face'	gesehen	/gə'ze:ən/	'seen'
Versehen	/fɛʀ'ze:ən/	'error'	versehen	/fɛʀ'ze:ən/	'to provide'
Zerstörung	/tsɛʀ'ʃtø:ʀʊŋ/	'destruction'	zerstören	/tsɛʀ'ʃtø:ʀən/	'to destroy'

These unstressed prefixes appear in a series of adverbs and conjunctions also; some examples:

be-	bereits	/bɛ'ʀaɪts/	'ready'
emp-	empor	/ɛm'pɔʀ/	'high, upwards'
ent-	entgegen	/ɛnt'ge:gən/	'against'
ge-	genug	/gɛ'nu:k/	'enough'

The prefix *miß-* ('mis-') takes primary stress in nouns but not in verbs, unless another prefix intervenes:

Mißbrauch	/'mɪsˌbʀaʊx/	'misuse'	mißbrauchen	/mɪs'bʀaʊxən/	'to misuse'
Mißtrauen	/'mɪsˌtʀaʊən/	'mistrust'	mißtrauen	/mɪs'tʀaʊən/	'to mistrust'

but

Mißbehagen	/'mɪsbəˌha:gən/	'displeasure'
mißbehagen	/'mɪsbəˌha:gən/	'to displease'
Mißverständnis	/'mɪsfəʀˌʃtɛntnɪs/	'misunderstanding'
mißverstehen	/'mɪsfəʀˌʃte:ən/	'to misunderstand'

A similar situation is found with the prefix *un-* (negative). It takes primary stress in nouns, e.g.

Unfall	/'ʊnˌfal/	'accident'
Ungeheuer	/'ʊŋgəˌhɔʏəʀ/	'monster'
Unsinn	/'ʊnˌzɪn/	'nonsense'

and in adjectives, unless another prefix intervenes, or if the adjective has the suffixes *-bar*, *-lich*, *-sam*:

ungenau	/'ʊŋgəˌnaʊ/	'inexact'
ungläubig	/'ʊŋˌglɔʏbɪx/	'unbelieving'

but

unbedeckt	/ʊmbə'dɛkt/	'uncovered'
unvorhergesehen	/ʊnfɔʀ'hɛʀgəze:ən/	'unforeseen'
unbrauchbar	/ʊm'bʀaʊxbaʀ/	'useless'
unglaublich	/ʊŋ'glaʊblɪx/	'unbelievable'
unaufhaltsam	/ʊnaʊf'haltzam/	'irresistible'

Note, however, that Bithel (1952: 344) points out a contrast between two stress patterns of *unerhört*:

/ˈʊnɛʀhø: ʀt/ 'not granted' /ʊnɛʀˈhø: ʀt/ 'unheard of'

And Wiese (2000: 294) between two patterns for *unmenschlich*:

/ˈʊnmɛnʃlɪx/ 'non-human' /ʊmˈmɛnʃlɪx/ 'inhuman'

Finally, there is a third set of prefixes that are variable and often contrastively so, including *durch, hinter, über, um, unter, voll, wider, wieder*; these and other similar prefixes will be dealt with under *Contrastive Word Stress* below (**4.1.4**). In the meantime, the following examples with *-sicht* and infinitive forms with *-sehen* conform to *Regular Initial Primary Stress*:

Durchsicht	/ˈdʊʀxˌzɪxt/	'perusal'	durchsehen	/ˈdʊʀxˌze:ən/	'to look through'
Übersicht	/ˈy:bəʀˌzɪxt/	'overview'	übersehen	/ˈy:bəʀˌze:ən/	'to look over'
Umsicht	/ˈʊmˌzɪxt/	'circumspection'	umsehen	/ˈʊmˌze:ən/	'to look around'

The teen numbers are pronounced as regular compounds, e.g.

vierzehn /ˈfi:ʀˌtse:n/ 'fourteen'

but longer numbers are stressed as phrases even though written as compounds, e.g.

vierundzwanzig /ˈfi:ʀʊnˈtsvantsɪx/ '24' (cf. *Kiel und Danzig* /ˈki:l ʊnt ˈdantsɪx/)
vierhundert /ˈfi:ʀˈhʊndəʀt/ '400' (cf. *vier Hunde* /ˈfi:ʀ ˈhʊndə/ 'four dogs')
vierhundertundzwanzig /ˈfi:ʀˈhʊndəʀtʊnˈtsvantsɪx/ '420'
(cf. *vier Hunde und Katzen* /ˈfi:ʀ ˈhʊndə unt ˈkatsən/ 'four dogs and cats')

4.1.2 Late Primary Stress

The vast majority of words with late primary stress are words of foreign origin (**4.1.2.3**), but there are two categories of 'native' German words that also demonstrate this pattern: a series of adverbs and conjunctions (**4.1.2.1**), and sets of hybrid words that have a 'native' stem with a foreign ending (**4.1.2.2**).

4.1.2.1 A Series of Adverbs and Conjunctions

There are many adverbs with prefixes that are stressed with nouns and verbs (see examples below), but are usually unstressed as 'straight' adverbs. For instance, all adverbs with the prefixes *her-* and *hin-*:

herab	/hɛʀˈap/	'(coming) down'	heran	/hɛʀˈan/	'(coming) towards',	etc.
hinab	/hɪnˈap/	'(going) down'	hinan	/hɪnˈan/	'(going) towards',	etc.

Other examples of such adverbs/conjunctions include

an-	anstatt	/anˈʃtat/	'instead'
bis-	bisher	/bɪsˈhɛʀ/	'till now, hitherto'
durch-	durchaus	/dʊʀxˈaʊs/	'thoroughly'
gegen-	gegenüber	/gegənˈy:bəʀ/	'opposite'
gerade-	geradeaus	/ gɛˌʀa:dəˈaʊs/	'straight on'
immer-	immerhin	/ˌɪməʀˈhɪn/	'after all'

in-	inzwischen	/ɪnˈtsvɪʃən/	'meanwhile'
so-	sofort	/zoˈfɔʀt/	'immediately'
über-	überall	/ybəʀˈal/	'everywhere'
unter-	unterwegs	/ʊntəʀˈve:ks/	'on the way'
viel-	vielleicht	/fiˈlaɪçt/	'perhaps'
voll-	vollkommen	/fɔlˈkɔmən/	'completely'
vor-	voraus	/fɔʀˈaʊs/	'beforehand, in advance'
wo-	wofür	/voˈfy:ʀ/	'for which; what for?'
zu-	zuerst	/tsuˈɛʀst/	'first (of all)'
etc.			

and also these locatives

daran /daʀˈan/ 'at, on, to it/them' darauf /daʀˈaʊf/ '(up)on it/them', etc.
hieran /hiəʀˈan/ 'on, about this' hierauf /hiəʀˈaʊf/ 'on this; hereupon', etc.
bergab /ˌbɛʀkˈap/ 'downhill' bergauf /ˌbɛʀkˈaʊf/ 'uphill'
flußabwärts /ˌflu:sˈapvɛʀts/ 'downstream' flußaufwärts /ˌflu:sˈaʊfvɛʀts/ 'upstream',
etc.

Nevertheless, when these words act as the first element of compound nouns, verbs and adjectives, the principle of *Regular Initial Primary Stress* still operates; for example:

herabziehen	/hɛʀˈapˌtsi:ən/	'to pull down'
hinzufügen	/hɪnˈtsu:ˌfy:gən/	'to add'
davonlaufen	/daˈfɔnˌlaʊfən/	'to run off, to abscond'
etc.		
bereitwillig	/bɛˈʀaɪtˌvɪlɪç/	'ready and willing'
emporragen	/ɛmˈpɔʀˌʀa:gən/	'to rise high'
entgegenkommen	/ɛntˈge:gəŋˌkɔmən/	'to come and meet'
geradelegen	/gɛˈʀa:dəˌle:gən/	'to straighten'
gegenüberstellen	/gegənˈy:bəʀˌʃtɛlən/	'to place opposite, to contrast'
Voraussicht	/fɔʀˈaʊsˌzɪçt/	'foresight, prescience'
vorbeieilen	/fɔʀˈbaɪˌaɪlən/	'to hurry past'
zurückstellen	/tsuˈʀʏkˌʃtɛlən/	'to put back, to postpone'
Zusammenhang	/tsuˈzamənˌhaŋ/	'connection'

4.1.2.2 Hybrids

The second case *Late Primary Stress* is that of hybrids, i.e. words of German origin that end in a final stressed syllable derived from another language. There are two kinds: first, place names with the Slavic ending *-in:*

Berlin /bɛʀˈli:n/
Stettin /ʃtɛˈti:n/
Zeppelin /tsɛpəˈli:n/

Bithel (1952: 350, 358) gives a few other examples.

Secondly, words with an ending of French origin containing *-ei*, *-lei* and *-age*, like *Metzgerei, Liebelei, Stellage*; these suffixes all require primary stress. But as Bithel (1952:

186) points out, this '*-ei* is from O. Fr. *i.e.* (<Lat. *-ita*).' It usually indicates a business or its location, or by extension a personal characteristic:

Metzgerei	/ˌmɛtsgəˈʀai/	'butcher's'
Bäckerei	/ˌbɛkəˈʀai/	'bakery'
Wäscherei	/ˌvɛʃəˈʀai/	'laundry'
Wichtigtuerei	/ˌvɪxtɪxˌtuːəˈʀai/	'pomposity'
Angeberei	/ˌaŋgeːbəˈʀai/	'tale telling'
etc.		

He adds: 'Actually the ending in some nouns is *-erei*, not *-ei*; *-ei* was often added to nouns in *-er:*, ... *Lauferei* ("running about") is formed from the verb *laufen*, rather than from the noun *Läufer. Dieberei* ("thievery") must be from *Dieb*, *Schweinerei* ("mess") from *Schwein.*' All these cases have primary stress on the final syllable.

He also maintains that the final *-lei* in *Liebelei* ('love affair' from *Liebe* 'love') has a French origin. This is replicated in other words like *Jubelei* ('jubilation' from *jubeln* 'to cheer') and *Mogelei* ('cheating' from *mogeln* 'to cheat'), again with the final syllable taking primary stress.

His final example of hybrids are words of German origin taking the French *-age* ending with final primary stress: *Stellage* ('stand, frame' from *Stelle* 'a place') and *Takelage* ('ship's rigging' from *Takel* 'tackle').

4.1.2.3 Lehnwörter and Fremdwörter

We turn now to the foot in words of fully foreign origin. Wängler (1967: 190)[3] refers to the helpful distinction between loanwords (*Lehnwörter*), which have accommodated to the regular German phonological pattern of *Regular Initial Primary Stress*, i.e. the trochaic foot, and foreign words (*Fremdwörter*) most of which are from French and have retained the French tendency for iambic feet, which we have called *Late Primary Stress.* He gives

Kairo	/ˈkaiʀo/	'Cairo'
Rokoko	/ˈʀoːkoko/	'Rococo'

as examples of loanwords, with *Regular Initial Primary Stress.* Other examples include

Lehnwörter (with a trochaic foot)			as against *Fremdwörter* (with an iambic foot)		
Kino	/ˈkiːno/	'cinema'	Büro	/byˈʀoː/	'office'
Kaffee	/ˈkafe/	'coffee'	Café	/kaˈfeː/	'café'
Turban	/ˈtuːʀban/	'turban'	urban	/uʀˈbaːn/	'urbane'
etc.					

Most *Fremdwörter* are characterized by late stress, usually the very final syllable, or the penultimate if the final syllable is weak, with /ə/. This pattern clearly arises from the fact that so many *Fremdwörter* have French as their origin, including words of classical origin that have entered German through French; some more examples:

Bibliothek	/bɪblɪoˈteːk/	'library'
Idee	/iˈdeː/	'idea'
Kamel	/kaˈmeːl/	'camel'
Religion	/ʀelɪgɪˈoːn/	'religion'

A second set of examples display their Classical origins as 'pseudo-compounds', illustrated by their second element, which takes *Late Primary Stress;*

-chron	/-ˈkʀo:n/	synchron
-gramm	/-ˈgʀa:m/	Programm, Telegramm
-graph	/-ˈgʀa:f/	Fotograph, Telegraph
-krat	/-ˈkʀa:t/	Aristokrat, Demokrat
-log	/-ˈlo:k/	analog, Dialog
-loge	/-ˈlo:gə/	Phililoge, Psychologe
-nom	/-ˈno:m/	Astronom, Ökonom
-nym	/-ˈnʏm/	Synonym, Pseudonym
-path	/-ˈpa:t/	Telepath
-phon	/-ˈfo:n/	Megaphon, Telephon/Telefon
-sphäre	/-ˈsfɛ: ʀə/	Atmosphäre, Hemisphäre
-skop	/-ˈsko:p/	Mikroskop, Teleskop
-soph	/-ˈzo:f/	Philosoph
-tom	/-ˈto:m/	Anatom
-typ	/-ˈtʏp/	Prototyp

A third set of examples of *Fremdwörter* is constituted of a stem and a stressed suffix:

-abel	/-ˈa:bəl/	variabel, diskutabel
-age	/-ˈa:ʒə, -ˈa:ʃ/	Spionage, Etage
-al	/-ˈa:l/	egal, Kapital
-an	/-ˈa:n/	momentan, spontan
-and	/-ˈant/	Konfirmand, Doktorand
-ant	/-ˈant/	interessant, Fabrikant
-anz	/-ˈants/	Eleganz, Finanz
-ar	/-ˈa:ʀ/	Altar, Bibliothekar
-är	/-ˈɛ:ʀ/	Sekretär, regulär
-at	/-ˈa:t/	Resultat, Kandidat
-ell	/-ˈɛl/	kommerziell, Flanell
-ent	/-ˈɛnt/	Moment, evident
-enz	/-ˈɛnts/	Tendenz, Essenz
-esk	/-ˈɛsk/	grotesk, Kafkaesk
-ett	/-ˈɛt/	brünett, Kotelett
-ette	/-ˈɛtə/	Etikette, Serviette
-eur	/-ˈø:ʀ/	Friseur, Redakteur
-ie	/-ˈi:/[4]	Akademie, Philosophie
-ier	/-ˈi:əʀ/	Barbier, Offizier
-ieren	/-ˈi:əʀən/	interessieren, spazieren
-ik	/-ˈi:k/[5]	Musik, Politik
-ismus	/-ˈi:smʊs/	Anglizismus, Sozialismus; also the plural form,
-ismen	/-ˈi:smən/	Anglizismen
-ist	/-ˈi:st/	Anglist, Journalist
-iv	/-ˈi:f/	aktiv, produktiv
-ment	/-ˈmɛnt/[6]	Dokument, Instrument
-os	/-ˈo:s/	grandios, vituos
-ös	/-ˈø:s/	nervös, religiös
-tät/	/-ˈte:t/	Majestät, Elektrizität

-tion	/-ˈtsjo:n/	Funktion, Nation
-ur	/-ˈu:ʀ/	Fraktur, Rasur
-urg	/-ˈu:ʀk/	Dramaturg, Metallurg

Here are a couple of examples with final weak /ə/:

Aprikose /apʀiˈko:zə/ 'apricot'
Gardine /gaʀˈdi:nə/ 'curtain'

In the exceptional case of the combination of the two weak final syllables *-ika*, primary stress falls on the antepenultimate syllable:

Amerika /aˈmɛʀikə/
Harmonika /haʀˈmɔnikə/
(This also applies in other instances where the antepenultimate happens to be the initial syllable, i.e. *Regular Initial Primary Stress*:
Afrika /ˈafʀikə/
Paprika /ˈpapʀika/)

Most borrowings from English happen to conform to *Regular Initial Primary Stress*, which is typical of Germanic languages, e.g.

Bambus	/ˈbambʊs/	'bamboo/s'
Dschungel	/ˈdʒʊŋgəl/	'jungle'
Pony, ponies	/ˈpo:ni, ˈpo:nis/	'pony, ponies
Training	/ˈtʀe:nɪŋ/	'training'
Manager	/ˈmanadʒəʀ/	'manager'
boxen	/ˈbɔksən/	'to box'
kicken	/ˈkɪkən/	'to kick'
etc.		

The distinction between *Lehnwörter* and *Fremdwörter* has created occasional contrasts. Bithel (1952: 181, 360) draws attention to *Tenor* /ˈte:nɔr/, a legal term for the content of a document, and /te:ˈno:r/, the musical term for a male voice. Wiese (1996: 278) also cites *Konsum* as another contrast, between /ˈkɔnzʊm/, a 'supermarket' (especially in the former DDR) and /kɔnˈzu:m/ 'consumption'; Bithel (1952: 367) notes that 'Words beginning with *Kon-*, which may be Lat. or Fr. *con-*, have sometimes initial, sometimes final stress' and cites a number of examples including *Konsul* /ˈkɔnzʊl/ (presumably, therefore, from Latin) and *Konfekt* /kɔnˈfɛkt/ (presumably, from French). It seems that German has taken occasional advantage of this potential for contrast in foot pattern.

4.1.3 Switching Feet

The foot type is changed by a set of stress-imposing suffixes. The distinction, for instance, between stressed final *-ik* /-ˈi:k/ and unstressed final *-ik* /-ɪk/ is overridden when the suffix *-er* indicating personal agency is added. The suffixal combination is rendered unstressed but imposes primary word stress on the preceding syllable, requiring a change of foot type in the stem:

Musik	/mu'zi:k/	produces	Musiker /'mu:zɪkəʀ/
Physik	/fy'zi:k/		Physiker /'fy:zɪkəʀ/
Politik	/pɔli'ti:k/		Politiker /pɔ'lɪtɪkəʀ/
Mathematik	/matema'ti:k/		Mathematiker /mate'ma:tɪkəʀ/

Similarly

Chemie	/xe'mi:/	produces	Chemiker /'xe:mikəʀ/
Drama	/'dʀa:ma/		Dramatiker /dʀa'ma:tikəʀ/

But, of course, there is no change where final *-ik* is unstressed:

Linguistik	/lɪŋ'gwɪstɪk/	Linguistiker /lɪŋ'gwɪstɪkəʀ/
Technik	/'tɛxnɪk/	Techniker /'tɛxnɪkəʀ/
etc.		

A second instance is that of the combination of stressed *-an-/-en-* + unstressed *-er* or *-isch*. Primary stress shifts to *-an-* :

Afrika	/'afʀika/	produces	Afrikaner /afʀi'ka:nəʀ/; also /afʀi'ka:nɪʃ/
Amerika	/a'mɛʀika/		Amerikaner /amɛʀi'ka:nər/; /amɛʀi'ka:nɪʃ/
Japan	/'ja:pan/		Japaner /ja'pa:nəʀ/; / ja'pa:nɪʃ/
Mexico	/'mɛksiko/		Mexikaner /mɛksi'ka:nər/; /mɛksi'ka:nɪʃ/
Republik	/ʀepʊ'bli:k/		Republikaner /ʀepʊbli'ka:nəʀ/; /ʀepʊbli'ka:nɪʃ/
Italien	/i'ta:ljən/		Italiener /ita'lje:nəʀ/; /ita'lje:nɪʃ/

(Note that in many cases, *-ien* does not produce a shift in primary stress in inflected words:

Australien	/aʊ'stʀa:ljən/	Australier	/aʊ'stʀa:ljəʀ/; /aʊ'stʀa:lɪʃ/
Belgien	/'bɛlgjən/	Belgier	/'bɛlgjəʀ/; /'bɛlgɪʃ/
Indien	/'ɪndjən/	Inder	/'ɪndəʀ/; /'indɪʃ/
etc.)			

A third instance is that of the combination of stressed *-es-* + unstressed-*e*/*-isch* and stressed -os-/-ös- + unstressed-*e*/*-isch*:

China	/'xi:na/	produces	Chineser /xi'ne:zəʀ/; /xi'ne:zɪʃ/
Malta	/'malta/		Malteser /mal'te:zəʀ/; /mal'te:zɪʃ/
Portugal	/'pɔʀtʊgal/		Portugieser /pɔʀtʊ'gi:zəʀ/; /pɔʀtʊ'gi:zɪʃ/
Frankreich	/'fʀaŋkʀaɪx/		Franzose /fʀan'tso:zə/; /fʀan'tsø:zɪx/

A fourth instance is that of the combination of stressed *-at-/-al-* + unstressed *-isch*:

Asien	/'a:zjən/	produces	Asiat /a'zja:t/; a:'zja:tɪʃ/
Musik	/mu'zi:k/		musikalisch /muzɪ'ka:lɪʃ/

A fifth and more complicated case is that of *-or-* when followed by (unstressed) *-en*, *-in*, *isch*. Words of foreign origin with final *-or* have either become *Lehnwörter* with *initial primary word stress*, e.g. *Debitor*, *Kreditor*, *Konditor*, *Auditor*, *Professor*, *Testator*, *Autor*, *Doktor*, *Motor*, while others have primary stress on *-or* itself, as French, with *Late Primary Stress*, e.g. *Humor*, *Kontor*, *Major*, *Meteor*, *Rumor*, *Tresor*. Also the case of the two words spelled as *Tenor* was noted above. These differences are all overridden with the addition of the three suffixes listed above; primary word stress falls on *-or-* as exemplified below:

plural: Kreditoren /krɛdɪˈto:rən/; Autoren /aʊˈto:rən/; Professoren /prɔfɛˈso:rən/
feminine: Doktorin /dɔkˈto:rɪn/; Professorin /prɔfɛˈso:rɪn/
adjective: meteorisch /me:teˈo:rɪʃ/; motorisch /mo:ˈto:rɪʃ/

However, it should be noted that *Tenor* with final stress ('male singer') becomes either *Tenore* or *Tenöre* in the plural, maintaining stress, however, on *-or/ör-*.

A sixth case involves a small group of words with final *-ig*. This suffix does not usually require a change of stress placement, but in a few cases it imposes stress on the immediately preceding syllable, seemingly to emphasize a change of meaning:

leben, lebend /ˈle:bən, ˈle:bənt/ 'to live', 'living' produces lebendig /leˈbɛndix/ 'alive, lively'
wahrhaft /ˈva: ʀhaft/ 'true' produces wahrhaftig /vaʀˈhaftɪx/ 'real, genuine'

Wiese (1996: 198) emphasizes 'that the pair *leb+end* vs. *leb+end+ig* ... is totally unique. No other participle allows an affixation of *-ig*, so that *lebendig* is highly exceptional ...'

4.1.4 Contrastive Foot Pattern

A few contrasts through word stress have already been noted: *Konsum* /ˈkɔnzʊm/ and /kɔnˈzu:m/, and *Tenor* /ˈte:nɔʀ/ and /teˈno: ʀ/; *Mißtrauen/mißtrauen* /ˈmɪsˌtʀaʊən/ (noun) and /mɪsˈtʀaʊən/ (verb); *unerhört* /ˈʊnɛʀhø: ʀt/ and /ʊnɛʀˈhø: ʀt/; and *unmenschlich* /ˈʊnˌmɛnʃlɪx/ and /ʊmˈmɛnʃlɪx/.

A number of others involve the contrast between a set of prefixes to verbs that can take either primary or secondary stress. The prefixes consist of five prepositions that can be either separable or inseparable from the verb stems. The separable prefix functions rather like an adverb and often bears a more concrete (locative) meaning; it takes primary stress and constitutes the main foot before the verb, which becomes a subordinate foot; whereas a more abstract meaning is associated with inseparable prefixes, which take a secondary stress, leaving primary stress on the verb, and consequently a reversal of foot status.

The set consists of five prefixes and are illustrated as follows:

separable (main + subordinate foot)		*inseparable* (subordinate + main foot)	
durchfahren	/ˈdʊʀxˌfa: ʀən/	durchfahren	/ˌdʊʀxˈfa: ʀən/
'to drive through without stopping'		'to traverse'	
durchschauen	/ˈdʊʀxˌʃaʊən/	durchschauen	/ˌdʊʀxˈʃaʊən/
'to look over, through (e.g. a book)'		'to see though (e.g. lies)'	
hintergehen	/ˈhɪntəʀˌge:ən/	hintergehen	/ˌhɪntəʀˈge:ən/
'to go behind'		'to deceive, double-cross'	
hinterlegen	/ˈhɪntəʀˌle:gən/	hinterlegen	/ˌhɪntəʀˈle:gən/
'to place (something) at the back'		'to deposit'	
übersetzen	/ˈy:bəʀˌzɛtsən/	übersetzen	/ˌy:bəʀˈzɛtsən/
'to set (something) across, over'		'to translate'	

übertreten 'to step over'	/ˈy:bəʀˌtʀe:tən/	übertreten 'to overstep'	/ˌy:bəʀˈtʀe:tən/
umfahren 'to run (somebody) over'	/ˈʊmˌfa:ʀən/	umfahren 'to drive around (something)'	/ˌʊmˈfa:ʀən/
umschreiben 'to paraphrase'	/ˈʊmˌʃʀaɪbən/	umschreiben 'to re-write'	/ˌʊmˈʃʀaɪbən/
unterschreiben 'to write underneath'	/ˈʊntəʀˌʃʀaɪbən/	unterschreiben 'to sign'	/ˌʊntəʀˈʃʀaɪbən/
unterstellen 'to take shelter (from rain)'	/ˈʊntəʀˌʃtɛlən/	unterstellen 'to subordinate, insinuate'	/ˌʊntəʀˈʃtɛlən/

The set would not be complete without *voll-* and *wider-* even though there are no direct contrasts like those above; the difference in word stress, however, mirrors the same kind of difference in meaning, e.g.

vollfüllen 'to fill full'	/ˈfɔlˌfy:lən/	vollziehen 'to fulfil'	/ˌfɔlˈtsi:ən/
widerhallen 'to echo, resound'	/ˈvi:dəʀˌhalən/	widerspiegeln 'to reflect, mirror'	/ˌvi:dəʀˈʃpi:gəln/

One further instance of contrastive stress involves compound adjectives with level (or double) primary stress, i.e. two main feet; in contrast to the more usual sequence of primary + secondary stress, i.e. main + subordinate foot. Examples that are frequently cited are

bildhübsch /ˈbɪltˈhʏpʃ/ 'as pretty as a picture'
bildschön /ˈbɪltˈʃø:n/ 'very beautiful (as a picture)'
nagelneu /ˈna:gəlˈnɔʏ/ 'brand new'
grassgrün /ˈgʀa:sˈgʀy:n/ 'as green as grass'
steinalt /ˈʃtaɪnˈalt/ 'very old'

This has potential for contrastive stressing, i.e. contrastive foot status, as evidenced in these two examples:

blutarm /ˈblu:tˈaʀm/ 'very poor'
steinreich /ˈʃtaɪnˈʀaɪx/ 'very rich'

in contrast with the usual stress pattern of compounds, producing:

/ˈblu:tˌaʀm/ 'anaemic'
/ˈʃtaɪnˌʀaɪx/ 'rich in stone'

4.1.5 Varying Feet

Languages live and change, and some changes are discernible in patterns of stress in German. There is evidence historically, as Bithel (1952: 246, 282, 363) observes, that a number of words 'with obscured etymology' are now established with shifted stress on account of analogy or, possibly, rhythm accommodating to the preferred trochaic foot structure with anacrusis. He cites, for instance,

Forelle	/fɔ'ʀɛlə/	'trout'
Holunder	/hɔ'lʊndəʀ/	'elderberry'
Hornisse	/hɔʀ'nɪsə/	'hornet'
Lawine	/la'vi:nə/	'avalanche'
Scharteke	/ʃaʀ'te:kə/	'trash literature'
Schlaffitchen	/ʃlaf'fɪtxən/	'collar'
schmarotzen	/ʃma'ʀɔtsən/	'to sponge on others'
Wacholder	/va'xo:ldəʀ/	'juniper tree'

Bithel (1952: 361–362) gives examples of contemporary fluctuation in stress placement, e.g. *Pastor*, *Januar*, *Februar* and the grammatical terms *Aktiv*, *Dativ*, *Genetiv*, *Konjunktiv*, *Passiv* (first or final syllable), and *Kilo-* and *Zenti-* words (either initial or on the second element of the compound).

Wiese (2000: 278) lists the following examples of 'words which can be found with either initial or final stress':

Dromedar	'dromedary'
Ballast	'ballast'
Leopard	'leopard'
Marzipan	'marzipan'
Motor	'engine'

Wängler (1967: 191) draws attention to popular disregard for contrastive separable and inseparable prefixes with some verbs. He cites *durchschneiden* and *umfassen* to illustrate his observation; both verbs have contrastive potential:

	separable	*inseparable*
durchschneiden	'to cut in two'	'to cut, cleave, sever'
umfassen	'to re-set, re-mount'	'to clasp, encompass'

He points out that, colloquially, people prefer initial stress; stressing the verb stem sounds rather 'official'[7] – a phonological contrast in register.

There is a degree of variability with adjectives prefixed with *un-*. *Unmöglich* has a modern standard form with primary stress on *-mög-*, but for pragmatic or rhetorical effect, stress can be shifted to *un-* (Weise 2000: 123); Bithel (1952: 246) points out that this is a reversal of history, for the older pronunciation with initial stress gave way so often to the rhetorical stressing, 'that in the end the rhetorical form displaces the original historical form: e.g. *un'endlich*, *uner'reicht*, *un'glaublich*, *un'möglich*, *un'sterblich* ...are now the standard forms'. Bithel (1952: 293) also refers to 'rhythmical shifting' to account for *unbrauchbar* /'ʊmbʀaʊxbaʀ/ as well as /ʊm'bʀaʊxbaʀ/, as given above; he provides many more examples (1952: 343–346). (There is no variability when *un-* itself is prefixed by *ver-* to create compound verbs, e.g. *ver'unglücken*, *ver'unreinigen*, etc.) *Alltag* /'altak/ 'weekday' produces *alltäglich* as both /'altɛglɪx/ 'workaday' and /al'tɛglɪx/ 'day by day' (Bithel 1952: 349).

4.1.6 Foot Network of Words in German

The two basic foot types of German words can be displayed as a summary in a system network. Cases of contrastive stress are separated into the two distinctive shapes as two distinctive words, whereas cases of variable stress belong to both shapes.

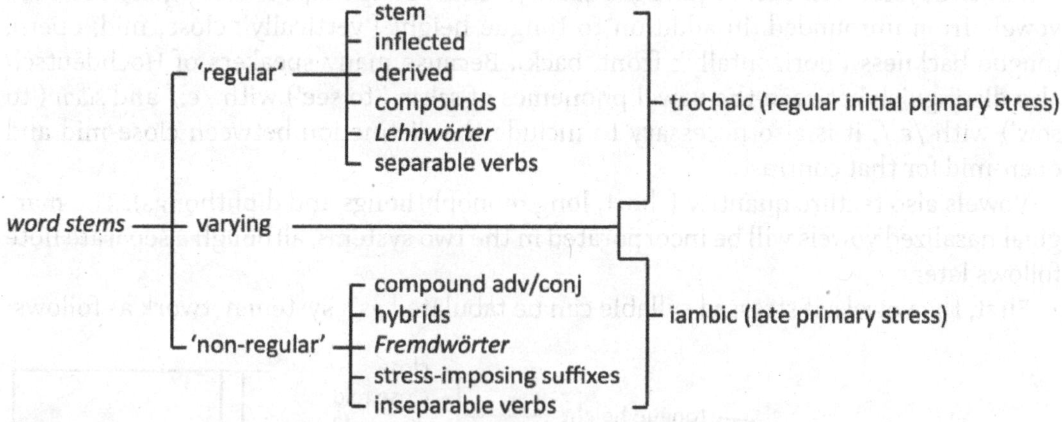

Figure 4.1 Network of prosodic shapes of the foot in German words

4.2 Syllable Structures, Nuclei and Margins

Structures often vary according to the prosodic status of a syllable. In German, syllables are characterized prosodically by primary, secondary and no stress; however, the structure of syllables with primary and secondary stress is essentially identical, since a form can be either a main foot or a subordinate foot as the second element of a compound. For instance, *Schritt* can be either the main foot or a subordinate foot in a compound like *Fortschritt*, with the structure CCVC in both cases:

Schritt /ˈʃʀɪt/ 'step'
Fortschritt /ˈfɔʀtˌʃʀɪt/ 'progress'

There is, on the other hand, a considerable difference between the possible structures of stressed and unstressed syllables; so it is necessary to present them separately. Furthermore, the structure of stressed syllables also depends on whether the vowel is long or short. In addition, there is a set of nasalized vowels in *Fremdwörter* of French origin; they are marginal in the sense that many speakers of *Hochdeutsch* render them with Germanized alternative pronunciations; furthermore, their occurrence and their distribution is extremely limited. As a consequence, four types of syllable structure need to be presented:

Type 1: stressed with short vowels,
Type 2: stressed with long vowels,
Type 3: unstressed, and
Type 4: nasalized.

4.2.1 Syllable Nucleus Systems

As in English, it is necessary to distinguish between those vowels that function as the nucleus of a stressed syllable and those that function as the nucleus in unstressed ones. Two separate systems are required as a consequence.

The two systems further require the quality feature of lip shape to distinguish rounded vowels from unrounded, in addition to tongue height ('vertically': close, mid, open), tongue backness ('horizontally': front, back). Because many speakers of Hochdeutsch also distinguish between the vowel phonemes of *sehen* ('to see') with /e:/ and *säen* ('to sow') with /ɛ:/, it is also necessary to include the distinction between close-mid and open-mid for that contrast.

Vowels also feature quantity (short, long monophthongs and diphthongs). The marginal nasalized vowels will be incorporated in the two systems, although a separate note follows later.

First, the vowels of stressed syllable can be tabulated as a system network as follows:

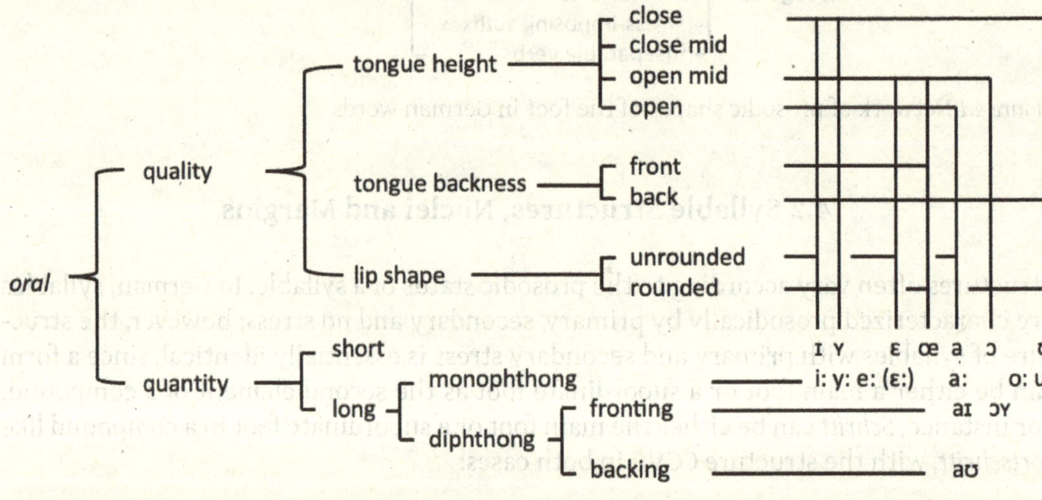

Figure 4.2 A system network of strong vowels in German

In unstressed syllables, only short vowels and a small range of syllabic consonants appear. Some of the short vowels are reduced forms of long vowels in the unstressed syllables of words that have entered German as either *Lehnwörter* or *Fremdwörter.*

/i/ veilleicht /fiˈlaɪxt/; Idee /iˈde:/
/ɪ/ tätig /ˈtɛtɪx/; Ärztin /ˈɛʀtstɪn/
/e/ Kanapee /ˈkanape/; egal /eˈga:l/
/ɛ/ empor /ɛmˈpɔʀ/; Verein /fɛʀˈaɪn/
/a/ Heimat /ˈhaɪmat/; Drama /ˈdʀa:ma/
/ɔ/ Kontrolle /kɔnˈtʀɔlə/
/o/ Auto /ˈaʊto/; Autos /ˈaʊtos/
/ʊ/ unerwartet /ʊnɛʀˈvaʀtət/; Übung /ˈy:bʊŋ/
/u/ Armut /ˈaʀmut/; Universität /univɛʀsiˈte:t/

/y/ Physik /fy'zi:k/; Büro /by'ʀo:/
/ʏ/ System /sʏs'te:m/
/ø/ Ökologie /økolo'gi:/
/ə/ berufen /bə'ʀu:fən/; Name /'na:mə/

It should be noted that unstressed /ɪ/ only appears in closed syllables in (unstressed) suffixes; that /ɛ/ only appears in closed syllables in (unstressed) prefixes; that /ɔ, ʏ/ only occur in closed syllables in *Lehnwörter* or *Fremdwörter*; and that /ə/ never appears initially in a word or syllable; it has no equivalent stressed form. (The occurrence of [ɐ] to represent unstressed <-er> as in *Sommer* is considered under *r*-sounds below.)

Syllabic consonants function as the nucleus of an unstressed syllable where there is a close transition between the consonant and a preceding syllable-final homorganic obstruent; this is dealt with in detail under **4.4 Simplifications** below.

Nasalized Vowels. Nasalized vowels occur in a number of French *Fremdwörter* in stressed syllables; *Duden* gives the following examples:

/ɛ̃:/ Timbre /'tɛ̃:bʀə/
/ã:/ Abonnement /abɔnə'mã:/
/õ:/ Fond /fõ:/
/œ̃:/ Parfum /paʀ'fœ̃:/

However, it should be noted how these nasalized vowels also get 'Germanized' (*eingedeutscht*) as either a short vowel followed by a nasal by speakers in the northern areas of Germany, or a long vowel followed by a nasal in the southern areas (see, e.g. Martens and Martens 1961: 90–92):

/ɛ̃:/ becomes /am/ in *Timbre* /'tambʀə/, or /a:m/: /'ta:mbʀə/
/ã:/ becomes /ɔŋ/ in *Abonnement* /abɔnə'mɔŋ/, or /o:n/: /abɔnə'mo:n/
/õ:/ becomes /ɔŋ/ in *Fond* /fɔŋ/, or /o:n/: /fo:n/
/œ̃:/ becomes /œŋ/ in *Parfum* /paʀ'fœŋ/, or /y:m/ in *Parfüm* /paʀ'fy:m/

Duden also acknowledges a number of unstressed nasalized vowels, with these examples:

/ɛ̃/ *timbrieren* /tɛ̃'bʀi:əʀən/
/ã/ *Pensee* /pã'ze:/
/õ/ *Fondue* /fõ'dy:/

Again, a process of Germanization is detectable whereby these short vowels lose their nasalization and are followed by a nasal:

/ɛ̃/ becomes /am/ in *timbrieren* /tam'bʀi:əʀən/
/ã/ becomes /aŋ/ in *Pensee* /paŋ'ze:/
/õ/ becomes /ɔn/ in *Fondue* /fɔn'dy:/

Finally, the severe limitation of their distribution should be noted: nasalized vowels, whether stressed (and long) or unstressed (and short), only ever occur in open syllables, never in closed syllables.

We turn now to the four syllable structures themselves.

4.2.2 Syllable Structures

The structures vary according to the number of consonants in their final margin (or coda):

Type 1: stressed syllables with short vowels cannot be open, i.e. they must be followed by a consonant or a consonant cluster consisting of up to four consonants;
Type 2: stressed syllables with long vowels may be open or closed with up to three consonants;
Type 3: unstressed syllables may be open or closed with up to two consonants (or three with a non-syllabic consonantal suffix); and
Type 4: syllables with nasalized vowels can only be open, i.e. with no consonants following.

Syllable structures can be shown in the following network where C represents a consonant and # represents no consonant:

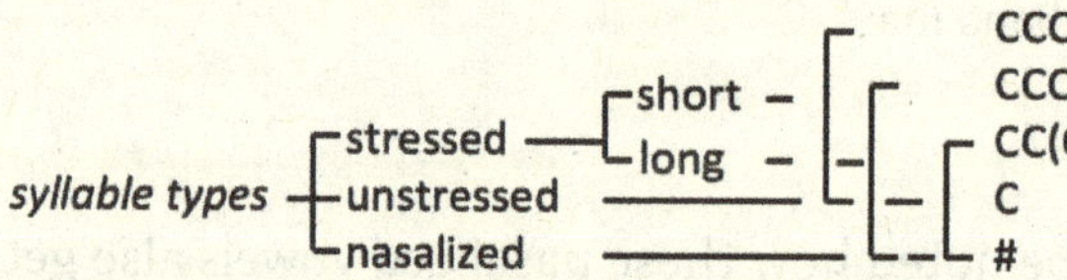

Figure 4.3 Network of syllable structures in German

This network can be elaborated more specifically as separate, polysystemic, networks for the four types of syllable structure. Each syllable type has its own vowel system; there are consequently four vowel systems in *Hochdeutsch.*

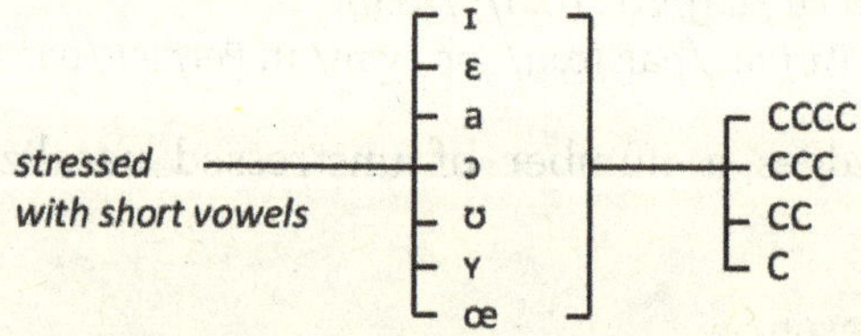

Figure 4.4 Network of the short vowel system with final margins in stressed syllables

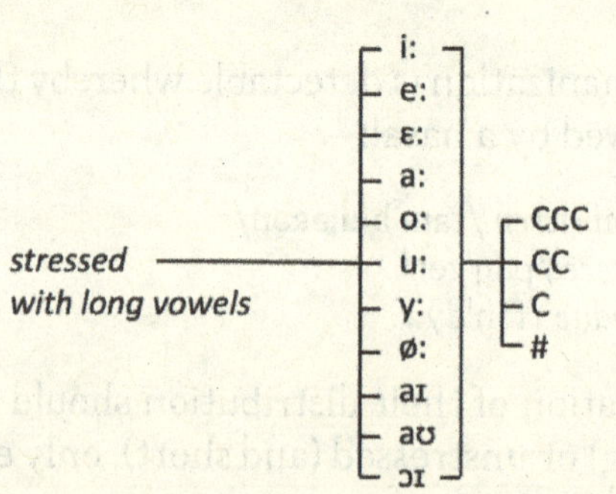

Figure 4.5 Network of the long vowel system with final margins in stressed syllables

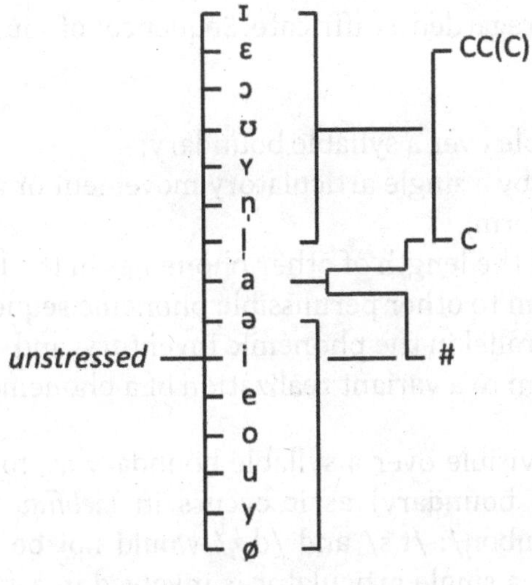

Figure 4.6 Network of the unstressed vowel system with final margins

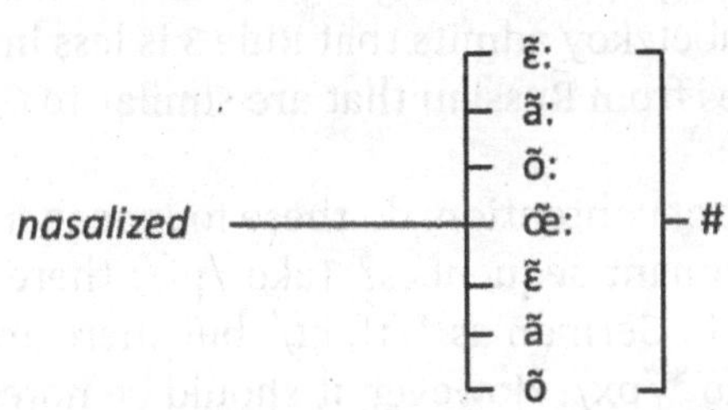

Figure 4.7 Network of the nasalized vowel system, with no final margins

4.2.3 Issues in the Inventory of Consonantal Phonemes

We have maintained that the four types of syllable structure are determined by vowels systems and syllable-final margins and it to these latter that we now turn. However, first, we need to consider four issues in the inventory and phonemic status of consonantal articulations as they impinge on the structure of syllable-final margins: the status of combinations like /pf/ and /ts/ as either sequences or as single affricate phonemes; the phonemic status of the phonetic realizations of [ç, x, χ]; likewise of *r*-type articulations; and, fourthly, cases of neutralization (*Aufhebung* 'cancellation, suppression').

Affricates. Trubetzkoy (1958/1967), *Duden*, Wängler (1961), Hall (1992), Ladefoged and Maddieson (1996), treat /pf, ts, tʃ/ and the infrequent case of /dʒ/ as single affricate consonant phonemes, whereas Martens and Martens (1961), Moulton (1962) and Kohler (1999) do not. Martens and Martens (1961: 212–229) treat these four sequences as typical plosive+fricative sequences that also includes /ps, ks, kv/. Wiese (2000: 13–14; 261–266) treats /pf, ts/ as affricates, and also /tʃ, dʒ/, but wishes to describe /ps, ks/ also as affricates; however, his criteria for establishing such sequences as affricates are suspect on both phonetic and phonological grounds and do not conform to Trubetzkoy's (1958/1967: 50–55) classic set of rules.

That classic set of six rules to establish a sequence of sounds as 'monophonematic' covers all manner of sequences, but it includes the criteria by which the sequence plosive+fricative may be regarded as affricate. Sequences of sounds can only be regarded as single phonemes if

1 they are not divisible over a syllable boundary;
2 they are produced by a single articulatory movement or a gradual decomposition of an articulatory form;
3 they do not exceed the length of other phonemes in the language concerned;
4 they do not conform to other permissible phoneme sequences;
5 they establish a parallel in the phonemic inventory; and
6 they do not conform to a variant realization of a phoneme.

/pf, ts, tʃ, dʒ/ are not divisible over a syllable boundary as, for instance, /p.f/ (where [.] represents a syllable boundary) as it occurs in *Liebfrau* /ˈliːpˌfraʊ/ and /t.ʃ/ in *Rechtschreibung* /ˈʀɛxtʃʀaɪbʊŋ/; /t.s/ and /d.ʒ/ would not be possible in German. All four are homorganic, i.e. a single articulator is involved in each sequence: lower lip in /pf/, tongue tip in /ts/, tongue front in /tʃ, dʒ/. Rule 2 therefore excludes /ps, ks, kv/ as potential affricates. Trubetzkoy admits that Rule 3 is less important but nevertheless illustrates it with examples from Russian that are similar to German /ts, tʃ/ in contrast to /ks/.

Rule 4 is the main point of contention: do these four sequences, /pf, ts, tʃ, dʒ/, follow the pattern of other consonant sequences? Take /pf/: there are no possible syllable-initial or -final sequences in German as */tf, kf/, but there are /ps, pʃ/ in a few words, mostly *Fremdwörter*, and no */px/. However, it should be noted that /ps, pʃ/are limited not only in frequency, but also in distribution; for instance, they cannot combine with /l, r/ in initial position, nor with nasals in medial or final position. On the other hand, /pf/ not only has a notably higher frequency in the language, but also a wider distribution: just as /p/ and /f/ can be followed by /l, r/, so can /pf/:

Plan, prüfen
Flanke, früh
Pflanze, Pfründe

And just as /p/ and /f/ can be preceded by a nasal in medial or final position so can /pf/:

Rampe
Senf
Kampf, schimpfen

In the case of /ts/, the sequences /ps, ks/ exist, but as noted above, they tend to be infrequent in the German lexicon and belong mainly to *Fremdwörter* in initial position and are very limited in distribution: no combinations with other consonants in initial, medial or final position. There are no sequences of */tf, tx/.

/tʃ/ is limited to *Fremdwörter* in initial position, although there is greater frequency in medial and final positions, including even the word *Deutsch*. /dʒ/ is wholly limited to *Fremdwörter*; there are no other sequences with /ʒ/.

Rule 5 applies to /pf, ts/, as they match other consonants in distribution, including /tsv/ matching /kv/ in initial position: Zweck /ˈtsvɛk/, Quetsche /ˈkvɛtʃə/. It applies only to a lesser extent to /tʃ, dʒ/ because of their lower frequency and distribution, mainly because of their occurrence in *Fremdwörter.* Rule 6 applies to all the noted sequences and so does not carry any particular weight.

Trubetzkoy's six detailed and comprehensive rules distinguish /pf, ts, tʃ, dʒ/ as authentic affricates as opposed to the other sequences. It would also be necessary to distinguish between affricates and identical phonemic sequences where there is a morpheme boundary, as in genitive forms such as *Rats* ('of advice'). Furthermore, historical considerations might be considered, as the High German Consonant Shift Phase 2 in the eighth century produced /pf/ from /p/, and /ts/ from /t/. Finally, native German speakers' perceptions might also contribute as they perceive /pf, ts, tʃ, dʒ/ as single consonants, especially as /ts/ is orthographically a single letter and /tʃ, dʒ/ likewise in a number of *Fremdwörter.*

In this presentation, /pf, ts/ will be regarded as regular single affricate consonant phonemes, and /tʃ, dʒ/ as marginal single affricate consonant phonemes – transcribed with 'condensed symbols' as single phonemes in the transcription of words: / pf, ʦ, ʧ, ʤ/. Other plosive+fricative sequences are transcribed simply as a sequence of separate symbols. Affrication as single consonants has implications for the distribution of consonants in clusters in syllable-initial and -final positions.

Ch-sounds. Opinion in the literature is also divided over the issue of the <ch> sounds of German. *Duden*, Martens and Martens, Moulton, Wängler and Kohler all treat [ç] and [x] as separate consonants; Wiese describes three articulations: [ç, x, χ]; and Hall handles the sounds as variants of a single consonant phoneme /x/. The distribution of [ç] is widely agreed upon: it occurs after front non-open vowels (/i:, ɪ, e:, ɛ, y:, ʏ, ø:, œ/), front closing diphthongs (/aɪ, ɔɪ/), and the consonants /n, l, r/, and before /i:, e:/ in a few *Fremdwörter* like *China, Chemie* and /ə/ in the derivational suffix *-chen* ('diminutive'), e.g. *Mädchen.* After other vowels, the point of articulation adjusts to the height of the tongue, from a velar position after back close vowels, e.g. *Buch* [bu:x], to a uvular position after open vowels, *Bach* [ba:χ]. Hall (45) cites just one example of [x] in initial position, before the vowel /a/, in *Chassidismus* /xasiˈdi:smʊs/ 'Hasidism'. Accordingly, the principles of complementary distribution and phonetic similarity apply and suggest that this variation of sounds constitute a single consonant phoneme. However, authors frequently raise the question of this status by referring to apparent contrasts which involve the *-chen* suffix [-çən] seemingly matching the sequence [-xən]; Moulton (32) cites four examples to support the notion of the separate identity of these two consonants:

Tauchen [ˈtaʊçən] 'little rope' — tauchen [ˈtaʊxən] 'to dive'
Kuhchen [ˈku:çən] 'little cow' — Kuchen [ˈku:xən] 'cake'
Frauchen [ˈfʀaʊçən] 'little woman' — hauchen [ˈhaʊxən] 'to breathe'
Mamachen [ˈmamaçən] 'little Mum' — bestachen [bəˈʃtaxən] 'stabbed'

Wiese (2000: 69, 217) disputes this argument by recognizing the first set with the *-chen* suffix [-çən] as compounds consisting of two lexical items, and the second set as single word stems with affixes, citing Bloomfield (1933) in support. In other words, the <ch> in the first set is the initial consonant of the *second* item, whereas the <ch> in the second is the final consonant of the word stem (see also Kohler 1999: 86). Hall (1992: 42–46) also agrees and comments on *Kuhchen* as a marginal word 'that is hardly ever used'! Indeed, they all appear to be contrived in an attempt to prove a point. In fact, Martens and Martens, Wängler and Kohler do not cite any contrasts. In this presentation, these *ch*-sounds are represented as a single phoneme and symbolized by /x/, as Hall does.

r-sounds. There is considerable discussion among scholars about the range of phonetic realizations, and considerable disagreement too. Two preliminary issues must first be resolved: the various phonetic realizations which have been noted, and the various relevant distributional positions within syllables.

The various phonetic realizations that have been noted are listed below, using only IPA symbols (converting idiosyncratic symbols accordingly):

voiced alveolar (apical) trill:	[r]
voiced alveolar (apical) flap:	[ɾ]
voiced uvular trill/flap:	[ʀ]
voiced uvular fricative:	[ʁ]
voiceless uvular fricative:	[χ] (carrying the aspiration of voiceless plosives)
voiced approximant:	[ʀ̞]
vocalized, syllabic:	[ɐ]
vocalized, non-syllabic:	[ɐ̯]

Relevant distributional positions within syllables are listed below, together with authors' suggested phonetic realizations:

Table 4.1 Allophonic variations of the phoneme /ʀ/

	initial single *rot*	initial cluster *Brot*	inter-vocalic *bohren*	before C *Wort*	final *Ohr*	*-er* unstressed *Bohrer*
Duden	ʀ	ʀ	ʀ	ʀ	ɐ̯	ɐ
Martens	r/ʀ	r/ʀ	r/ʀ	r/ʀ	ɐ̯	ɛɐ̯
Moulton	r/ʀ	r/ʀ	r/ʀ	ʀ/ɐ̯	ʀ/ɐ̯	ɐ
Wängler	r/ʀ	r/ʀ	r/ʀ	r/ʀ	r/ʀ	ʀ̞
Kohler	ʁ	ʁ, χ	ʀ̞	ɐ	ɐ	ɐ
Hall	r/ʀ/ʁ	r/ʀ/ʁ	r/ʀ/ʁ	ɐ̯	ɐ̯	ɐ
Wiese	ʁ/ʀ̞	ʁ/ʀ̞	ʀ̞	ɐ	ɐ	ɐ

As Wiese noted (2000: 170), no other consonant in German has such a large set of allophonic realizations. Nor, one might add, such a large set of descriptions. What is clear, however, is that the general principles of complementary distribution and free variation apply, to suggest a single phoneme. The principle of phonetic similarity needs further comment since two variations of the *r*-sound are vocalic, rather than consonantal. Yet, even in this respect, the tongue position of [ɐ] is not far from the tongue position of uvular articulations from which it is clearly derived. Therefore, in other words, all three major criteria for establishing the *r*-sounds as allophones of a single phoneme are met.

Martens and Martens, Moulton, Wängler and Hall all opt to symbolize the phoneme as /r/; Kohler prefers /ʁ/, and Wiese /ʀ/. It seems sensible to recognize the most widely used articulation in modern *Hochdeutsch* for its primary symbol as a phoneme: /ʀ/; the only oddity of doing so is probably transcribing unstressed *-er* as /əʀ/. /ʀ/ would have to be 'interpreted' allophonically as in, e.g. *Duden* above.

Neutralization. The fourth issue regarding the transcription of German consonants concerns the cases of neutralization within the obstruent system. The obstruent system consists of 6 plosives: /p, t, k, b, d, g/; 8 fricatives: /f, s, ʃ, x, h, v, z, ʒ/; and 4 affricates: /pf, ʦ, ʧ, ʤ/. They are all units within their systems because they maintain contrasts that are responsible for the differentiation of words and their meanings. However, they do not maintain contrasts in all positions within a syllable; in other words, their contrastive potential is restricted, and where it is restricted, their contrast potential is said to be 'neutralized' (or '*aufgehoben*', 'cancelled', 'suppressed').

Trubetzkoy (1958/1967: 69–75) describes four different kinds of neutralization, but only two are relevant to German. The first is where a contrasting pair of consonant phonemes is replaced by a sound that is not identical to the phonetic forms of either of the pair. This is case of the neutralization of /p - b/, /t - d/ and /k - g/ after syllable-initial sibilant fricatives. There is no contrast after initial /ʃ/; the /p - b/ contrast, for instance, is not maintained in this phonological context, but what appears in its place is a sound that is neither the fortis aspirated voiceless [pʰ] nor the lenis non-aspirated voiced [b], but a lenis non-aspirated voiceless [b̥]; similarly with /t – d/, [d̥]. Trubetzkoy (1958/1967: 69–75) called the replacement sound an 'archiphoneme'. However, conventionally, the voiceless phoneme is used in transcription: *Spatz* /ʃpats/; *Stadt* /ʃtat/.

This kind of neutralization is retained in the newer vocabulary that allows clusters with initial /s/:

/sp/ Spezies, Spirans
/st/ Stil, Stoiker ('stoic')
/sk/ Skelett, Skizze

and

/ʃk/ Schkeuditz, Schkopau (two place-names in Germany)

where the 'archiphonemes' are, phonetically lenis: [b̥, d̥, g̊].

The second kind of neutralization is where one of the contrastive pair of phonemes appears and the other does not. The most well-known case is that of the non-appearance of voiced obstruents in syllable-final position (*Auslautverhärtung*), despite standard spelling. The 'archiphoneme' functions as a phoneme by contrasting with other phonemes while allowing no contrast between fortis voiceless and (lenis) voiced forms. Syllable-final <b, d, g, v, s, ge> are pronounced with their equivalent fortis voiceless counterparts. Examples include:

lieb 'dear' with final /p/; but *Liebe* 'love' with medial /b/
Rad 'wheel' with final /t/; but *Räder* 'wheels' with medial /d/
Tag 'day' with final /k/ (or /x/); but *Tage* 'days' with medial /g/
tätig 'busy' with final /x/; but *tätiger* 'busier' with medial /g/

brav 'good, honest' with final /f/; but *Bravo* with medial /v/
los 'loose' with final /s/; but *lose* 'movable' with medial /z/
orange 'orange (colour)' with final /ʃ/; but *Orange* 'orange (fruit)' with medial /ʒ/.

This syllable-final 'process' of fortis voiceless articulation applies mid word with following consonants in suffixes and compounds, e.g.

Liebling 'darling' with /p/
Radfahren 'cycling' with /t/
täglich 'daily' with /k/ (or /x/)
Tätigkeit 'activity' with /x/
Bravheit 'good, honest behaviour' with /f/
losarbeiten 'to work loose' with /s/
orangefarben 'orange coloured' with /ʃ/

It should also be noted that this second kind of neutralization takes place in a situation analogous to the first context mentioned above: the contrast /f – v/ is neutralized by 'archiphonemes' as phonemes in their own right: /v/ only occurs after initial /ʃ/, and /f/ only occurs after initial /s/:

Schweiz /ʃvaɪts/ 'Switzerland'
Sphäre /ˈsfɛːʀə/ 'sphere'

The clustering of consonants in syllable final-position is complicated by two other factors: morphological suffixation, and the segments that join the two elements of compounds, the so called *Fugenvokal* or *-konsonant*.

Morphological suffixation is either syllabic, i.e. with a vowel, usually /ə/, e.g. *Pferd+e/+en* ('horse, horses, horses, dat.'), or non-syllabic consisting only of a consonant or two, e.g. *Sommer+s* ('of summer'), *Auto+s* ('cars'), *gib+t* ('(he/she/it) gives'), *gebt* ('(you, pl) give'), *gibst* ('(you, sg) give'), and /-n/ in *Sommer+n* ('summers', dat.) and words like *vor+n*. Such non-syllabic consonantal suffixes have the capacity to increase the complexity of syllable-final consonant clusters, especially with the genitive singular and *du* forms of verbs. In the tables below, cases with morphological suffixation with be marked with| before the suffix.

Secondly, there is the case of non-syllabic consonantal 'jointing' of the two elements of a compound. Not all compounds require this 'jointing' mechanism, however, e.g. *Fugemaschine* 'jointing machine' (<*Fuge* + *maschine* 'joint' + 'machine'). On the other hand, others do, usually displaying a relic of a historical genitive form with either /-n-/ or /-s-/ (see Bithel 1952: 295), e.g. *Fugenvokal* (<*Fuge* +n+ *Vokal*; 'jointing vowel'), *Hilfsmittel* (<*Hilf-* +s+ *Mittel*; 'help' + 'means' = 'device, remedy'). This latter case produces a final cluster /-lfs/, which does not otherwise occur. In the tables below, cases with this *Fugenkonsonant* /s/ will be shown up as /s-/, e.g. /lfs-/ marking the consonant as syllable-final, but not word-final.

4.2.4 Syllable-final Margins

Each syllable type has its own system of final consonantal clustering (**4.2.2**):

Type 1: stressed syllables (either primary or secondary) with short vowels must take a consonant, with a full total of four;
Type 2: stressed syllables (either primary or secondary) with long vowels may be either open, with no consonant following, or closed with up to three consonants following;
Type 3: unstressed syllables may be either open or closed with up to two consonants, or three with a suffix;
Type 4: nasalized syllables with either primary or secondary stress are only open, and therefore will not figure in this particular section.

The sequences within final consonant clusters respect the degrees of sonority (*Schallfülle*, Jespersen 1932: 190–193) in reverse order. The consonants with the greatest degree of sonority, according to Jespersen and illustrated in German, are *r*-sounds and then laterals and nasals. The hierarchy for the consonants stands as follows, adapted slightly for German. Although /ʀ/ is realized as a flap, trill and fricative as well as an approximant, it occupies the degree of greatest sonority among the consonants. The voiceless obstruent group of articulations are collapsed into one group as they were phonologically for English (see **1.3**).

2 Voiced *r*-sounds
3 Voiced laterals
4 Voiced nasals
5 Voiced fricatives
6 Voiced plosives
7 Voiceless obstruents

It is therefore to be expected that if the first consonant in a final cluster has degree 7, any following consonant is confined to other consonants with degree 7. And that is found to be the case, as illustrated in the data charts below. Since consonants with degrees 5 and 6 are excluded in final position, the next relevant consonants are those with degrees 3 and 4. /ʀ/ with degree 2 is followed by any consonant with a lower degree of sonority; /l/ with degree 3 cannot be followed by /ʀ/ but may be by nasals and voiceless obstruents; nasals with degree 4 cannot be followed by either /ʀ/ or /l/ but are followed by voiceless obstruents only. Hence there are more consonant clusters with an initial resonant consonant.

Permissible syllable-final consonant clusters will be illustrated first from the two non-nasalized types of stressed syllable structure; in fact, it is only necessary to use Type 1 with the short stressed vowels, since they have the largest inventory of possibilities, with up to four consonants. Type 2 with the stressed long vowels select accordingly, up to three. Final clusters in unstressed syllables are very much simpler and should be treated separately. There are no final clusters in syllables with nasalized vowels. Data charts for these three syllable types provide the evidence for the networks that follow.

Type 1/2 syllables have the following final single consonants and clusters of two (- = not a possible sequence; blank = highly unlikely or no token):

Table 4.2 Data charts for final margins of syllables type 1 and 2

<table>
<tr><th>single</th><th>+p</th><th>+t</th><th>+k</th><th>+f</th><th>+s</th><th>+ʃ</th><th>+x</th><th>+ pf</th><th>+ʦ</th><th>+m</th><th>+n</th><th>+l</th></tr>
<tr><td>p knapp</td><td>-</td><td>Abt</td><td></td><td></td><td>Schnaps</td><td>hübsch</td><td></td><td></td><td></td><td>-</td><td>-</td><td>-</td></tr>
<tr><td>t Bett</td><td></td><td></td><td></td><td></td><td>Bett|s</td><td></td><td></td><td></td><td></td><td>-</td><td>-</td><td>-</td></tr>
<tr><td>k Rock</td><td></td><td>Akt</td><td>-</td><td></td><td>Fuchs</td><td></td><td></td><td></td><td></td><td>-</td><td>-</td><td>-</td></tr>
<tr><td>f Stoff</td><td></td><td>Luft</td><td></td><td>-</td><td>Stoff|s</td><td></td><td></td><td></td><td>seufz-</td><td>-</td><td>-</td><td>-</td></tr>
<tr><td>s daß</td><td></td><td>Lust</td><td></td><td></td><td>-</td><td></td><td></td><td></td><td></td><td>-</td><td>-</td><td>-</td></tr>
<tr><td>ʃ wasch</td><td></td><td>wäsch|t</td><td></td><td></td><td>Tisch|s</td><td>-</td><td></td><td></td><td></td><td>-</td><td>-</td><td>-</td></tr>
<tr><td>x Dach</td><td></td><td>Macht</td><td></td><td></td><td>Dach|s</td><td></td><td>-</td><td></td><td></td><td>-</td><td>-</td><td>-</td></tr>
<tr><td>pf Kopf</td><td></td><td>hüpf|t</td><td></td><td></td><td>Kopf|s</td><td></td><td></td><td>-</td><td></td><td>-</td><td>-</td><td>-</td></tr>
<tr><td>ʦ Spatz</td><td></td><td>sitz|t</td><td></td><td></td><td></td><td></td><td></td><td></td><td>-</td><td>-</td><td>-</td><td>-</td></tr>
<tr><td>ʧ deutsch</td><td></td><td>eingedeutsch|t</td><td></td><td></td><td></td><td></td><td></td><td></td><td></td><td>-</td><td>-</td><td>-</td></tr>
<tr><td>m Lamm</td><td>Lump</td><td>Amt</td><td></td><td></td><td>Wams</td><td>Ramsch</td><td></td><td>Kampf</td><td>-</td><td>-</td><td>-</td><td>-</td></tr>
<tr><td>n Bann</td><td>-</td><td>Hand</td><td>-</td><td>Senf</td><td>Hans</td><td>Wunsch</td><td></td><td></td><td>Tanz</td><td>-</td><td>-</td><td>-</td></tr>
<tr><td>ŋ lang</td><td>-</td><td>sing|t</td><td>Bank</td><td></td><td>läng|s</td><td></td><td>Mönch</td><td></td><td></td><td>-</td><td>-</td><td>-</td></tr>
<tr><td>l voll</td><td>Kalb</td><td>kalt</td><td>Kalk</td><td>Wolf</td><td>Hals</td><td>falsch</td><td>Milch</td><td></td><td>Holz</td><td>Halm</td><td>Köln</td><td>-</td></tr>
<tr><td>ʀ Herr</td><td>Korb</td><td>Start</td><td>stark</td><td>Dorf</td><td>ander|s</td><td>Marsch</td><td>durch</td><td></td><td>Herz</td><td>Form</td><td>vor|n</td><td>Kerl</td></tr>
</table>

clusters of three, based on permissible clusters of two:												
	+p+t	+p+s	+t+s	+k+t	+k+s	+f+t	+f+s	+s+t	+ʃ+t	+x+t	+x+s	
p	-	-	Haupt|s					Papst				
t			-					-	-			
k			Akt|s	-	-			Axt				
f			Geschäfts-					hoff|st				
s								-	-			
ʃ								wäsch|st	-			
x			nacht|s					lach|st		-	-	
pf								hüpf|st				
ts								-				
tʃ	-								-			
m	pump|t	Mumps	Amt|s					nimm|st		-	-	
n	-	-	Lands-	-	-	Ankunft	Hanf|s	Kunst	wünsch|t	-	-	
ŋ	-	-	-	lenk|t	link|s	-	-	Pfingst-	-	tünch|t	Mönch|s	
l	salb|t	Kalb|s	Gestalt|s	folg|t	Volk|s	hilf|t	Hilfs-	Wulst	fälsch|t		Elch|s	
ʀ	stirb|t	Korb|s	Pferd|s	Markt	Marx	Werft	Dorf|s	Wurst	herrsch|t	Furcht	Storch|s	
	+ pf+t	+ pf+s	+ts+t	+m+t	+m+s	+n+t	+n+s	+l+t	+l+s			
p	-	-		-	-	-	-	-	-			
t			-	-	-	-	-	-	-			
k				-	-	-	-	-	-			
f	-	-	seufz|t	-	-	-	-	-	-			
s			-	-	-	-	-	-	-			
ʃ			-	-	-	-	-	-	-			

x			ächz|t	-	-	-	-	-	-			
pf	-	-		-	-	-	-	-	-			
ts			-	-	-	-	-	-	-			
tʃ			-	-	-	-	-	-	-			
m	schimpf|t	Kampf|s	-	-	-	-	-	-	-			
n	-	-	tanzt	-	-	-	-	-	-			
ŋ	-	-	-	-	-	-	-	-	-			
l			walz|t	qualmt	Qualm|s ?		Köln|s	-	-			
ʀ			Arzt	barm|t	Worms	warn|t	Horn|s	perl|t	Kerl|s			

and clusters of four, based on permissible clusters of three, but only possible with final /-st/ or genitive /-s/:

	-p+st	-pf+st	-t+st	-k+st	-f+st	-ʃ+st						
p	-	-										
t			-									
k				-								
f					-							
s						-						
ʃ						-						
x												
pf		-										
ts			-									
tʃ						-						
m	pump|st	schimpfst										
n			send|st									

ŋ				denk|st								
l	selb|st		hält|st	folg|st	hilf|st	fälsch|st						
ʀ	Herbst		art|st	berg|st	darf|st	herrsch|st						
**												
	-x+st	-m+st		-n+st	-l+st	-k+t+s	-f+t+s	-s+t+s				
p												
t												
k												
f												
s												
ʃ												
x	-											
pf												
ts												
tʃ												
m		-										
n	tünch|st		-			-						
ŋ		-		-								
l		film|st			-			Wulst|s				
ʀ	horch|st	barm|st		Ernst	quirl|st	Markt|s	Werft|s					

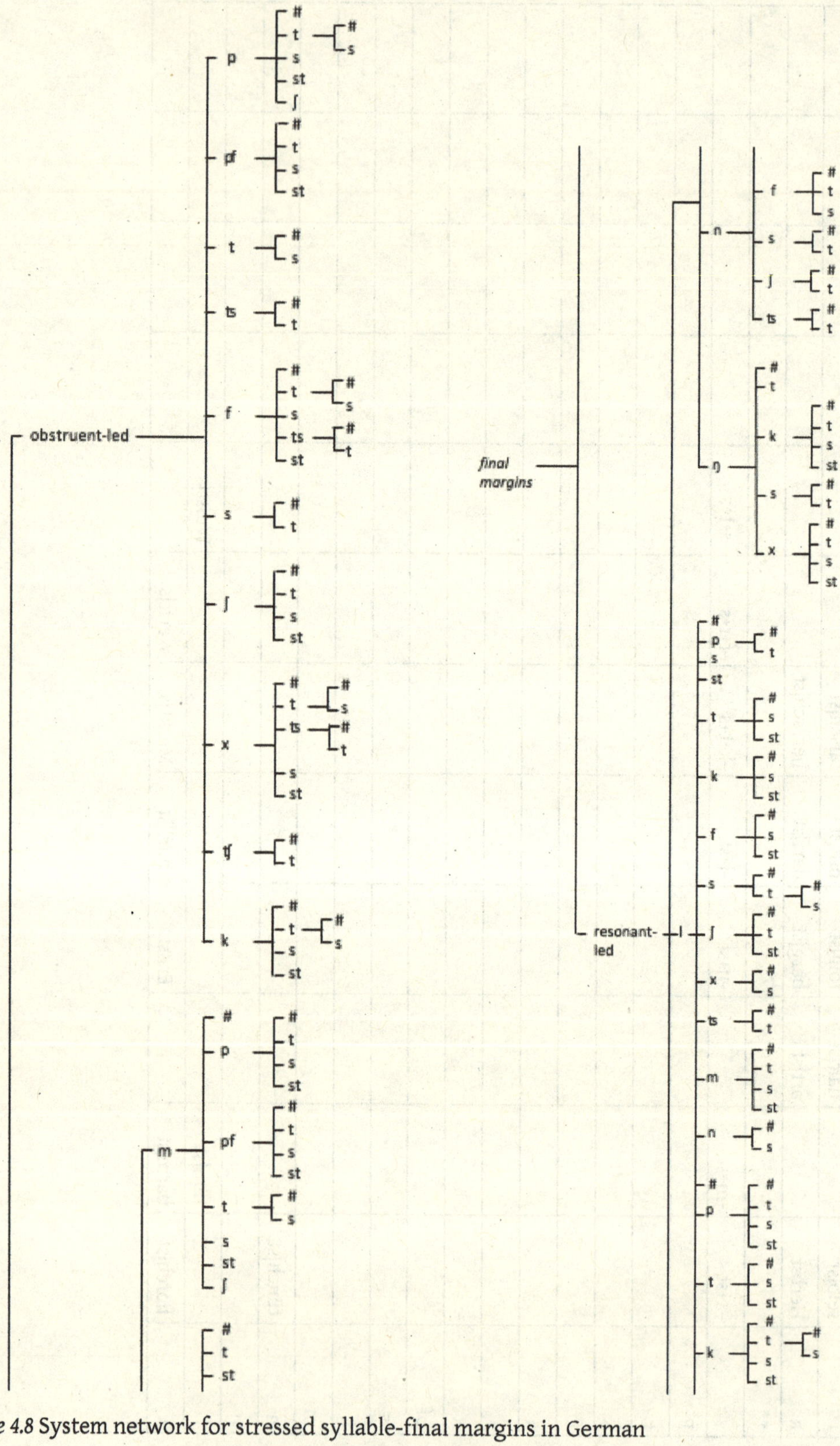

Figure 4.8 System network for stressed syllable-final margins in German

The genitive singular suffix /-s/ does render possible a five-consonant cluster with *des Herbsts* ('of the autumn') and *Ernsts* ('Ernst's') which might well occur in rapid colloquial speech; similarly, it could extend *Obst* to *Obsts* ('of the fruit') in Type 2 structures. However, not all scholars regard such extensions as acceptable.

Apart from this last consideration, a system network of consonant clusters as final margins in German stressed syllables can be presented as follows. Final /-st/ is presented as a combined sequence, but genitive /-s/ as a singleton. The network is overt and explicit, to make it as comprehensible as possible, with a division between obstruent-led and resonant-led clusters.

Type 3 final clusters in unstressed syllables present a much simpler system. First of all, it should be noted that not all unstressed vowels can take a final margin; it was noted above that /ɪ, e, o, u, y, ø/ do not; they only occur in open unstressed syllables. Others, on the other hand, must do so, namely: /ɪ, ɛ, ɔ, ʊ, ʏ/; they only occur in closed unstressed syllables; while /a, ə/ occur in both. The following table shows what is permissible as final margins in unstressed syllables:

Table 4.3 Data charts for final margins of syllable type 3

	+t	+s	+ʃ	+x	+m	+n	+ŋ	+l	+ʀ		
ɪ		Arktis	englisch	billig		Ärztin					
ɛ					empor				Erfolg		
a	Heimat	China|s									
ɔ						Kontrolle					
ʊ		Stoizismus					Übung				
ʏ		System									
ə	hattet	Obstes			Atem	hatten		Mittel	Lied|er		
	+t+s	+st	+m+s	+n+t	+n+s	+l+t	+l+s	+l+n	+ʀ+t	+ʀ+s	+ʀ+n
ɪ											
ɛ				entweder							
a	Heimats-			Heiland							
ɔ											
ʊ											
ʏ											
ə		hattest	Atems	Abend	ersten|s	wandelt	Handel|s	wandeln	andert	Winter|s	andern
	+n+t+s	+l+st		+l+n+t	+ʀ+st						
ɪ											
ɛ											
a	Heiland|s										
ɔ											
ʊ											
ʏ											
ə	abend|s	wandelst		wandelnd	wanderst						

These possibilities can be presented in a system network as follows:

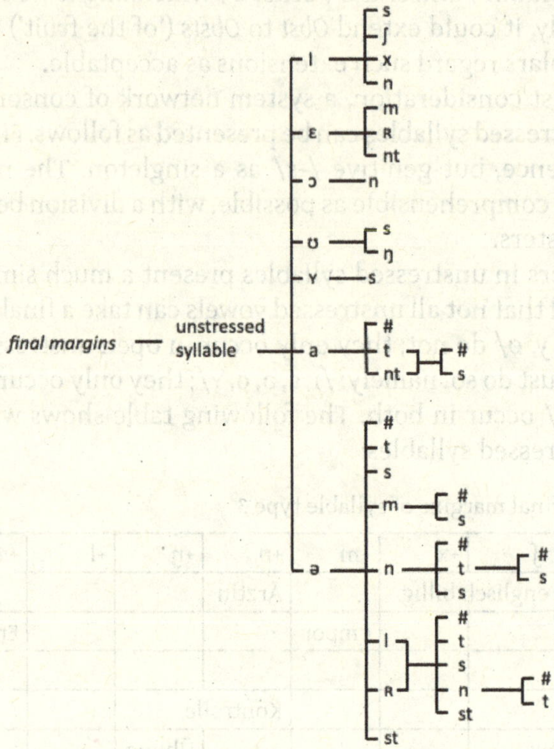

Figure 4.9 System network for unstressed syllable-final margins in German

We noted above that Type 4 nasalized syllables are open syllables with no coda.

4.2.5 Syllable-initial Margins

Finally, the structure of syllable-initial margins. These are considerably simpler than the systems for syllable-final structures on three accounts: clusters extend to three consonants at most and not four (or even five); there are no sequences of resonants in initial clusters; and there are no inflectional modifications at the beginnings of words.

Syllable-initial margins may be zero or contain up to three consonants. Zero onset of stressed syllables is marked phonetically by the glottal stop [ʔ], the so called *harter Vokaleinsatz*, as in *Achtung* /ˈ[ʔ]axtʊŋ/, *verachten* /fɛʀˈ[ʔ]axtən/. It is not, as a rule, marked in unstressed syllables, e.g. *sehen* is not *[zeːʔən] but /zeːən/; *Durcheinander* is not *[dʊʀxʔaɪnʔandəʀ], but is pronounced without any glottal stops.

As for phonemic onsets, the following consonants appear in initial margins, though not in final margins: voiced obstruents (/b, d, g, v, z, ʒ, ʤ/), /h/ and /j/; on the other hand /ŋ/ does not appear initially. The resonants /m, n, l, r, j/ may occur alone or only as final items in initial clusters. The sequence within a cluster otherwise regularly follows the features of the sonority hierarchy, with obstruents preceding resonants. A distinction has to be made once again between regular words of traditional German origin and those which are 'irregular', either *Lehnwörter* or *Fremdwörter*. The consonants /s, ʒ, ʧ, ʤ/

only feature in syllable-initial margins in *Lehnwörter* and *Fremdwörter*, e.g. *Skizze, Genie, Tscheche, Dschungel.* The other consonants are illustrated in the following examples:

Table 4.4 Data chart for syllable-initial margins

single		+p	+t	+v	+m	+n	+l	+R	+p+l	+p+R	+t+R
/p/	Paar	-	-	-	-	-	Plan	Prall	-	-	-
/b/	bar	-	-	-	-	-	blasen	braten	-	-	-
/pf/	Pfarrer	-	-	-	-	-	Pflanze	Pfropf	-	-	-
/f/	fahren	-	-	-	-	-	flach	Frage	-	-	-
/v/	wahr	-	-	-	-	-	-	Wrack	-	-	-
/t/	tarnen	-	-	-	-	-	-	trat	-	-	-
/d/	da	-	-	-	-	-	-	Draht	-	-	-
/ʦ/	zart	-	-	zwar	-	-	-	-	-	-	-
/ʃ/	Schar	Spar-	Star	schwarz	schmal	Schnabel	Schlaf	Schrat	Spleiße	Sprache	Strahl
/z/	sah	-	-	-	-	-	-	-	-	-	-
/k/	Karte	-	-	Quark	-	Knabe	klar	Kram	-	-	-
/g/	Garten	-	-	-	Gmund	Gnade	Glas	Grad	-	-	-
/x/	-chen	-	-	-	-	-	-	-	-	-	-
/m/	Mahr	-	-	-	-	-	-	-	-	-	-
/n/	Narr	-	-	-	-	-	-	-	-	-	-
/l/	lahm	-	-	-	-	-	-	-	-	-	-
/r/	Rahm	-	-	-	-	-	-	-	-	-	-
/j/	Jahr	-	-	-	-	-	-	-	-	-	-

The system of syllable-initial margins of regular words might look like this, where capital *V* indicates that /ʃp, ʃt/ has the option of preceding a vowel as well as /l, R/:

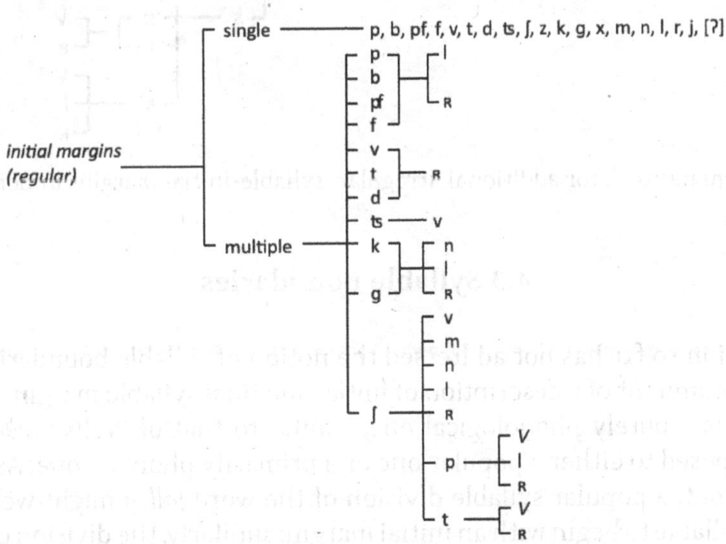

Figure 4.10 System network for regular syllable-initial margins in German

The syllable-initial margins of *Lehnwörter* and *Fremdwörter* may additionally consist of the following possibilities:

/ps/ Psalm
/pʃ/ Pschorr
/pn/ Pneumatik
/ks/ Xaver
/s/ City
/sp/ Spezies
/spr/ sprayen
/st/ Stil, Stoiker
/str/ streamen
/sk/ Skelett, Skoda, Skat
/skl/ Sklave
/skr/ Skrupel
/sm/ Smoking
/sn/ Snob
/sl/ Slalom
/ʒ/ Jalousie
/ʧ/ tschüß
/ʤ/ Dschunke

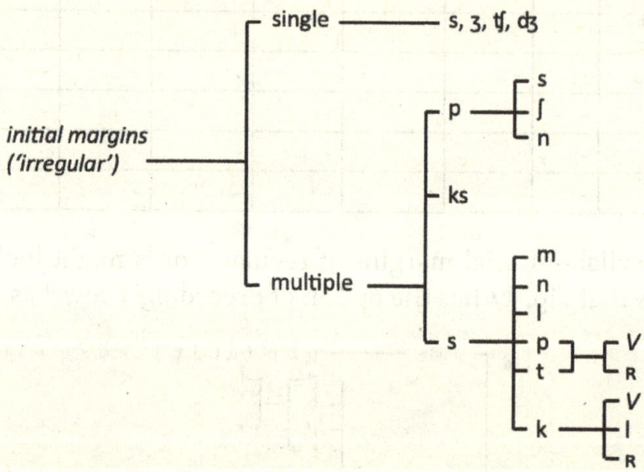

Figure 4.11 System network for additional 'irregular' syllable-initial margins in German

4.3 Syllable Boundaries

The presentation so far has not addressed the notion of syllable boundaries, which is a necessary concomitant of a description of initial and final syllable margins. The position adopted here is a purely phonological one, similar to that of Wells (1990: xix–xx) for English, as opposed to either a popular one or a primarily phonetic one. As Wiese (2000: 35–37) points out, a popular syllable division of the word *fallen* might well be /fa.lən/, preferring a syllable to begin with an initial margin; similarly, the division of *reisen* might well be /ʀaɪ.zən/, but what about *reißen* as /ʀaɪ.sən/? In the last case, the final syllable would begin with /s/ which is not permissible in regular German words (as opposed to *Lehnwörter* and *Fremdwörter*). The phonological answer is to regard the boundary as falling between /s/ and /ə/; this preserves the general rule that /s/ may occur regularly in syllable-final margins but not in initial margins, and this means that the boundary, phonologically speaking, falls as /ˈʀaɪs.ən/. This then would equally apply to *fallen* and *reisen* as /ˈfal.ən/ and /ˈʀaɪ.zən/. In other words, phonological syllable boundaries respect the distribution of phonemes in regular monosyllables.

Many other examples could be taken, but two are chosen to highlight the phonological nature of boundaries, rather than popular or purely phonetic. First of all, compare *Physik* and *System*: both take 'late primary stress'; the boundary in *Physik* must fall immediately after <y> (/y/) rather than after <s> (/z/) because otherwise the first syllable would end in a voiced obstruent */fyz.ˈiːk/, which is not permissible in regular monosyllables, hence /fy.ˈziːk/. On the other hand, the boundary in *System* must fall as /sʏs.teːm/, because /ʏ/ occurs only in unstressed syllables that are closed, and initial /st-/ is not permissible in regular monosyllables, */sʏ.ˈsteːm/.

The second example focusses on the glottal stop as the zero onset of a stressed syllable. Compare *vereisen* ('to freeze') and *verreisen* ('to go on a journey'): both take the unstressed prefix *ver-*, but in the former, it precedes a syllable with zero onset which is articulated with [ʔ], yielding syllable boundaries as /fɛʀ.ˈaɪz.ən/, whereas the latter has syllable boundaries as /fɛʀ.ˈʀaɪz.ən/.

In conclusion, Wiese's (2000: 35) examples of optional syllabification can be simply resolved phonologically as follows:

erstens /ˈɛrst.əns/
Fenster /ˈfɛnst.əʀ/
Elster /ˈɛlst.əʀ/
Ängste /ˈɛŋst.ə/
edles /ˈeːt.ləs/
regnen /ˈreː.gnən/
extra /ˈɛks.tra/ (or possibly: /ˈɛkst.ra/, but unlikely because of the principle of onset maximization; see Wiese 2000: 52–53).

There is also no requirement to consider single intervocalic consonants as 'ambisyllabic' (as /l/ in *fallen*) as he maintains, even though there might be phonetic justification for it. Pike (1947: 246) argued for the distinction between phonetic and phonemic syllables (see above **1.3**), and this applies to German too.

4.4 Simplifications

Simplifications are the result of the easing of articulatory movements, which in most cases does not result in loss of meaning. Each language simplifies in its own way, and so simplification processes belong to the phonology of a language (see **1.4**). Simplifications affect words, phrases, clauses and sentences, in various degrees according to style and tempo. Jespersen (1932: 169–177), Bithel (1952: 188–217) and Hall (1992: 138–157) provide the most detailed coverage of simplification processes in German words; they involve elision and assimilation. Hall distinguishes both a relaxed style of speech and a rapid casual style of conversation from a more careful style; there are, no doubt, also many finer degrees of style. He illustrates the three styles as follows, with, however, the symbols used in this presentation:

	Wir haben in Bonn einen Film gesehen
careful:	viʀ 'ha:bm̩ ɪn'bɔn aɪnn̩ 'fɪlm g'ze:ən
relaxed:	viʀ 'ha:bm̩ ɪm'bɔn aɪn 'fɪlm g'ze:ən
casual:	vɐ 'ha:m ɪm'bɔn n̩ 'fɪlm g'ze:n

Elision in German words affects consonants, vowels and whole syllables; even in Hall's illustration of careful speech, the elision of /ə/ is noted twice: the instances of /m̩/ and /n̩/. In the more casual speech, the consonants /ʀ, b/ are elided, the vowel /aɪ/ and whole syllables are elided.

Assimilation is illustrated above even in careful speech: the /-ən/ of *haben* has not only lost its vowel, but /n/ has been adjusted to the bilabial articulation of the preceding /b/; a case of progressive assimilation. In the more relaxed style, the /n/ of *in* before *Bonn* is adjusted likewise, but in this case to the following /b/; a case of regressive assimilation.

In this presentation, space prevents a description of simplifications beyond careful and relaxed speech.

Elision. The elision of consonants mainly affects /t/ 'trapped' between other consonants: Jespersen cites *Hauptman* as /ˈhaʊpˌman/, *Nachttisch* as /ˈnaxˌtɪʃ/, and phrases like *recht gut* as /ˈʀɛx'gu:t/, *hast du?* as /ˈhas du/, etc.; Hall cites *festlich* as /ˈfɛslɪx/, *Häftling* as /ˈhɛflɪŋ/, etc.

The elision of vowels mainly affects /ə/, especially in final /-ən, -əl/ following homorganic obstruents in close transition, yielding either a syllabic nasal or lateral: *treten* /ˈtre:tən/ becomes /ˈtre:tn̩/, *Boden* /ˈbo:dən/ becomes /ˈbo:dn̩/, *Reisende* /ˈʀaɪzəndə/ becomes /ˈʀaɪzn̩də/, etc. See also below under *Assimilation* for other nasal possibilities. A syllabic lateral emerges from such words as

Mittel	/ˈmɪtl̩/	vermitteln	/fɛʀˈmɪtl̩n/
Handel	/ˈhandl̩/	handeln	/ˈhandl̩n/
Schlüssel	/ˈʃlʏsl̩/	wechseln	/ˈvɛksl̩n/
Diesel	/ˈdi:zl̩/	rieseln	/ˈʀi:zl̩n/

It should be noted that there is otherwise open transition between /l/ and any other preceding obstruent, as in English (see Chapter 2, **2.3**, p. 39), e.g. *Apfel* /ˈapfəl/, and so, technically, the /l/ is not syllabic (although some linguists treat this case, phonologically, as if syllabic, e.g. Hall 1992: 59, as ['apfl̩]).

The elision of whole syllables also affects /-ə/, which is frequently lost in such contexts as final in verb forms: *ich habe* /ɪx 'ha:p/ and *habe ich?* /ˈha:b.ɪx/ ; and in *es* as in *wie geht es?* as /vi 'ge:t s/, and *mache es gut* as /ˈmax s 'gu:t/. It also affects unstressed /a/ in *dar-* adverbs, so that *daran* /da'ʀan/ becomes /ˈdʀan/, *darauf* /ˈdʀaʊf/, *darum* /ˈdʀʊm/, etc.

Elision results also in the coalescence of prepositions and articles as two consecutive unstressed syllables: *in dem* becomes *im*; *in das*, *ins*; *bei dem*, *beim*, etc. However, if the article is stressed, elision does not take place, e.g. *in dem Moment* /ɪn ˈdeːm moˈmɛnt/ ('at *that* moment').

Assimilation. The principal example of assimilation in German is the adjustment of /n/ to its immediate environment. Assimilation is either phonemic, with the adjustment of a phoneme, in this case /n/, to another phoneme in the system, e.g. /m/; or phonetic, with the adjustment being an allophonic variation of /n/, e.g. [ɱ], as in *Senf* [zɛɱf]. Only phonemic instances of assimilation are considered in a presentation of word phonology. Assimilation is also either 'progressive', i.e. a phoneme affects the articulation of the following one, or 'regressive', i.e. a phoneme affects the articulation of the preceding one; occasionally, both happen in the same instance, what Jespersen (1932: 170) called *doppelseitige Assimilation* and Bithel (1952: 195) 'bilateral assimilation'. Progressive and regressive assimilation were illustrated in Hall's example above: the bilabial articulation of /b/ of *haben* affects, 'progressively', the following /n̩/, yielding /ˈhaːbm̩/; while the /b/ of *Bonn* can affect, 'regressively', the preceding /n/, yielding /ɪm ˈbɔn/.

Progressive, phonemic, assimilation is further illustrated in the following examples:

Lippen /ˈlɪpən/ becomes /ˈlipm̩/
Leben /ˈleːbən/ becomes /ˈleːbm̩/
Abend /ˈaːbənt/ becomes /ˈaːbm̩t/
lecken /ˈlɛkən/ becomes /ˈlɛkŋ̍/
Wagen /ˈvaːgən/ becomes /ˈvaːgŋ̍/

Regressive, phonemic, assimilation, likewise in these examples:

/ˈaɪn-/ becomes /ˈaɪm-/ in Einpacken, Einblick, einmal
/ˈaɪn-/ becomes /ˈaɪŋ-/ in Einkauf, Eingang

And in many other examples of prefixes with final /-n/: *an, gegen, in, neben, von, un, zwischen.*

Incidentally, Jespersen (1932: 170) provides *nebenbei* as an instance of bilateral assimilation, by which /-ən/ becomes /m̩/ following the elision of /ə/ and under pressure of preceding and following bilabial articulations. He might also have provided *Gegenkraft* as another example, to illustrate syllabic /ŋ/. Bithel (1952: 193–195) points out how these simplification processes have operated historically, producing *Imbiss, Himbeere* (= *Beere, die die Hinde gern frisst*), *Wimper* (from *wintbrâwe*); also the prefix *emp-* in *empfangen, empfehlen, empfinden*, in contrast to the prefix *ent-* before other phonemes, e.g. *entarten, entdecken, entgegen, entlang*, etc.

Simplifications with syllabic nasals and lateral require amendments to the system network proposed above for unstressed syllable-final margins in German, to accommodate the following: *leben, lebend, abends, treten, erstens, Heiland, Heilands, Handel, Handels, wandeln, wandelnd, wandelt, wandelst.*

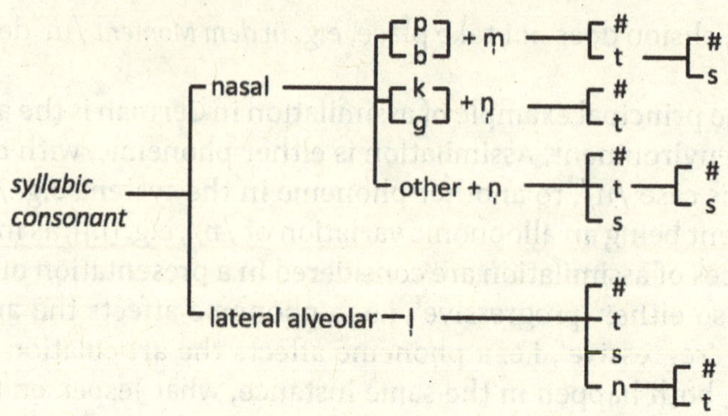

Figure 4.12 System networks with syllabic consonants following obstruents in unstressed syllable-final margins in German

4.5 Conclusion

Naturally, by looking at the characteristics of the word phonology of another language, the **non-universal** dimension of Systemic Phonology is highlighted. Although German belongs to the same language family as English and has a number of phonological features in common, the foot types and systems are different, as are the syllable types and structures, the 'rules' for syllabification and the details of simplifications.

Nevertheless, the **hierarchy** of ranks of feet, syllables and phonemes is shared with English, although we have only considered allophonic features in an incidental way. The **polysystemic** principle has been prominent again: the foot potential of *Fremdwörter*, distinctive syllable types and structures, strong and weak vowel systems, nasalized vowels and consonant margins, including neutralization features. We introduced data charts to provide the evidence for **system networks.** The German simplification system network illustrated the **syntagmatic** dimension, by the articulatory impact of one segment on neighbouring ones in assimilation and epenthesis.

Chapter 5

Word Phonology of Welsh

5.1 Introduction

Welsh is spoken extensively in Wales, by about 700,000 people in a total population of approximately 3 million. It is also spoken in Argentina by as many as 5,000 people as a result of Welsh emigration from the mid-nineteenth century into areas of Patagonia (BBC 2014), and also, in smaller numbers, in USA, Canada and the rest of UK, again as a result of migration. Welsh is a Celtic language, in the Brythonic branch, which also includes Breton and Cornish. It is an official language in Wales alongside English.

Welsh has a number of notable features. It is a verb-subject-object (VSO) language. It has a distinctive word class of verb-nouns, some of which also operate within larger verbal groups to form the equivalent of modals and the passive. Prepositions are conjugated like verbs. Possessive pronouns consist of elements preceding and following a noun. In phonology, there is a very strong tendency to maintain penultimate stress whatever suffixes are added to a word; initial consonants are subject to change ('mutation') in certain syntactic contexts, including definite reference with feminine nouns; and the phonotactics of vowels and final consonants within a syllable or word is intriguingly elaborate.

A sociolinguistic feature of Welsh is that there is no single standard accent in Wales. However, the collection of accents in the North of Wales have enough common factors to suggest, in general terms, a North-Walian accent (see, e.g. Kelly 1992), and similarly, a collection of accents in the South have enough common factors to suggest a South-Walian accent. Several studies show a gradation of phonetic and systemic features between Northern and Southern accents, with the South-West being the simplest system of all (see Rees 2018 and his cited bibliography). It is commonly heard that North-Walians claim that their accent is the purest because it is the richest in terms of systemic inventories. It is also the case that the percentages of Welsh speakers in the populations of the North is very much greater than those in the South; nevertheless, the populations of the South are greater in numbers. It is therefore necessary to either develop two separate system networks for the North and the South, or combine them in such a way that the South system is shown to be a reduction of the North system.

The description of Welsh phonology that underlies this new presentation in terms of Systemic Phonology is based upon the following scholarly work: Awbery (1984; 2009), Ball and Jones (1984), Ball and Williams (2001),[1] Clee (2017), Hannahs (2009; 2013), Iosad (2017), Kelly (1992), Mayr and Davies (2011), Rees (2018) and Williams (1989), as well as local informants.

In the Argentinian province of Patagonia, Welsh has been spoken continuously since the first Welsh settlers landed in 1865. As more Welsh settlers arrived in the nineteenth century, their language community became well established. Although the settlers originated from all parts of Wales, it appears that elements of the South-Walian accents prevailed even though the Northern syntactic and lexical items of the Welsh Bible were preserved. Use of the language declined in the first half of twentieth century under pressure from government language policies and the inward migration of Spanish-speaking workers attracted into a relatively prosperous economic environment. However, a revitalization of the language began with the centennial celebrations of 1965, and continued with eisteddfod events, the remarkable impact of a dedicated, highly respected Welsh missionary, Mair Davies in the Welsh chapels (see Davies 2012), and the Welsh Language Project managed locally since 1997 but financed principally from Wales (Arwel 2016; see also Johnson (2009; 2010) and Coupland and Garrett (2010)). The impact of this revitalization has led to a re-evaluation of the significance of Patagonian Welsh within the Welsh language community in Wales, which justifies its inclusion in this present study; see **5.8 Spanish Influences**, as a separate study, below.

5.2 Foot Structures of Words in Welsh

Our starting point again is the rank of foot in the phonological hierarchy as in English and German, but as we shall see the system and its phonetic expression are quite different. North- and South-Walian accents share a common prosodic pattern of word shapes. There are four prosodic shapes that the foot takes for words in their citation forms, as exemplified below, which are then followed by a description of compound words (**5.2.2**). But the phonetic realization of the Welsh foot needs attention first.

5.2.1 Phonetic Realization of the Foot in Welsh

The basic form of the Welsh foot is trochaic: a stressed syllable followed by a single, less stressed, syllable. As in stress realizations in English and German, all three prosodic features are involved but their distribution in Welsh is quite different. Whereas the initial, stressed, syllable retains the loudness feature, which is reinforced by the lengthening of any following consonants, the second less stressed syllable acquires the features of higher pitch and greater duration. This different distribution of the prosodic features contributes to a distinctive sense of Welsh rhythm. See Williams (1989), Kelly (1992) and Ball and Williams (2001: 169–185) for details of experimental data.

The foot may also be a single stressed syllable, as in monosyllabic words. It combines the characteristic features of loudness, pitch rise and duration of the Welsh foot onto that one syllable.

In words of three syllables, the final two syllables normally fulfil the trochaic structure of the foot. If the initial syllable contains a short vowel with no final margin, it is unstressed, i.e. a light syllable. If, however, the initial syllable contains a long vowel or has a final margin, or both, the syllable is heavy and is credited with secondary stress. As such it constitutes a separate, 'subordinate' foot. The final foot is always the main foot in Welsh, containing primary stress.

In words of four syllables, the first two follow the trochaic pattern and so they constitute a subordinate foot. Again, the first syllable of the subordinate foot takes secondary stress, allowing the final foot to remain the main foot.

In words of five or more syllables, the pattern follows the trisyllabic form if the number of syllables is uneven; otherwise, the pattern follows the pattern with an even number of syllables.

We were careful to describe the trochaic foot as stressed syllable followed by a 'less stressed' syllable, rather than by a weak syllable. Because the second syllable carries part of the prosodic form, it maintains a certain level of stress that cannot be designated phonetically as unstressed. Hence, unlike in English or German, scholars have proposed another level of stress, tertiary. This has phonological significance since the vowel system in tertiary stressed syllables differs from that in unstressed ('light') syllables. Examples of these different possibilities appear below.

It should also be noted that, again unlike in English and German where there is a tendency for vowel quality in unstressed syllables to become more centralized, this is distinctly not the case in Welsh. In fact, in Welsh the central vowel /ə/ features in the system of vowels in stressed syllables, and is actually forbidden in an unstressed final syllable.

The foot structure in Welsh words remains constant whatever morphological additions are made. This can be seen in these examples.

cân	/ˈkaːn/	'song, poem'	(one foot: primary stress)
caniad	/ˈkanjad/	'song'	(one foot: primary + tertiary stress)
caniadau	/kaˈnjadaɨ/	'songs'	(one foot: weak + primary + tertiary stress)
caniadaeth	/kaˈnjadaɨθ/	'music'	(one foot: weak + primary + tertiary stress)
canu	/ˈkanɨ/	'to sing'	(one foot: primary + tertiary stress)
cantor	/ˈkantɔr/	'singer'	(one foot: primary + tertiary stress)
cantorion	/kanˈtɔrjon/	'singers'	(two feet: secondary + primary + tertiary stress)
caniedydd	/kaˈnjɛdɨð/	'song-writer'	(one foot: weak + primary + tertiary stress)
caniedyddion	/ˌkanjɛˈdəðjɔn/	'song-writers'	(two feet: secondary + weak + primary + tertiary stress)
cytgan	/ˈkətgan/	'chorus'	(one foot: primary + tertiary stress)
cytganau	/kətˈganaɨ/	'choruses'	(two feet: secondary + primary + tertiary stress)
datgan	/ˈdatgan/	'to declare, state'	(one foot: primary + tertiary stress)
datganu	/datˈganɨ/	'to recite'	(two feet: secondary + primary + tertiary stress)
datganiad	/datˈganjad/	'declaration, recital'	(two feet: secondary + primary + tertiary stress)
datganiadau	/ˌdatgaˈnjadaɨ/	'declarations, recitals'	(two feet: secondary + weak + primary + tertiary stress)
datgeiniad	/datˈgeinjad/	'narrator'	(two feet: secondary + primary + tertiary stress)

5.2.2 The Phonology of the Foot in Welsh

There are three main prosodic shapes of the foot, and a fourth that occasionally arises through loan words from English.

1 *Monosyllables*

Monosyllables, naturally, receive primary stress. This includes not only lexical items in citation forms, but grammatical items also in citation forms and when used emphatically. In these cases, the foot is a single stressed syllable. (It should also be noted that in connected speech, grammatical items usually lose their stress, and often their syllabicity.)

2 *Regular polysyllables*

The general rule is that the penultimate syllable in the vast majority of polysyllabic words is stressed, no matter what the morphological structure of the word may be, as exemplified in **5.2.1** above; more examples:

/ˈdarɬɛn/ *darllen* 'to read'	/ˈkanɔl/ *canol* 'central'
/darˈɬɛnur/ *darllenwr* 'reader'	/kaˈnɔlvan/ *canolfan* 'centre'
/darɬɛnˈaduɨ/ *darllenadwy* 'readable'	/kanɔlˈvanaɨ/ *canolfannau* 'centres'

In this case, the foot is the normal trochaic sequence of one stressed syllable followed by tertiary stress; thus, a regular disyllabic word consists of single foot. Then, as explained above, the first syllable of a regular trisyllabic word is either a 'heavy' syllable (with two moras, e.g. a long vowel or vowel with a final consonant) with secondary stress, as in

/ˌdarˈɬɛnur/ *darllenwr* 'reader'

or a 'light' syllable, unstressed, as in

/kaˈnɔlvan/ *canolfan* 'centre'

The foot structure of words with four syllables consists of two feet (see Hannahs 2013: 47–51), as in

/ˌdarɬɛˈnaduɨ/ *darllenadwy* 'readable' /ˌkanɔlˈvana/ *canolfannau* 'centres'

The final foot is always the main foot and preceding feet are subordinate within the phonological word.

3 *Final stressed (irregular) polysyllables*

There are certain words of Welsh origin that regularly require stress on their final syllable, which constitutes the main foot; preceding syllables follow the pattern explained in 2 above. A comprehensive listing is found in Griffiths and Jones (1995). Many of them are quasi-compounds, e.g.

- emphatic pronouns: /məˈviː/ *myfi* 'myself'
- compound adverbs, adjectives and prepositions: /hɛbˈlau/ *heblaw* 'besides' (*heb* 'without' + *llaw* 'hand')

- certain compound verbs beginning with *ym-* : /əmˈhɛl/ *ymhel* 'to meddle' (*ym* 'reciprocal' + *hel* 'to hunt'). However, there are cases where there is a contrast in stress placement that leads to a contrast in meaning: /əmˈla:ð/ *ymlâdd* 'to tire oneself' and /ˈəmlað/ *ymladd* 'to fight'; /əmˈðuɨn/ *ymddwyn* 'to bear (a child)' and /ˈəmðuɨn/ *ymddwyn* 'to behave' (Ball and Williams 2001: 166–167, 177).
- compounds of *gwneud, gweld*: /ˌailˈʷneɨd/ *ail-wneud* 'to re-do'; /ˌkəvˈwɛld/ *cyfweld* 'to interview'
- nouns ending with the suffix *-âd, -had*: /ˌkanjaˈta:d/ *caniatâd* 'permission'; /ˌparˈha:d/ *parhad* 'continuation'
- 'loose' compound (see below under *Compounds*) formed with the prefixes *di-*, *cyd-*, *cyn-*, *cam-*, *gor-*, *hunan-* : /diˈðiu/ *di-dduw* 'godless'; /ˌhɨnanˈdɨ:b/ *hunan-dyb* 'selfishness'. However, a contrast can be demonstrated between the loose compound /ˌdiˈvla:s/ *di-flas* 'tasteless' with final stress and the regular polysyllabic stress of /ˈdɪvlas/ *diflas* 'distasteful'. Similarly, between *cyn-* /kɨn-/ 'former, ex-' as in /ˌkɨnˈʷraig/ *cyn-wraig* 'ex-wife' and *cyn-* /kən-/ 'first, early' as in /ˈkənvɨd/ *cynfyd* 'ancient world'.

Others display diachronic coalescence of two consecutive vowels becoming a diphthong, e.g.

- verb-nouns ending in *-au, -oi, -eu*: /ˌmuinˈhaɨ/ *mwynhau* 'to enjoy'; /ˌparaˈtɔi/ *paratoi* 'to prepare'; /kəvˈleɨ/ *cyfleu* 'to imply'
- adjectives ending in *-aus, -eus, -ous, -aeg, -eig*: /kəvˈleɨs/ *cyfleus* 'convenient'; /kəmˈraig/ *Cymraeg* 'Welsh (language)'; /kəmˈreig/ *Cymreig* 'Welsh'; also /kəmˈra:ɨs/ *Cymraes* 'Welsh woman'

4 *Loan words*

Loan words from English tend to preserve the stress pattern of the original form, which might involve an 'alien' foot structure of stressed syllable followed by two less stressed, e.g.

/ˈkɪlɔgram/ *cilogram* 'kilogram'
/ˈparagraf/ *paragraff* 'paragraph'

However, when these words take on suffixes, they 'revert' to the pattern of *regular polysyllables*:

/ˌkɪlɔˈgramaɨ/ *cilogramau* 'kilograms'
/ˌparaˈgrafaɨ/ *paragraffau* 'paragraphs'

Here are other examples with suffixes that display shift to the foot structure of regular polysyllables:

/aˈpe:l/ *apêl* 'appeal'; /aˈpe:laɨ, ape:lˈiadɨ/ *apelau, apeliadau* 'appeals'
/ˌkaŋgaˈru:/ *cangarŵ* 'kangaroo'; /ˌkaŋgaˈru:ɔd/ *cangarŵod* 'kangaroos'
/ˌəmbaˈrɛl/ *ymbarél* 'umbrella'; /ˌəmbaˈrɛlaɨ, əmbaˈrɛlas/ *ymbarelau/ymbarelas* 'umbrellas'

Compounds

In addition to the 'quasi-compounds' listed in 3 above, which consist basically of a prefix and a stem, there are 'proper' compounds that are usually classified as either strict or loose, according to their stress pattern. These compounds consist of two lexical items, the first qualifying the second. Strict compounds are fused tightly into single lexical items, orthographically, as in

/ˈbragdɨ/ *bragdy* 'brewery' (< *brag* + *tŷ* 'malt' + 'house')
/ˈfɛrmdɨ/ *ffermdy* 'farmhouse' (<*fferm* + *tŷ* 'farm' + 'house')

There is one primary stress, in its regular penultimate place. The /t/ of *tŷ* becomes voiced under the influence of the preceding voiced consonant, a case of 'progressive assimilation'. Other examples display what is known as 'provection', the devoicing of a voiced obstruent, as in

/wɨˈnɛprɨd/ *wynepryd* 'countenance' (<*wyneb* + *pryd* 'face' + 'form, aspect'; /b/→/p/)
/aˈbatɨ/ *abaty* 'abbey' (<*abad* + *tŷ* 'abbot' + 'house'; /d/→/t/)
/kɔˈstauki/ *costawci* 'mastiff' (<*costawg* + *ci* 'surly' + 'dog'; /g/→/k/) (see Hannahs 2013: 153)

In these cases, there is again a single primary stress, and in its regular penultimate place.

'Loose' compounds, on the other hand, take two stresses, one on each element, secondary and primary, and are orthographically separate. Examples are taken from Ball and Williams (2001: 168)

/aˌdɛrɨn ˈdɨ/ *aderyn du* 'blackbird' (<*aderyn* + *du* 'bird' + 'black')
/ˌkadair ˈvaur/ *cadair fawr* 'armchair' (<*cadair* + *fawr* 'chair' + 'big')
/ˌkadair ˈɛsmʊiθ/ *cadair esmwyth* 'easy chair' (<*cadair* + *esmwyth* 'chair' + 'comfortable')

The first element receives a secondary stress, the final element the primary, in line with the foot sequence of subordinate + main, mentioned above.

It is pointed out that, just as in English, such compounds are distinguished from phrases by the strength of stressing:

/aˈdɛrɨn ˈdɨ/ *aderyn du* 'a black bird'
/ˈkadair ˈvaur/ *cadair fawr* 'a big chair'
/ˈkadair ˈɛsmʊiθ/ *cadair esmwyth* 'a comfortable chair'

with primary stresses on both words in each phrase, requiring two main feet in sequence.

The stress pattern of loose compounds, therefore, entirely depends on the syllabic nature of the final element; if the final element is monosyllabic, primary stress will fall on this final syllable; if the final element is polysyllabic, primary stress will fall in its regular penultimate place. This can also be demonstrated with place names:

/ˌɬanˈdaːv/ *Llandaf* 'Llandaff'
/ˌɬanˈgɔɬɛn/ *Llangollen*
/ˌɬanəˈmauðʊi/ *Llanymawddwy*
/ˌɬanəmˈðəvri/ *Llanymddyfri* 'Llandovery'
/ˌabɛrˈθau/ *Aberthaw*

/ˌabɛrˈtawɛ/ *Abertawe* 'Swansea'
/ˌabɛrgəˈnɔlwɨn/ *Abergynolwyn*
/ˌabɛrˌgwɨnˈgrɛgɪn/ *Abergwyngregyn*

5.3 Syllable Types and Structures

It is important to distinguish between the types of syllables because they determine the system of vowels that can appear in them. It seems, in the first place, useful to distinguish six types: the three primary cases of stress presented above, and three corresponding unstressed types:

1. Stressed monosyllables (primary)
2. Stressed penultimate syllables of regular polysyllables (primary), including stressed syllables (i.e. secondary) that precede primary stressed syllables
3. Stressed final syllables of irregular polysyllables (primary)
4. Unstressed final syllables of regular polysyllables (tertiary)
5. Unstressed syllables preceding a primary stress (weak)
6. Unstressed monosyllables (weak)

Syllables have a structure consisting of a vowel – whether short, long or diphthongal – as the peak (or 'nucleus'), in open syllables (without a final consonant) and closed syllables (with a final consonant). There are no phonological syllabic consonants in this presentation; see the relevant discussion below under **5.4.3 Final Margins.** Syllables have systems of consonants in initial and final position consisting of either a singleton or double and triple clusters.

Syllables may consist of a single vowel:

/iː/ *i* 'to'

with a single initial consonant:

/siː/ *si* 'murmur'

with a double initial consonant cluster:

/briː/ *bri* 'fame'

and, but rarely, with a triple initial consonant cluster:

/spriː/ *sbri* 'spree, fun'

Also, with a single final consonant:

/iːs/ *is* 'below'
/siːr/ *sir* 'county'

With a double final consonant cluster:

/sɪkr/ *sicr* 'sure'

And, occasionally, with a triple final consonant cluster:

/ɬɛstr/ *llestr* 'vessel, dish'

5.4 Syllable Margin Systems

Consonants and consonant clusters form both onsets and codas of syllables, but their systems differ.

In initial position syllables may have zero, single, double and triple consonants. There appears to be no restriction on vowels that can open syllables.

5.4.1 Initial Margins in Citation

All consonants may appear as singletons initially except /ŋ, χ/, although each of these re-appear in initial position in mutation forms (see below). /θ, ð, l, r/ only occur very rarely in initial position in basic word forms, but do so regularly in mutation forms (see **5.4.2** below). The permissible two-member combinations in 'basic' (i.e. non-mutated) words are shown in the chart below. In these 'data charts', the evidence is provided to justify the system networks that follow. For simplicity's sake, English glosses are omitted.

Table 5.1 Preliminary evidence of initial margins in Welsh

	single	+l	+r	+j	+w	+nasal
p	*pa*	*pla*	*prae*	*pioden*	*pwerus*	
b	*bae*	*blaen*	*braen*	*bioleg*	*bwaog*	
t	*tal*	*tlawd*	*traws*			
d	*dal*		*draw*	*diodydd*	*dweud*	
k	*cae*	*claer*	*crair*	*cieidd-dra cweir*		*cnaif*
g	*gair*	*glan*	*grawn*	*giachod*	*gwaun*	
f	*ffa*	*fflach*	*ffraeth*	*ffieiddio*		
v	*faint*		*fry*	*fiola*		
θ	*thus*					
ð	*ddoe*					
s	*saer*	*slumyn*			*swatio*	*smala, snisin*
ʃ	*siarad*					
χ	-				*chwa*	
h	*hau*				*hwiangerdd*	
ɬ	*llan*			*llieiniau*		
l	*lan*					
r̥	*rhan*			*rhieni*		
r	*rŵan*					
j	*iâ*					
w	*wedi*					
m	*mae*			*mieri*		
n	*na*					
ŋ	-					

It will observed that /θ, ð, ʃ/ do not combine with any consonant in a cluster; that /l, r, n, j, w/ do not occur as the first member of a cluster but regularly do so as the second;

that /ɬ, r̥, m/ only take /j/ as a second element, and /χ, h/ only take /w/ as second element, even though /χ/ may not occur as a singleton.

There is an isolated case of three-consonant clusters involving the initial sequence of /gw-/, as in *gwlad* 'country, land', *gwraig* 'wife', *gwneud* 'to do, make'. There are three possible interpretations to this case: either as a labialized /g/ as /gʷ/, or as a glide (or semivowel) /gw/, or even possibly as an extra-short unstressed vowel /gŭ/. This feature is confined to cases involving clusters with /l, r, n/; all members of the three clusters are rounded, but there is open rounded 'transition' between /g-/ and /l, r, n/ in contrast to the closed transition of *glwth* /glu:θ/ 'couch' and *grwn* /grʊn/ 'ridge (in a field)', which are rounded on account of the following rounded vowel. Accordingly, the cluster system includes, with additional examples:

gwl	*gwlân*	'wool'
gwr	*gwrando*	'to listen'
gwn	*gwnïo*	'to sew'

Clusters with initial /s-/ take voiceless plosives as their second member, in addition to the /l/ and the nasals illustrated above. Many of these cases derive from well-established loan words.

sp	*sbio*	'to spy'
st	*stwc*	'pail'
sk	*sgip*	'skipping rope'

There is a very limited set of three-member combinations, based on the /sp-, st-, sk-/ initial clusters, again mainly from well-established loan words, followed by /r/ and in one case with /w/.

spr	*sbri*	*'spree'*
str	*stryd*	*'street'*
skr	*sgrech*	*'screech'*
skw	*sgwâr*	*'square'*

The syllable-initial margin system for basic word forms in Welsh might be presented as follows:

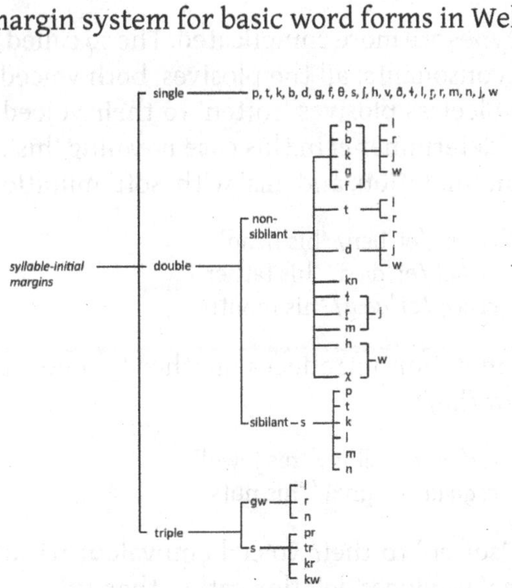

Figure 5.1 System network for syllable initial margins of basic word forms in Welsh

5.4.2 Initial Margins in Mutation

There is also a highly significant separate system of initial consonants in a range of syntactic environments, where certain initial consonants change ('mutate'). There are three types of consonant change ('mutations') and also one type of consonant addition to words with initial vowel, which is traditionally called 'aspiration', but is in fact a voiceless vowel onset. In the latter case, /h/ is added after certain pronouns and possessive determiners, e.g.

arian /ˈarjan/ 'money' *ei harian* /ei ˈharjan/ 'her money'

This also happens with *ugain* 'twenty' after *ar* 'on', e.g.

ugain /ˈɪgain/ 'twenty' *un ar hugain* /ˈɨ:n ar ˈhigain/ 'twenty one'

For a full discussion of all the relevant syntactic environments, a grammar of Welsh should be consulted, e.g. Morris-Jones (1913), Griffiths and Jones (1995).

The three types of consonant mutations affect three different ranges of consonants. The simplest type is the so called 'spirant mutation' where the three voiceless plosives become equivalent voiceless fricatives, under certain kinds of syntactic environment. One is, again, the effect of the possessive determiner *ei* 'her' preceding a noun:

pen /pɛn/ 'head' *ei phen* /ei ˈfɛn/ 'her head'
tad /ta:d/ 'father' *ei thad* /ei ˈθa:d/ 'her father'
ceg /ke:g/ 'mouth' *ei cheg* /ei ˈχe:g/ 'her mouth'

It will be observed that this 'spirant mutation' dramatically increases the number of instances of word-initial /θ/ and also introduces /χ/ as an initial singleton. It also introduces two new initial consonant clusters /θl/ from /tl/, and /χn/ from /kn/:

tlws /tlu:s/ 'jewel' *ei thlws* /ei ˈθlu:s/ 'her jewel'
cnau /knaɨ/ 'nuts' *ei chnau* /ei ˈχnaɨ/ 'her nuts'

The other mutation types are more complicated. The so called 'soft mutation' involves a much wider range of consonants: all the plosives, both voiced and voiceless, and /m, ɬ, r̥/. In this type, the voiceless plosives 'soften' to their voiced equivalents, for example after the possessive determiner *ei* in this case meaning 'his'. Note, therefore, that *ei* means 'her' with 'spirant' mutation, and 'his' with 'soft' mutation:

pen /pɛn/ 'head' *ei ben* /ei ˈbɛn/ 'his head'
tad /ta:d/ 'father' *ei dad* /ei ˈda:d/ 'his father'
ceg /ke:g/ 'mouth' *ei geg* /ei ˈge:g/ 'his mouth'

Note also that 'soft' mutation introduces another two new consonant clusters /dl/ from /tl/, and /gn/ from /kn/:

tlws /tlu:s/ 'jewel' *ei dlws* /ei ˈdlu:s/ 'his jewel'
cnau /knaɨ/ 'nuts' *ei gnau* /ei ˈgnaɨ/ 'his nuts'

The voiced plosives 'soften' to their voiced equivalent fricatives, but in the case of initial /g/, the 'softening' produces deletion rather than [ɣ]:

brawd /braud/ 'brother' *ei frawd* /ei ˈvraud/ 'his brother'
dant /dant/ 'tooth' *ei ddant* /ei ˈðant/ 'his tooth'
gardd /garð/ 'garden' *ei ardd* /ei ˈarð/ 'his garden'

This is also the case of the /gw/ clusters; /w/ is retained before the following consonant

gwlad /gwla:d/ 'country' *ei wlad* /ei ˈwla:d/ 'his country'
gwraig /gwraig/ 'wife' *ei wraig* /ei ˈwraig/ 'his wife'
gwnïad /gwnˈi:ad/ 'sewing' *ei wnïad* /ei wnˈi:ad/ 'his sewing'

Again, it will be observed, that this 'soft mutation' dramatically increases the number of cases of word-*initial* /ð/ and also introduces other initial clusters: /wl, wn, wr/.

The so called 'softening' of /m/ renders it /v/:

mam /mam/ 'mother' *ei fam* /ei ˈvam/ 'his mother'

while it renders /ɬ, r̥/ to their equivalent voiced resonants:

llaw /ɬau/ 'hand' *ei law* /ei ˈlau/ 'his hand'
rhieni /r̥iˈɛni/ 'parents' *ei rieni* /ei riˈɛni/ 'his parents'

'Soft mutation' dramatically increases the number of instances of word-initial /l, r/.

The syntactic environments for 'soft' mutation include the use of *yn* as a particle before the attribute of a relational process and the numerals *un* 'one' (with feminine nouns), *dau* 'two' (with masculine nouns), *dwy* 'two' (with feminine nouns), and with some very restricted cases with *saith* 'seven' and *wyth* 'eight'. For example

da /da:/ 'good' *mae'r bachgen yn dda* /... ða:/ 'the boy is good'
merch /mɛrχ/ 'girl' *mae hi'n ferch dda* /... vɛrχ ða:/ 'she is a good girl'
un ferch /ɨ:n vɛrχ/ 'one girl'
punt /pɨnt/ 'pound' *saith bunt* /saiθ bɨnt/ 'seven pounds'

However, 'soft' mutation does not happen after the particle *yn* nor after *un* with feminine words with initial /ɬ, r̥/. So, in such cases, /ɬ, r̥/ resist mutation:

llawen /ˈɬawɛn/ 'happy' *mae hi'n llawen* /mai hin ˈɬawɛn/ 'she is happy'
rhad /r̥a:d/ 'free' *yn rhad ac am ddim* /ən r̥a:d ak am ðɪm/ 'free and for nothing'
llong /ɬɔŋ/ 'ship' *un llong* /ɨ:n ɬɔŋ/ 'one ship'
rhodd /r̥o:ð/ 'gift' *un rhodd* /ɨ:n r̥o:ð/ 'one gift'

Thirdly, there is 'nasal mutation' that affects both voiceless and voiced plosives, but no other consonants. It is primarily associated with the unstressed possessive determiner *fy* /və/ 'my' and the preposition *yn* /ən/ 'in'. The voiceless plosives become their equivalent voiced nasal followed by /h/:

pen /pɛn/ 'head' *fy mhen* /vəm ˈhɛn/ 'my head'
tad /ta:d/ 'father' *fy nhad* /vən ˈha:d/ 'my father'
ceg /ke:g/ 'mouth' *fy ngheg* /vəŋ ˈhe:g/ 'my mouth'

It will be observed how in these instances there is a syllable break between the nasal and the following /h/, despite the spelling that suggests initial consonant clusters of nasal + /h/, which are not otherwise permitted in Welsh phonology. The situation is more complicated with initial consonant clusters involving voiceless plosives:

plant /plant/ 'children' *fy mhlant* /vəm ˈhlant/ 'my children'
tlysau /tləsai/ 'jewels' *fy nhlysau* /vən ˈhləsai/ 'my jewels'
clust /klɨ:st/ 'ear' *fy nghlust* /vəŋ ˈhlɨ:st/ 'my ear'

In careful speech, as transcribed above, a new consonant cluster is introduced through 'nasal' mutation: /hl/. The effect on clusters with /r/ is different; the /r/ effectively becomes voiceless /r̥/:

priod /ˈpri:ɔd/ 'spouse' *fy mhriod* /vəm ˈr̥i:ɔd/ 'my husband/wife'
troed /tro:ɨd/ 'foot' *fy nhroed* /vən ˈr̥o:ɨd/ 'my foot'
croen /kro:ɨn/ 'skin' *fy nghroen* /vəŋ ˈr̥o:ɨn/ 'my skin'

In these instances, speakers interpret the orthographic sequence <hr> as if <rh>, i.e. /r̥/.

In the case of voiced plosives, the mutation is directly to their nasal equivalents, without /h/.

barf /barv/ 'beard' *fy marv* /və ˈmarv/ 'my beard'
dant /dant/ 'tooth' *fy nant* /və ˈnant/ 'my tooth'
gardd /garð/ 'garden' *fy ngardd* /vəŋ ˈarð/ 'my garden'
gwlad /gwla:d/ 'country' *fy ngwlad* / vəŋ ˈwla:d/

The situation with consonant clusters follows the same pattern:

brawd /braud/ 'brother' *fy mrawd* /vəm ˈraud/ 'my brother'
draig /draig/ 'dragon' *fy nraig* /vən ˈraig/ 'my dragon'
glo /glo:/ 'coal' *fy nglo* /vəŋ ˈlo:/ 'my coal'

In the case of the rounded /gw/ as in *gwlad*, the rounding is retained in the following consonant, as it is in 'soft' mutation:

gwlad /gwla:d/ 'country' *fy ngwlad* /vəŋ ˈwla:d/ 'my country'
gwraig /gwraig/ 'wife' *fy ngwraig* /vəŋ ˈwraig/ 'my wife'

It will observed once again that whereas the orthography suggests 'impermissible' word-initial consonant clusters, syllable breaks prevent this in pronunciation.

It must be emphasized again that these phonological processes in mutation relate to a much wider range of syntactic environments than this presentation suggests. For a full grammatical presentation, a grammar of Welsh should be consulted, but these mutation processes remain constant.

The syllable-initial margins of words with mutation highlight the polysystemic principle of Systemic Phonology; they might be presented as follows:

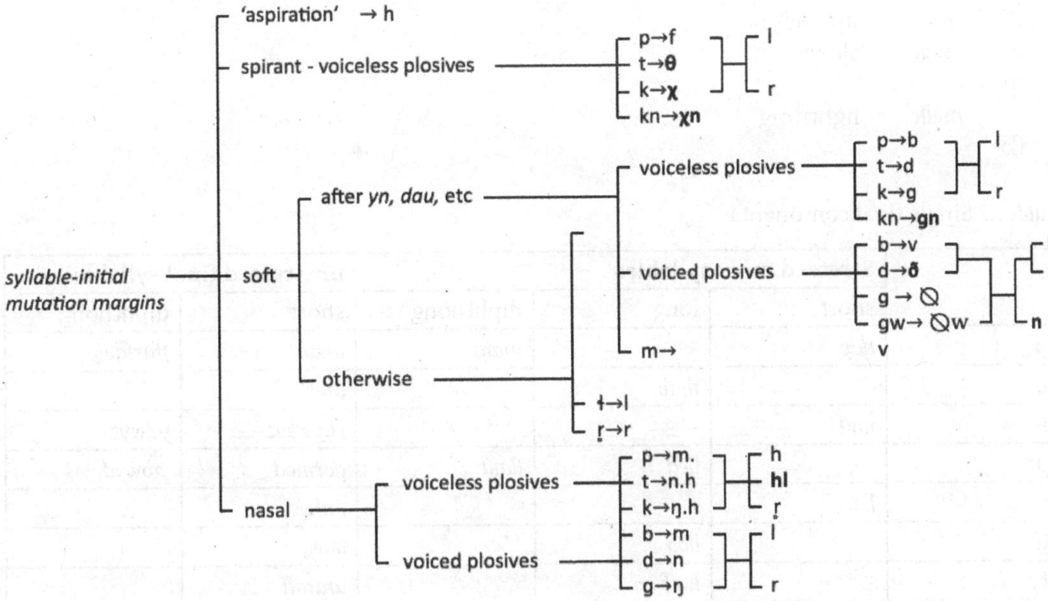

Figure 5.2 Systemic network of initial consonants in mutations, with significant differences from the basic system of Welsh, in **bold**

5.4.3 Final Margins

In syllable-final position, all consonants can appear as singletons, except /h, r̥/, and also /j, w/ if they are not reckoned as final elements of diphthongs. /ʃ/ only occurs finally in recent loan words from English; see below **5.7 Recent English Borrowings.** /ʧ/ occurs in a few words like *cwtsh*, borrowed from Middle English *couche* (whence Modern English *couch*); likewise *saetsh*[2] 'sage', *coetsh* 'pram'.

Syllable-final consonants have a profound phonotactic effect on the structures of syllables in Welsh, as they determine the type of vowel that may precede them, as is shown in the following 'data chart', in which – indicates 'impermissible'; blank indicates 'not attested'; and brackets indicate 'rare'. As above, the data charts are intended to provide the evidence for the system networks that follow.

Two-member clusters have the same profound effect on the structure of syllables. If the two members are both voiceless obstruents, the preceding vowel is long in the North, but short in the South. The first member is a fricative and the second a plosive. Obstruent clusters are illustrated in the following chart, showing that not all potential clusters are permitted.

fp	-	
ft	*wfft*	'for shame'
fk	-	
θp	-	
θt	-	
θk	-	
sp	*cosb*	'penalty'

st *trwst* 'uproar'
sk *cwsg* 'sleep'
ɬp -
ɬt *mel̩lt* 'lightning'
ɬk -

Table 5.2 Single final consonants

	Stressed monosyllables			unstressed final syllable[3]	
	short	long	diphthong	short	diphthong
p	*hap*	-	*maip*	*anap*	*ffurfdeip*
b	-	*mab*		*ateb*	
t	*mat*	-		*rhywsut*	*ydwyt*
d	-	*lled*	*llaid*	*gormod*	*abwyd*
k	*llac*	-		*anlwc*	
g	-	*llog*		*adeg*	
f	-	*hoff*		*argraff*	
v	-	*haf*		*araf*	
θ	-	*llath*	*llaeth*	*popeth*	*cytuniaeth*
ð	-	*lladd*	*hawdd*	*mynydd*	*lluniaidd*
s	-	*mis*	*maes*	*aros*	*adlais*
ʃ	*(brwsh)*				
ʧ	*(cwtsh)*				
χ	-	*llach*	*lluwch*	*bellach*	*cyfuwch*
h	-	-	-	-	-
ɬ	-	*llall*		*Ebrill*	*byrbwyll*
l	*lol*	*hil*	*haul*	*afal*	*gadael*
r̥	-	-	-	-	-
r	*mor*	*môr*	*caer*	*agor*	*ansoddair*
j	-	-	-	-	-
w	-	-	-	-	-
m	*llam*	-	*twym*	*ystum*	*bolrwym*
n	*llan*	*glân*	*llawn*	*calon*	*arwain*
ŋ	*lleng*	-		*ffyrling*	

Potential two-member combinations within clusters occur with other than voiceless obstruents. These clusters are all only preceded by short vowels and certain diphthongs, in both North and South; hence the need for a distinction between the two types of final clusters. Examples are given in the following 'data chart', in which, in this case, brackets indicate repetition of examples already cited in the chart.

Table 5.3 Two-member final margins

	Preceded by				Followed by			
	-vl fric	-l	-r	-nasal	+ vl fric	+l	+r	+nasal
p	*cosb*	*help*	*llarp*	*lamp*				
b						*pobl*	*llwybr*	*llwybr*
t	*mellt*		*llewpart* *maint*					
d			*bord*	*llond*		*cenedl*	*lledr*	*gwadn*
k	*cwsg*		*darn*	*llanc*				
g							*llwgr*	
f								
v	*lleddf*	*celf*	*berf*			*sofl*	*llwfr*	*llafn*
θ			*porth*				*ewythr*	
ð			*gardd*					
s			*cwrs*	*owns*				
ʃ								
χ		*cylch*	*merch*				*ochr*	
h	-		-					
ɬ								
l	*(sofl)*							
r̥	-	-	-			-	-	-
r	*(ochr)*							
j	-	-	-			-	-	-
w	-	-	-			-	-	-
m		*helm*	*fferm*			*aml*		
n	*(llafn)*		*bwrn*					
ŋ								

It should be noted in this present context, that the English word *starch* is rendered in modern Welsh as *startsh*,[4] with a combination of two final consonants.

It might be thought that final /l, r, n/ following an obstruent or nasal constitutes a syllabic consonant, as in English. Indeed, according to Awbery (1984, 2009; see also Hannahs 2009), Welsh speakers in the South tend either to insert an epenthetic vowel ('svarabhakti') of the same quality as the preceding (stressed) vowel, thus creating an extra syllable, as with *aml* 'often' as /ˈamal/, or simplify a cluster such as in *possibl* 'possible' to /ˈpɔsɪb/ and *anadl* 'breath' to /ˈanal/ (but retain /d/ if an inflection is added: *anadlu* /aˈnadli/ 'to breathe'). Both these South-Walian 'solutions' preserve the stress patterning of regular polysyllables.

Hannahs (2009: 22, 27, 29) also refers to a case of metathesis with final /-θr/ in words like *ewythr* 'uncle' and *dieithr* 'strange', which change to /ˈewɨrθ/ and /ˈdiːarθ/. This is another strategy to avoid realizing an extra final syllable.[5] One other strategy in respect to /v/ in words like *cefn* 'back' and *ysgafn* 'light (weight)' is to vocalize it [u]: /ˈkɛun/, /ˈəskaun/, rather like its common weakening in final position as in *cyntaf* 'first' /ˈkənta/.

However, Welsh speakers in the North tend to keep a close transition between the obstruent and final /l, r, n/, which nevertheless appears to correspond to similar English syllabic consonants. But the stress pattern of words like *anadl*, *cenedl* and *possibl* (/ˈanadl/, /ˈkɛnɛdl/, /ˈpɔsɪbl/) suggest conformity to regular polysyllables as two syllables only. Furthermore, the choice of vowel in *llyfr* as /ɪ/ rather than /ə/ indicates that it must be treated as a stressed monosyllable (see **5.5.2.1** below).

The distinction was drawn in **1.3** between phonetic and phonological syllables and this seems to be relevant in this context: the sequence /-nadl/, /-nɛdl/ and /-sɪbl/ may well be two syllables from a phonetic point of view, but they *function* as a single syllable in Welsh word phonology. As a consequence, /ˈanadl/, /ˈkɛnɛdl/ and /ˈpɔsɪbl/ maintain the stress patterning of regular polysyllables. Furthermore, in Welsh poetry, words with final /l, r, n/ in clusters, like *ofn* 'fear', are treated as a single syllable metrically.

All this helps to explain what happens to three-member combinations of a similar kind in syllable-final clusters in Welsh: /-str/, as in *ffenestr* 'window', *llestr* 'dish', *meistr* 'master'. South-Walian speakers 'simplify' the cluster by either eliding the final /r/ as /ˈfɛnɛst/ or inserting an epenthetic vowel as in /ˈɬɛstɛr/ and /ˈmeistɪr/; in both cases, the stress patterning of regular polysyllables is preserved. North-Walian speakers also tend to elide /r/ in *fenestr*, but maintain close transition in *llestr* and *meistr*, which may then be regarded as a stressed monosyllable. With inflections, the sequence /-str-/ is retained: *fenestri* /fɛˈnɛstri/ 'windows'. Furthermore, *calendr* /ˈkalɛndr/ 'calendar' also maintains primary stress on the penultimate, as in regular polysyllables.

The complete system network for syllable-final margins can be presented as follows.

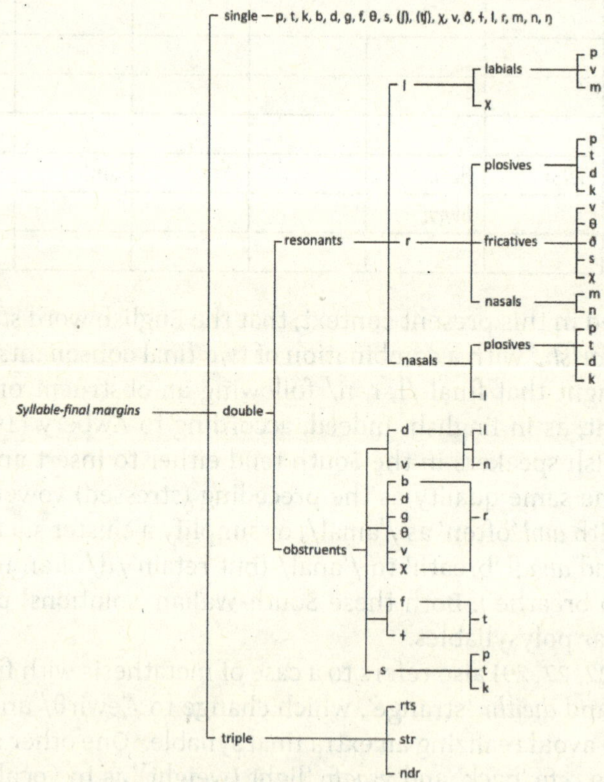

Figure 5.3 System network for syllable-final margins

Syllable division of sequences of consonants in word-medial positions is determined largely by permissible final and initial consonant margins. For instance, the sequence /-χg-/ is not permissible as either a final or an initial cluster, and so the syllable division occurs between the two consonants, as in *bachgen* /ˈbaχ.gɛn/ 'boy'; /χ/ is a permitted final margin, and /g/ a permitted initial margin. Other examples include:

/ˈkʊm.ni/ *cwmni* 'company'
/ˈham.ðɛn/ *hamdden* 'leisure'
/ˈkən.tav/ *cyntaf* 'first'
/əŋ.ˈhɨ:d/ *ynghyd* 'together'
/ˈr̥ag.vɪr/ *Rhagfyr* 'December'

In other instances, where there are possible alternatives to syllable division, pronunciation usually makes the division clear. For instance, the sequence /-dn-/ could be divided as either /-d.n-/ or as /-dn.-/ because the latter is a permissible final cluster. However, speakers, when asked to identify the two syllables of *cadno* 'fox' pronounce the word as /ˈkad.nɔ/. Similarly, the following examples:

/ˈar.dal/ *ardal* 'district'
/ˈkəv.nɔd/ *cyfnod* 'time'

Single medial consonants are usually 'credited' to the following syllable, unless they are 'forbidden' as syllable-initial singletons. For example:

/ˈa.gɔr/ *agor* 'to open'

but

/ˈaŋ.ɛn/ *angen* 'need'

5.5 Syllable Nucleus Systems

It is difficult to separate Welsh vowel categories from syllable-final margins, because they are interdependent. Certain classes of vowels require certain syllable-final margins; or in other words, syllable-final margins demand certain vowel classes to precede them. There is a hint of this interdependence in the initial presentation of final singletons above. However, before a description of the vowel categories, a discussion of the transcription of the vowels is necessary.

5.5.1 Transcribing the Vowels of Welsh

There are major difficulties in determining a comprehensive conventional set of symbols for transcribing the vowels of Welsh. The most obvious difficulty is the distribution of Welsh dialects and whether the pronunciation system of one dialect can serve as a national standard. The principal contenders are standard Northern and Southern accents, but although linguists point out that there are major dialect areas within both, there is common ground in descriptive work to suggest that Northern and Southern standard accents can be recognized. The two accents differ *systemically*, in that the inventory of contrastive vowels is different; they differ *phonetically*, in that phonetic realizations of many vowels differ; and they differ *distributionally*, in that some vowels may occur in certain environments in the North, but not in the South. Furthermore, the vowel system itself is relatively complex, involving short and long monophthongs, and short and long diphthongs; it is also changing by generational shift and by the effect of bilingualism with English with the importing of words from English in UK, and with Spanish in Patagonia, Argentina.

The main systemic difference is that the North includes close central vowels of the type [ɨ] and diphthongs that close towards [ɨ]. The main phonetic difference is that the contrastive distinction between pairs of vowels is based primarily on quantity in the North, e.g. [iː/i] but equally on quality as well as quantity in the South, e.g. [i/ɪ] (see Ball and Williams 2001: 29–40). The end point of closing diphthongs is transcribed differently accordingly, e.g. [ai] in the North and [aɪ] in the South. The distributional differences include short vowels occurring before syllable coda [ɬ] in the North, but corresponding long vowels in that environment in the South. However, it is noticeable that due to generational shift, the incidence of the long vowel is now generally confined to the South West; hence in this presentation, the North-Walian version is adopted as being the fullest inventory, but point out where the South-Walian version differs. There are several other distributional differences that will be detailed later under syllable structures.

Iosad (2017) argues strongly for the phonological status of length (quantity) in the variety of South-west Welsh he described, but this would apply to all accents. Whereas Jones (1984) recognizes the phonetic distinction between long and short vowels, he eschews the length mark in his transcription system. However, many linguists (Awbery 1984, 2009; Griffiths and Jones 1995; Hannahs 2013; Iosad 2017) employ marks for length and distinct symbols for quality differences, rather like linguists describing the vowel system of British English since Gimson (1962). Jones 1984, Awbery 1984, 2009 and Griffiths and Jones 1995) choose [i, u, ɨ] to indicate the endpoint of closing diphthongs, although Hannahs (2013) takes the equivalent lax vowel symbols in two cases, [ɪ, ʊ], but keeps [ɨ]. Ball and Williams (2001), Mayr and Davies (2011) and Rees (2018), on the other hand, recommend the symbol [ɪ] for the short vowel.

There are two other significant differences of a phonetic nature: the diphthong symbolized by many as /əi/ is treated as /ei/ by Awbery and Griffiths and Jones as a more modern rendering; and the recognition of long first elements in the North of three central-closing diphthongs: /aːɨ, oːɨ, uːɨ/ does not apply in the South.

Hence, the transcription system we adopt is as follows:

short vowels
/ɪ, ɛ, a, ɔ, ʊ, ɨ, ə/
long vowels
/iː, eː, aː, oː, uː, ɨː/
front-closing diphthongs
/ei, ai, ɔi, ʊi/
back-closing diphthongs
/ɪu, ɛu, au, əu, ou, ɨu/
central-closing diphthongs
/eɨ, aɨ, ɔɨ/ also /aːɨ, oːɨ, uːɨ/

The South-Walian inventory consists of 20 distinct vowels; the North-Walian 29. Northern /ɨ, ɨː, ɨu/ and the six central closing diphthongs are rendered in the South as /ɪ, iː, ɪu/ and as /ei, ai, oi/ and /ai, ɔi, ʊi/ respectively.

5.5.2 The Distribution of the Vowel Systems in Syllable Structures

The syllable structures are immensely more complicated than those of English and German, where a system of strong vowels operates in all primary and secondary stressed syllables, and a separate system of weak vowels in unstressed ones, with only little overlap. The only major restriction to that simple configuration is that short vowels are confined to closed syllables.

However, in Welsh, vowel selection must take account of not only stress and open and closed syllables, but also position of stressed syllables in a word (see **5.3 Syllable Types and Structures**) and the kinds of consonants that follow. There are severe restrictions as to which vowels may precede voiceless plosives and which diphthongs that may occur in stressed penultimate syllables, to mention just two examples. The vowel /ə/ has its own idiosyncratic distribution, which is quite different from its English and German counterparts. Neutralization of long and short vowels also is a feature in a number of syllable types. And as already noted, there are also a number of differences between the systems of South- and North-Walian Welsh.

We will consider monosyllables first, which are naturally stressed, apart from a few grammatical items – *yr, y, yn, dy, fy* /ər, ə, ən, də, və/ 'the (pre-vocalic), the (pre-consonantal), in, your (singular), my', which will be presented later under *Unstressed monosyllables.* The order of presentation of the vowel systems within syllable types and structures follows the sequence introduced in **5.3** above.

5.5.2.1 Stressed Monosyllables

The short central vowel /ə/ does not occur in stressed monosyllables. All other vowels occur in syllables closed with /n, l, r/. Only long vowels occur in open syllables and syllables closed with voiced plosives and all fricatives. Only short vowels occur in syllables closed with the voiceless plosives and /m, ŋ/. As already noted, the general trend is also for short vowels to precede /ɬ/. In the South, short vowels occur before all consonant clusters; however, in the North, long vowels occur before obstruent clusters (fricative + plosive), and short vowels before all other clusters. These restrictions are illustrated in the following 'data chart'.

The system includes words of English origin that have been long assimilated into the Welsh language, but it becomes more complicated with the more recent introduction of words from English that retain their English phonological values. These latter will be dealt with in a separate section **5.7 Recent English Borrowings**.

In the data chart below, non-permitted combinations are marked with -; a blank = unattested; N = North only; S = South only; (_) = rare. Principal orthographical equivalents are given as a guide to pronunciation, since the spelling system is transparent in most cases. However, in one notable exception, <ae> in final monosyllables represents long /aːɨ/ and in the final syllable of polysyllables short /aɨ/, but /ei/ elsewhere, in the North; <ae> represents /ai/ in any final syllable as its Southern equivalent, and /ei/

elsewhere; e.g. *aelodaeth* 'membership' is /eɨˈlɔdaɨθ/ in the North and /eiˈlɔdaiθ/) in the South. One other apparent exception concerns the letter <y>, although it is more or less consistent in phonological terms: in lexical items, <y> represents North /ɨ, ɨː/, South /i, iː/ in final syllables, whether stressed or unstressed, but otherwise /ə/, whether stressed or unstressed. However, in monosyllabic grammatical words (see **5.5.2.6** below), it represents /ə/ only.

Table 5.4 Distribution of vowels in stressed monosyllables

	Orthog[6]	open	-n,l,r#	-p,t,k#	-s#	-ɬ#	-m,ŋ#	-C#	-ob+ob#	-C+C#
iː	*i, î*	*mi*	*mil*	-	*mis*	-	-	*llif*	*N gwisg*	-
ɪ	*i*	-	*prin*		*S thus*	*ill*	*chwim*	-	*S gwisg*	*imp*
eː	*e, ê*	*lle*	*llên*	-	*lles*	-	-	*llef*	*N llesg*	-
ɛ	*e*	-	*llen*	*het*	*nes*[7]	*gwell*	*trem*	-	*S llesg*	*merch*
aː	*a, â*	*tra*	*glân*	-	*glas*		*ffrâm*	*lladd*	*N gwallt*	-
a	*a*	-	*llan*		-	*llall*	*mam*	-	*S gwallt*	*camp*
oː	*o, ô*	*llo*	*lôn*	-	*nos*	-	-	*llog*	*N cosb*	-
ɔ	*o*	-	*llon*		*(clòs)*	*coll*	*llong*	-	*S cosb*	*torch*
uː	*w, ŵ*	*llw*	*cŵn*	-	*tlws*	-	-	*rhwd*	*N cwsg*	-
ʊ	*w*	-	*cwr*	*lwc*	-	*twll*	*cwm*	-	*S cwsg*	*lwmp*
N ɨː	*u, û,* *y, ŷ*	*llun*	-	*llus*	-		*(bûm)*	*mud*	*dysg*	-
N ɨ	*u, y*	-	*llyn*		-	*hyll*	*grym*	-	-	
ə		-	-	-	-	-	-	-	-	-
ei	*ei*	*tei*	*ceir*	-	-	*lleill*	-	*(eid)*	*(gweisg)*	*beirdd*
ai	*ai*	*llai*	*llain*	*maip*	*llais*	*naill*	*saim*	*llaid*	*braisg*	*maint*
ɔi	*oi*	*troi*	*cloir*	*cloit*	*clois*			*cloid*	*cloist*	
ɪu	*iw*	*lliw*	*niwl*							
ɛu	*ew*	*llew*	*mewn*	*cewc*				*ewch*		
au	*aw*	*llaw*	*llawn*	*crawc*	*haws*			*awch*	*trawst*	*dawns*
ou	*ow*	*(S clou)*	*clown*					*clowch*		*owns*
əu	*yw*									
N ɨu	*uw, yw*	*Duw*	*clywn*					*uwd*	*uwch*	
N eɨ	*eu, ey*	*creu*						*dweud*		*teyrn*
N aɨ	*au*	*llau*	*haul*					*gwaudd*		
N aːɨ	*ae*	*cae*	*hael*	*aet*	*llaes*	*gwaell*[8]	*aem*	*gwaed*	*aech*	*aent*
N ɔɨ	*ou*									
N oːɨ	*oe*	*ddoe*	*coel*		*coes*	*troell*	*cloem*	*coed*	*bloesg*	*cloent*
N uːɨ	*wy, ŵy*	*llwy*	*llwyr*		*dwys*	*pwyll*	*rhwym*	*llwyd*	*rhwysg*	*hwynt*

5.5.2.2 Stressed Penultimate in Regular Polysyllables

Regular polysyllables require primary stress on the penultimate syllable and secondary stress on any preceding 'heavy' syllable. In the North, only short vowels occur in closed stressed syllables whatever the following consonant or cluster is, and only long vowels in open syllables, i.e. those that are followed by a vowel, e.g. *lliain* /'ɬi:ain/. This is also the pattern being established in the South, although traditionally, short and long vowels contrasted with each other before /n, l, r/. Awbery (1984, 2009) gives examples of short and long vowels in similar environments:

carreg /ˈkarɛg/ 'stone' *arall* /ˈa:raɬ/ 'other' *cadair* /ˈka:dɛr/ 'chair'
enill /ˈɛnɪɬ/ 'to win' *meddwl* /ˈme:ðʊl/ 'to think'

However, in the South, many now pronounce all these and similar words with a short vowel, and follow the North-Walian pattern completely. Both the North and the South – both traditional and newly emerging tendencies – include /ə/ in stressed penultimate syllables, but exclude /ai, aɨ, a:ɨ, o:ɨ, u:ɨ/. Note that the only words with /ɔi/ are recent loans from English.

In the 'data chart' below, non-permitted combinations are marked with -, as opposed to blanks, which indicate that there happen to be no examples of otherwise permissible combinations; N = North only; S = South only; (_) = rare; (S ..) = now becoming rare in the South.

5.5.2.3 Final Stress in Irregular Polysyllables

As noted above (**5.2.1**), most examples of final stress in 'irregular' polysyllables are formed from prefixed stressed monosyllables. The incidence of vowels in these syllables, therefore, closely follows that of stressed monosyllables.

5.5.2.4 Final Tertiary Stressed in Regular Polysyllables

This concerns, basically, the second 'half' of the regular disyllabic foot. This is why the designation 'unstressed final syllables' used earlier, before this particular presentation, was regarded as temporary. It is important to note that these syllables are not unstressed, but carry part of the prosodic information of regular polysyllables. In fact, the power of tertiary stress is heard in the reduced form of a number of commonly used words in colloquial speech, in which it is the tertiary stressed syllable that is retained and not the initial primary stress, e.g. *eto* /ˈɛto/ 'still, again' becomes *'to.*

The main examples of final tertiary stressed in regular polysyllables are taken from basic lexical items, but also from the second element of 'strict' compounds and from suffixes, including inflected prepositions, which yield a number of cases with final /t/, deriving historically from the following pronoun *ti* 'you (sing.)'. The long/short vowel selection is neutralized, with a preference for the short. It is noticeable, however, that many South speakers prefer the long close vowels /i:, u:/. The long/short variations in diphthongs are also neutralized to the short form.

In the 'data chart' below, non-permitted combinations are marked with -, as opposed to blanks, which indicate that there happen to be no examples of otherwise permissible combinations; N = North only; S = South only; (_) = rare; (S ..) = now becoming rare in the South.

Table 5.5 Distribution of vowels in stressed penultimate in regular polysyllables

	orthog	open	-n,l,r-	-p,t,k-	-s-	-ɬ-	-m,ŋ-	-C-	-ob+ob-	-C+C-
iː	*i, ï*	*lliain*	*(Sllinell)*	-	-	-	-	*(S trigo)*	-	-
ɪ	*i*	-	*llinell*	*llipa*	*misol*	*dillad*	*gwingo*	*trigo*	*pistyll*	*lindys*
eː	*e, ë*	*lleol*	-	-	-	-	-	-	-	-
ɛ	*e*	-	*llenni*	*llety*	*mesur*	*gwella*	*trengi*	*ebol*	*gwesty*	*melltith*
aː	*a, ä*	*chwaon*	-	-	-	-	-	-	-	-
a	*a*	-	*llanw*	*llacio*	*caseg*	*gallu*	*camu*	*magu*	*asgell*	*llarpio*
oː	*o, ö*	*glöwr*	-	-	-	-	-	-	-	-
ɔ	*o*	-	*onnen*	*diota*	*noson*	*colled*	*ffromi*	*ogof*	*osgo*	*modrwy*
uː	*w, ŵ*	*pŵer*	-	-	-	-	-	-	-	-
ʊ	*w*	-	*hwnna*	*hwpo*	*mwswm*		*cwmwd*	*gwgu*		*mwnci*
N ɨː	*u, y, ŷ*	*buarth*	-	-	-	-	-	-	-	-
N ɨ	*u, y, ŷ*	-	*tunell*	*rhupunt*	*cusan*	*arddulli*	*pumed*	*udo*	*ustus*	*gwyllti*
ə	*y*	-	*mynydd*	*tyci*	*ysu*	*tywyllu*	*crymu*	*adnewyddi*	*ystum*	*cysgu*
ei	*ei*	*lleiaf*	*gweini*	*meitin*	*eisoes*	*peilli*	*deimwnt*	*ceibo*	*eistedd*	*meithrin*
ai	*ai*	-	-	-	-	-	-	-	-	-
ɔi	*oi*		*toiled*							
ɪu	*iw*	*caethiwo*	*niwloedd*		*briwsyn*			*lliwgar*		*lliwfrith*
ɛu	*ew*	*tewach*	*cewri*	*llewpart*		*rhewllyd*		*drewgi*		*mewngylch*
au	*aw*	*awel*	*mawnog*	*cawsog*			*nawmil*	*croesawgar*	*anhawster*	*llawnder*
ou	*ow*		*cedowrach*	*bilidowcar*	*trowsus*			*powdwr*		*godidowgrwydd*
əu	*yw*	*clywed*	*cywrain*		*trywsus*					
N ɨu	*uw, yw*	*rhywun*	*rhywle*		*rhywsut*			*duwdod*		*uwchradd*
N eɨ	*eu, ae*	*euog*	*euro*	*ffreutur*	*llaesu*			*meudwy*	*cyfleuster*	*blaengar*
N aɨ	*au*	-	-	-	-	-	-	-	-	-

N a:ɨ	*ae*	-	-	-	-	-	-	-	-	-
N o:ɨ	*ou, oe*	-	-	-	-	-	-	-	-	-
N ɔɨ	*oe*		*oeri*	N *jolihoeti*	*arloesi*	*troellog*	-	*poethach*	*moesgar*	*croesffordd*
N u:ɨ	*ŵy*	-	-	-	-	-	-	-	-	-
N ʊɨ	*wy*	*llwyaid*	*llwynog*	*llwyted*	*cwysi*	*pwyllog*	*twymo*	*llwydo*	*wystrys*	*pwynti*

Table 5.6 Distribution of vowels in final stress in irregular polysyllables

	orthog	open	-n,l,r#	-p,t,k#	-s#	-ɬ#	-m,ŋ#	-C#	-ob+ob#	-C+C#
iː	*i, î*	*myfi*	*ymdrin*	*di-glip*	*di-bris*	-	-	*ymhlith*	*N di-Grist*	-
ɪ	*i*	-					*di-ddim*	*gwib*	*S di-Grist*	*di-wifr*
eː	*e, ê*	*efe*	*amhêr*	-	*rhibidirês*	-	-	*annheg*	-	
ɛ	*e*	-	*ymhen*	*di-glec*	-	*ymhell*	*di-glem*	-		*ymweld*
aː	*a, â*	*di-dda*	*gwahân*	-	*di-flas*		*di-âm*	*ymladd*	*N di-wallt*	*mwynhânt*
a	*a*	-	*di-far*	*di-hap*	-	*di-wall*	*paham*	*(di-fflach)*	*S di-wallt*	*di-arf*
oː	*o, ô*	*efô*	*di-sôn*	-	*di-nos*	-	*paratôm*	*gwahodd*	*N di-gosb*	*paratônt*
ɔ	*o*	-	*ymron*	*di-flot*	-	*yngholl*	*lind-dilong*	-	*S di-gosb*	*di-wobr*
uː	*w, ŵ*	*randibŵ*	*di-ddŵr*	-	-	-	-	*di-rwd*	*N di-gwsg*	-
ʊ	*w*	-	*di-dwn*	*di-ffrwt*	-		*ynghlwm*		*S di- gwsg*	*di-dwrf*
N ɨː	*u, û, y, ŷ*	*mam-gu*	*cytûn*	-	*di-frys*	-	*canfûm*	*ynghyd*	*N di-ddysg*	-
N ɨ	*u, y,ŷ*	-	*ynghyn*	*di-sut*	-		*di-rym*	*di-wych*	*S di-ddysg*	-
ə	*y*	-	-	-	-	-	-	-	-	-
ei	*ei*	*mwynhei*	*mwynheir*					*Cymreig*		*di-feind*
ai	*ai*	*di-fai*	*di-ail*	*petait*	*di-gais*		*(di-glaim)*	*ychwaith*		*di-haint*
ɔi	*oi*	*ymdroi*	*paratoir*	*paratoit*	*paratois*			*paratoid*	*paratoist*	
ɪu	*iw*	*di-liw*			*di-iws*					
ɛu	*ew*	*di-flew*						*mwynhewch*		
au	*aw*	*heblaw*	*prynhawn*		*di-naws*			*yrhawg*		*di-sawdl*
ou	*ow*		*paratown*	*di-ddowt*				*paratowch*		*di-gownt*
əu	*yw*	-	-	-	-	-	-	-	-	-
N ɨu	*uw*	*di-Dduw*						*cyfuwch*		
N eɨ	*eu, ey*	*cyfleu*			*cyfleus*			*ymwneud*		

N aɨ	au, áu	amgáu	di-haul		parhaus					
N a:ɨ	ae	di-gae	ymlaen	petaet	Cymraes		petaem	mwynhaech		petaent
N ɔɨ	ou				cyffrous					
N o:ɨ	oe		di-boen	paratoet	di-foes		paratoem	erioed		
N u:ɨ	wy,ŵy	di-nwy	di-ffrwyn		di-bwys	di-bwyll	di-rwym	di-ffrwyth	di-frwysg	di-gwymp

Table 5.7 Distribution of vowels in tertiary stress

	orthog	open	-n,l,r#	-p,t,k#	-s#	-ɬ#	-m,ŋ#	-C#	-ob+ob#	-C+C#
iː	*i*	(*S torri*)	-	-	-	-	-	-	-	-
ɪ	*i*	*torri*	*Lladin*	*canit*	*megis*	*pennill*	*ffyrling*	*lledrith*	*athrist*	*eurbinc*
eː		-	-	-	-	-	-	-	-	-
ɛ	*e*	*godre*	*llawen*	*canet*	*llawes*	*llinell*	*lletem*	*cymhleth*	*moresg*	*llannerch*
aː		-	-	-	-	-	-	-	-	-
a	*a*	*llaca*	*llafar*	*atat*	*cymdeithas*	*arall*	*adlam*	*lleuad*	*llewpart*	*cadarn*
oː		-	-	-	-	-	-	-	-	-
ɔ	*o*	*llacio*	*llenor*	*wrthot*	*Llinos*	*difancoll*	*ohonom*	*tyllog*	*diosg*	*gosgordd*
uː	*w*	(*S tarw*)	-	-	-	-	-	-	-	-
ʊ	*w*	*tarw*	*llongwr*	*anlwc*	*meindlws*	*trobwll*	*degwm*	*cwmwd*	*llabwst*	*cynnwrf*
N ɨː		-	-	-	-	-	-	-	-	-
N ɨ	*u, y*	*canu*	*llafur*	*rhywsut*	*anghofus*	*cynull*	*burum*	*llonydd*	*locust*	*addurn*
ə		-	-	-	-	-	-	-	-	-
ei		-	-	-	-	-	-	-	-	-
ai	*ai*	*bragdai*	*llefain*		*mantais*	*eraill*		*llwyaid*	*engraifft*	*gofaint*
ɔi	*oi*	*morloi*								
ɪu	*iw*	*minlliw*		*anterliwt*						
ɛu	*ew*	*llwydrew*								
au	*aw*	*deunaw*	*riawr*		*cydnaws*			*deuawd*	*hytrawst*	*huawdl*
ou	*ow*									
əu		-	-	-	-	-	-	-	-	-
N ɨu	*uw, yw*	*menyw*						*cyfuwch*		
N eɨ	*eu, ey*	(*ynteu*)								
N aɨ	*au, ae*	*byrddau*	*cythraul*		*cadfaes*			*lluniaeth*		

N a:ɨ		-	-	-	-	-	-	-	-	-
N ɔɨ	*oe*	*echdoe*	*llugoer*		*eisoes*			*lleoedd*		
N o:ɨ		-	-	-	-	-	-	-	-	-
N uɨ	*wy*	*adwy*	*trylwyr*	*ydwyt*	*cynwys*	*byrbwyll*	*bolrwym*			*canwyd*
N u:ɨ		-		-	-	-	-	-	-	-

Table 5.8 Distribution of vowels in weak (unstressed) syllables in non-final position

	orthog	open	-n,l,r#	-p,t,k#	-s#	-ɬ#	-m,ŋ#	-C#	-ob+ob#	-C+C#
iː		-	-	-	-	-	-	-	-	-
ɪ	*i*	*llieiniau*	*llinellau*		*isafbwynt*	*dilledyn*	*cimychiaid*	*migyrnai*	*pistyllio*	*crintachlyd*
eː		-	-	-	-	-	-	-	-	-
ɛ	*e*	*lleoliad*	*llenyddol*	*lletyau*	*gwresogi*	*pellafoedd*	*cemegyn*	*pregethu*	*esgeulus*	*egnïol*
aː		-	-	-	-	-	-	-	-	
a	*a*		*llanerchau*	*ategol*	*gwasanaeth*	*galluog*	*camarwain*	*adennill*		*anfantais*
oː		-	-	-	-	-	-	-	-	
ɔ	*o*	*troëdig*	*aflonyddu*		*cyfosododd*	*collasant*	*siomedig*	*crochanau*	*gostyngiad*	*cofrestrfa*
uː		-	-	-	-	-	-	-	-	
ʊ	*w, ŵ*	*sŵoleg*	*cwningen*	*cwpanau*	*mwsoglau*		*cwmanog*	*crwbanod*	*cymalwstaidd*	*gwrthodaf*
N ɨː		-	-	-	-	-	-	-	-	
N ɨ	*u, y, ŷ*	*hualau*	*munudau*		*llusernau*	*cynulleidfa*	*llumanau*	*hudolus*	*clustogau*	*urddasol*
ə	*y*	-	*mynyddoedd*		*llysywen*		*llyngesau*	*llythyrau*		
ei	*ei, ae*	*daeareg*	*blaengarwch*		*deisebu*		*deimwntau*		*eisteddfod*	*meidroldeb*
ai		-	-	-	-	-	-	-	-	
ɔi	*oi*									
ɪu	*iw*	*diweddar*	*niwlogrwydd*							
ɛu	*ew*	*rheweiddio*	*rhewlifoedd*					*tewhau*		
au	*aw*	*athrawesau*			*nawseiddio*			*ymgnawdoli*	*anawsterau*	*cyflawnsaom*
ou	*ow*		*powlenni*							
əu	*yw*	*tywysydd*	*cywreindeb*		*trywsusau*					
N ɨu	*uw, yw*							*duwdodau*		*lluwchfeydd*
N eɨ	*eu, ey, ae non#*	*haearnaidd*	*ceunentydd*				*haematoleg*		*maestiroedd*	*blaendaliad*
N aɨ		-	-	-	-	-	-	-	-	

N aːɨ		-	-	-	-	-	-	-	-	
N ɔɨ	oe		*lloerennau*	*coetireodd*	*croesawu*	*troelledig*		*doethineb*	*croestyniad*	
N oːɨ		-	-	-	-	-	-	-	-	
N uɨ	*wy, ŵy*	*hwyaden*	*wylofain*		*pwysasoch*	*twyllodrus*	*rhwymedig*	*swyddogol*	*cymwysterau*	*gwyrdroi*
N uːɨ		-	-	-	-	-	-	-	-	

5.5.2.5 Non-final Unstressed Syllables

Finally, the two cases of zero ('weak') stress. First of all, instances of unstressed syllables that precede primary stress. Again the long/short vowel selection is neutralized, although the vowel in open syllables, i.e. before another vowel, has the quality of the 'long' equivalent; for instance *llieiniau* has [lli-] while *llinellau* takes /ɪ/. The long/short variations in diphthongs is also neutralized. /ai/ and /aɨ/ are not permitted because they only appear in final syllables.

In the 'data chart' below, non-permitted combinations are marked with -, as opposed to blanks, which indicate that there happen to be no examples of otherwise permissible combinations; *N* = North only; *S* = South only; (_) = rare; (S ..) = now becoming rare in the South.

5.5.2.6 Unstressed Monosyllables

Unstressed monosyllables are grammatical items that usually remain unstressed. However, they may occur stressed for emphatic or contrastive purposes, in which case they retain their vowel form, even if it contradicts the normal spelling conventions. They will be presented here in their normal unstressed form. Monosyllabic grammatical forms include:

> Prepositions: *am, ar, at, tan, dan, tros, dros, trwy, drwy, heb, i, o, wrth, gan, hyd, â, ag, yn, yng, ym, mewn, cyn, er, ger, rhag, rhwng, fel, ers, nes*
> personal pronouns: *i, fi, mi, ti, di, ef, fe, e, fo, o, hi, ni, chwi, chi, hwynt, hwy, nhw, fy, dy, ei, ein, eich, eu*
> articles: *y, yr*
> preverbal particles: *y, yr, a, ni, nid, na, nad, fe, mi*
> auxiliary verbs: *mae, maen, maent, yw, sy, sydd, oes, bydd, wyt*
> conjunctions: *a, ac, ai, ond, os, pe, na, nac*

Some grammatical items lose their syllabicity when preceded by a vowel.

Vowels in open syllables are pronounced short, but close vowels retain the quality of their 'long' equivalent; for instance, *i* and *nhw* have [i] and [u], whereas *nid* and *rhwng* have [ɪ] and [ʊ]. *e* and *o* are pronounced as [ɛ] and [ɔ], while *ef* is [ev], following the pattern before voiced obstruents. The vowel /ə/ is permitted in this system. Vowels preceding final /s/ are pronounced short.

In the chart below, non-permitted combinations are marked with -, as opposed to blanks, which indicate that there happen to be no examples of otherwise permissible combinations; N = North only.

Table 5.9 Distribution of vowels in unstressed monosyllables

	orthog	open	-n,l,r#	-p,t,k#	-s#	-ɬ#	-m,ŋ#	-C#	-ob+ob#	-C+C#
iː	*i*	*i, fi, etc.*	-	-	-	-	-	-	-	-
ɪ	*i*	-						*nid*		
eː	*e*	-	-	-	*S nes*	-	-	*ev,* *S heb*	-	-
ɛ	*e*	*e, pe*	*er, ger, fel*	-	*N nes*			*N heb*		*ers*
a	*a, â*	*a, â, na*	*ar, tan, etc.*	*ac, at*			*am*	*ag, nad, etc.*		
oː	*o*	*o, fo*	-	-	-	-	-	-	-	-
ɔ	*o*				*os, tros*					*ond*
uː	*w*	*nhw*	-	-	-	-	-	-	-	-
ʊ	*w*	-					*rhwng*			*wrth*
N ɨː	*y*	-	-	-	-	-	-	*hyd, bydd*		
N ɨ	*y*		*cyn*							
ə	*y*	*y, fy, etc.*	*yn, yr*				*ym, yng*			
ei	*ei*	*ei, eu*[9]	*ein*					*eich*[10]		
ai	*ai, ae*	*ai, mae*	*maen*							*maent*
ɔi										
ɪu	*yw*	*yw*								
ɛu	*ew*		*mewn*							
au										
ou										
əu										
N ɨu										
N eɨ										
N aɨ										
N aːɨ										
N ɔɨ	*oe*				*oes*			*oedd*		
N oːɨ										
N uɨ	*wy*	*trwy, hwy*		*wyt*						*hwynt*
N uːɨ										

5.6 System Networks for Vowels

Having shown the distribution of vowels in six different types of syllable, it begins to become clear that there is some overlap between them, but not enough to reduce them all into one integrated system. Hence, the polysystemic principle of Systemic Phonology applies in order to present four different systems according to different syllable types. It could also be applied to separate systems also for North-Walian and South-Walian accents, but since the differences are regular, an experiment in combining the two accents into one network is undertaken.

There is a more or less complete overlap of the vowel distributions in stressed monosyllables and final stressed syllables of irregular polysyllables, and so they constitute a single system. It is, however, different from the system involved in the primary and secondary stressed syllables of regular polysyllables, and so it constitutes its own separate system. Thirdly, the system of tertiary stresses in regular polysyllables is different again, and fourthly, the systems of vowel distribution in weak syllables in monosyllabic and polysyllabic words overlap to such an extent that they too can constitute their own separate system.

Here is an attempt to construct the system network of vowels in stressed monosyllables and final stressed syllables in irregular polysyllabic words. Naturally, what they have in common is primary stress at the very end of a word. System 1 presents this as below. Strictly speaking, Northern and Southern varieties should be represented separately in their networks and so further exemplify the polysystemic feature of Systemic Phonology, but in the interests of space, an attempt is made to combine them: *S* = South-Walian; *N* = North-Walian.

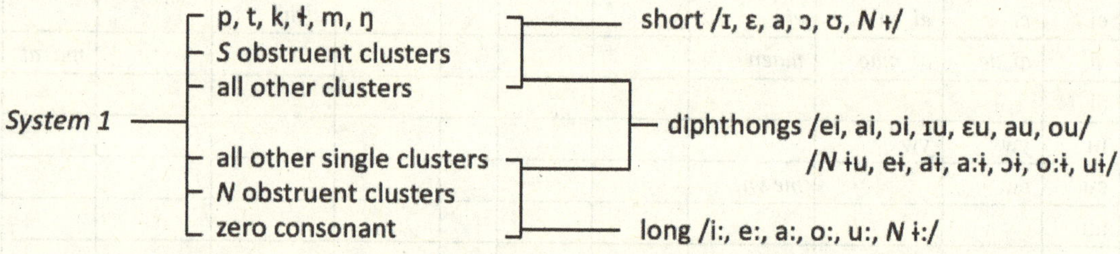

Figure 5.4 System 1 network for vowels in stressed monosyllables and final stressed syllables in irregular polysyllables

System 2 represents the vowel system of the primary stress in the penultimate syllable of regular polysyllables, which includes the vowels /ə, əu/ but excludes the distinction between long and short monophthongs and diphthongs ('neutralization') and the vowels /ai, ɔi, *N* aɨ, a:ɨ/. Long vowels occur in open syllables, i.e. before another vowel; short vowels appear elsewhere. Long *N* diphthongs /a:ɨ, o:ɨ, u:ɨ/ become indistinguishable from their short equivalences: /aɨ, ɔɨ, ʊɨ/.

System 2 also includes the vowel distribution in non-final unstressed syllables. This suggests that System 2 represents vowel distribution in all non-final syllables, whereas the other systems cover, between them, the various possibilities in final syllables, both polysyllabic and monosyllabic.

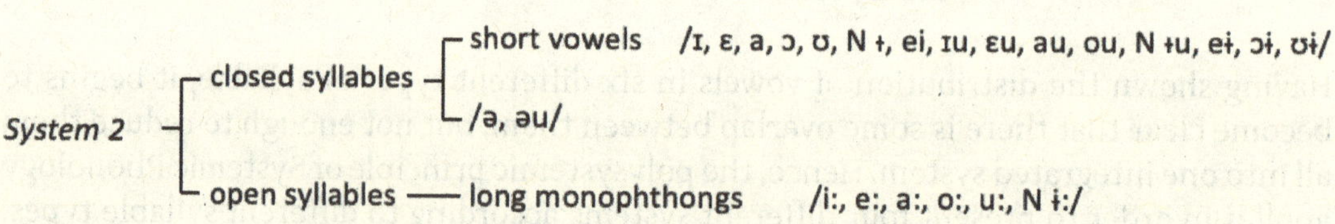

Figure 5.5 System 2 network for vowels in stressed penultimate syllables in regular polysyllables

It should be noted that /ɔi/ does, in fact, occur in recent borrowings from English, e.g. *toiled* 'toilet'; see **Recent English Borrowings** below.

System 3 represents the vowel system of the tertiary stress in the final syllable of regular polysyllables, which excludes /ə, ei, əu/, but includes all the short ('neutralized') monophthongs and diphthongs, including /ai, ɔi, *N* aɨ, a:ɨ/, which are 'forbidden' in penultimate syllables. In other words, System 3 combines the range of System 1 (final syllables with primary stress) with the limitation of the System 2 neutralization of regular polysyllables.

System 3 — /i, e, a, o, u, *N* ɨ/
— /ai, ɪu, ɛu, au, ou, *N* ɨu, eɨ, ɔɨ, ʊɨ/

Figure 5.6 System 3 network for vowels in tertiary stressed final syllables in regular polysyllables

System 4 represents the limited vowel system in unstressed monosyllables. Because of their nature as a relatively small number of grammatical words, many blanks appeared in its chart. It is similar to System 3, but it does include /ə, ei/ that are normally excluded from final syllables. There happen not to be any unstressed monosyllables with /ɔi, ɪu, au, ou, əu, N aɨ/.

System 4 — /i, e, a, ə, o, u, *N* ɨ/
— /ai, ei, ɛu, *N* ɨu, eɨ, ɔɨ, ʊɨ/

Figure 5.7 System 4 network for vowels in unstressed monosyllables

5.7 Recent English Borrowings

It is commonly the case that speakers of neighbouring languages who interact with each other either become bilingual or, if they remain monolingual, will borrow relevant items from the other language (Pike and Fries, 1949). English speakers have in this way acquired words like *cwm, crag, corgi, eisteddfod, bard, cawl, bara brith* from Welsh; but it is clearly the case that Welsh speakers in UK have borrowed far more items from English. Because Welsh speakers in UK are largely bilingual in the two languages, it is inevitable that they have 'imported' far more items than they have 'exported'. And they have imported such words with their Welsh accent of English, which has had profound repercussions on their phonology of Welsh.

Many loan words have long been established in Welsh vocabulary and have been assimilated into conventional Welsh phonology. However, it is noticeable that certain forms are heavily stocked with words from English. For instance, words with initial and final <sb>, <st> and <sg> are largely derived from English: *sbâr, sbectol, sbeit, sbio, sbort, sbri, asb; stabl, stad, staen, stâl, stamp, stapl, startsh* ('starch'), *stiw, stiwdio, stôl* ('stool'), *stori, storm, streic; sgip, sgôr, sgrin, sgwâr, sgwrs* ('discourse'), *sgyrt, desg.* English words with English initial <ch-> /tʃ-/ are usually rendered as Welsh <si-> /ʃ/: *sialc, siambr, siart, siec* (*'cheque'*), *simnai*; and finally with <-tsh>: *startsh.*[11] The English letter <j> has been introduced to render English /dʒ/: *jac-y-do, jam, jar, jôc, jwg.* English letter <x> /ks/ is rendered in Welsh as <cs>: *tacsi, bocs, tecstio.* English <z> is not used at all, apart from the solitary example of *cwiz* 'quiz'; /z/ is otherwise rendered as Welsh <s>: *sêl* ('zeal'), *sebra, sero, sinc* ('zinc'), *sw* ('zoo'), and the alternative, *cwis.* Welsh words with initial <l, r> are often derived from English: *lamp, lefel, letys, lili, lôn* ('lane'), *lori, lwc; radio, record, reis, roced, rownd, rwbel* ('rubble'), *rwber.* All these words all appear in Evans and Thomas (1953), apart from *cwiz.* The only new additional consonants in the Welsh phonology are /dʒ/ and this one instance of /z/.

Of the more recent borrowings, we have already noted words that have disturbed the conventional stress patterns of Welsh, as *cilogram* /ˈkɪlɔgram/ 'kilogram', *paragraff* /ˈparagraf/ 'paragraph', /aˈpeːl/ *apêl*[12] 'appeal', /ˌkaŋgaˈruː/ *cangarŵ* 'kangaroo',/ and /ˌəmbaˈrɛl/ *ymbarél* 'umbrella'.

Other borrowings have disturbed the phonotactic distribution of long and short monophthongs. This has resulted in long vowels appearing in contexts that were not permissible in conventional Welsh phonology as presented in **5.5.2** above, and short vowels equally appearing in opposite contexts.

Long vowels in English precede the voiceless plosives and /m/; they do not, of course, precede /ɬ, ŋ/, and so no such borrowings 'interfere' with this environment.

Table 5.10 Long vowels in new environments

		iː	eː	aː	oː	uː
before	p			*siâp*		*grŵp*
	t		*sêt*	*gât*		
	k	*tîc*			*strôc*	
	m	*tîm*	*gêm*	*ffrâm*	*crôm*	

Short vowels from English appear before voiced obstruents and all voiceless fricatives. No instances of borrowings with final /ð/ have been noted.

Table 5.11 Short vowels in new environments

		ɪ	ɛ	a	ɔ	ʊ	ɨ
before	b	*bib*		*ffab*	*còb*	*hẁb*	
	d	*sgìd*	*led*	*dad*	*od*	*mẁd*	
	g	*wig*	*pèg*	*bag*	*ffrog*	*mẁg*	
	f	*stiff*		*caff*	*toff*	*stwff*	
	v	*sbif*		*laf*			
	θ				*ffroth*		*myth*
	s		*ffres*	*màs*	*bòs*	*bws*	
	ʃ					*brwsh*	
	z	*cwiz*					
	χ			*fflach* 'flash'			
	dʒ		*slej*				

/ə, ei/ also appear in new environments in stressed monosyllables: *nyrs* ('nurse'), *rỳg* ('rug'), *ryc* ('ruck'), *syr* ('sir'), *sgyrt* ('skirt'); *cei* ('quay'), *lein* ('line'), *meic* ('mic'), *neis* ('nice'), *teim* ('thyme'), *teip* ('type').

Finally, /ɔi/ now appears in stressed penultimate syllables in regular polysyllables: *paranoia, toiled, boicot, asteroidau.* These are shifted into secondary stresses with inflections: *toiledau, boicotio*, as previously noted.

This short presentation on English borrowings is not intended to be in any way comprehensive, but it simply shows how English is affecting current Welsh phonology.

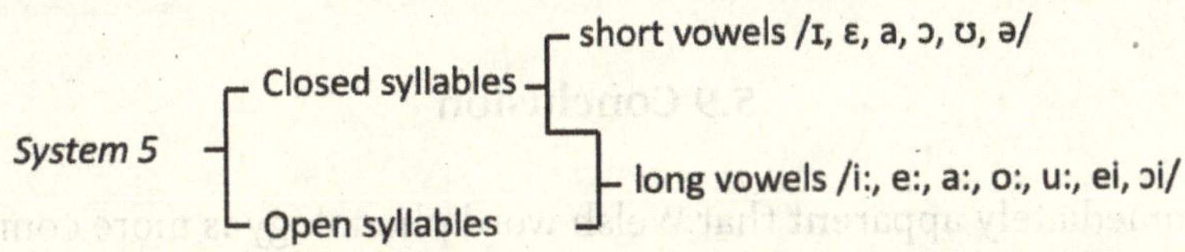

Figure 5.8 System 5 network, as a coexistent vowel system with recent English borrowings

5.8 Spanish Influences

As in the case of Welsh in UK with its dominant English neighbour, all Welsh speakers in Patagonia are bilingual with Spanish. This inevitably affects their accent. This is shown in the work of the two principal academic linguists who have described that accent, R.O. Jones (1976; 1984) and Rees (2021a; 2021b). Jones (1976) investigated phonetic realizations of /χ/, /ʃ/ and voiceless plosives and the vowel /ə/; and the status of /h/ (Jones 1984). Jones found that among his younger informants, /χ/ had become Argentine Spanish [x], /ʃ/ had given way to /sɪ/, the voiceless plosives had lost their aspiration, /h/ was unstable (see Coloma 2018), and /ə/ alternated with /ɪ/.

Jones's 'younger informants' are now contemporary with those Rees (op cit) calls 'heritage speakers', as distinct from adult and child learners. He confirms that there is a strong tendency among these elderly well established Welsh heritage speakers to pronounce /χ/ as [x], /ʃ/ as /s/, and to pronounce voiceless plosives as unaspirated as in Spanish and drop /h/. Rees also found that /r/ in the cluster /tr/ is now pronounced as tapped [ɾ] rather than the approximant [ɹ] common in Wales. The consonant systems are otherwise well maintained, although /r̥/ has become rare, being replaced by trilled /r/ (Rees, personal communication). The inventory of Patagonian Welsh consonants is, therefore, as follows, with deviations from the consonant systems noted above (**5.4**), marked in bold, including phonetic realizations, and infrequent items in brackets:

p **[p]**, b, t **[t]**, d, k **[k]**, g, m, m, ŋ, f, v, θ, ð, s, **(ʃ)**, **x**, **(h)**, ɬ, l, **(r̥)**, r, j, w

As for vowels, /ə/ is maintained, but North-Walian close central vowels and close centring diphthongs are not; there is a clear impression of the South-Walian vowel system prevailing, but with one element of North-Walian long diphthongs remaining: /a:i/ as in *gwaed* /gwa:id/ 'blood' (Rees, personal communication). Hence, Systems 1 to 4 (as in **5.6** above) are maintained minus the *N* element. Bell (2016) confirms the preservation of length contrasts despite any pressure from Spanish.

Rees, however, notes some changes among the younger generation of adult and child learners, notably the 'restoration' of /ʃ/ as a result of the impact of Welsh language teachers from Wales and acquaintance with /ʃ/ from Buenos Aires Spanish (Coloma 2018: 244–245). However, the influence of Spanish is recorded in learners' progressive but not yet complete acquisition of the language ('interlanguage') in the frication of intervocalic /b, d, g/, and the addition of /e/ before word-initial clusters of the type /sp-, st-, sk-/. Of course, it remains to be seen whether these and other 'interlanguage' features become 'fossilized' in a new accent of Patagonian Welsh.

5.9 Conclusion

It becomes immediately apparent that Welsh word phonology is more complicated and intricate than either English or German. In one important respect the methodology employed in this chapter for Welsh has differed from the methodology for English. In Welsh, there is no need to distinguish between basic forms in citation and complex forms with inflections and derivations, since the prosodic structure of any word, whether basic or complex, retains identical patterns; on the other hand, in English, prosodic patterns vary considerably depending on the nature of morphological affixes; even in German there are some changes in prosodic patterning between simple and complex forms – but there are none in Welsh. The structures at the **rank** of foot in the **hierarchy** require the main foot always to be final, and subordinate feet always to precede it. This, incidentally, highlights the **non-universal** aspect of Systemic Phonology.

The **polysystemic** principle of Systemic Phonology is called upon to a far greater degree in Welsh. In addition to differences of consonant systems in initial and final margins, Welsh requires an additional system to handle cases of word-initial mutation in relation to a large number of syntactical structures. There are therefore three essential consonant systems in Welsh. However, the polysystemic principle is applied to an even greater extent with its vowel systems: not two separate systems as a result of stress in syllables as in English and German, but four as a consequence of different types of syllable structure, location of syllables within a word and the phonotactics involving final margins, and a fifth to accommodate loan words from English and, potentially, a sixth from Spanish. The polysystemic principle in Systemic Phonology proves its immense worth in Welsh.

Welsh does not have a single standard accent, and therefore it was an opportunity to experiment with combined **system networks** for the vowels that identified North-Walian features regularly from South-Walian. This is only possible because of the regular systemic variations between the two main accents.

Bilingualism and contact with a dominant language has another kind of sociolinguistic impact. English has a dominance in the world and by and large it assimilates loan words into its own existing phonological patterns. German has a distinctive prosodic pattern for loan words, and, marginally, a set of nasalized vowels, principally as a result of contact with French. Welsh is adapting to the influence of its dominant neighbours, English and Spanish, and as a result, is developing co-existent phonological patterns (Pike and Fries 1949) to a far greater extent.

Chapter 6

Word Phonology in Tera

Tera is one of the 500 indigenous languages of Nigeria. It is a minority language spoken by over 100,000 people in the north east of the country, in the northern part of Gombe State and the eastern part of Borno. Most of the people acquire Hausa as their trade language and a smaller proportion acquire English as their language of education. Their own name for themselves and their language is *Nyimatli* /ɲimáɬi/. The language is classified as Afro-Asiatic, Chadic, Biu-Mandara, A, A.1, Western (Eberhard et al. 2019).

Linguistic work on Tera has principally been associated with Newman (1964; 1968; 1970; 1980). However, an orthographical version of the language was established much earlier with the publication by the British and Foreign Bible Society of *Labar Mbarkandu nu Yohanna Bula Ki*, a first translation of the *Gospel of John*, attributed to Gordon Beacham, a Canadian missionary, in 1930. This was accompanied by a catechism and a hymn book, but the use of Tera in Christian worship gradually gave way to the dominance of Hausa. A revival of interest in a written form of the language occurred in the 1990s with Ayuba Nyagham's *Ye Chituku ɓu̲ Me Nyimatli*,[1] and used quite extensively by the Tera writer and broadcaster Jauro Maila. In 2004, Isioma A Jideonwo, published her *Let's Develop Nyimatli Language*, and Maimuna Magaji, her *Tera-English-Hausa Dictionary* in 2018. In the meantime, the Nyimatli Language Project conducted a series of workshops from 2004 that included the creation of a new orthography, which resulted in the publication of *Reading & Writing Nyimatli* in a definitive edition (NLP 2015), along with a set of reading books, *Lagarkati Shogar Me Nyimatli*, and the Nigerian Bible Translation Trust published the complete New Testament, *Mewar Alqawarang*, in 2016. A more recent treatment of Tera pronunciation appeared in Tench (2007).

6.1 Phonological Features of Chadic Languages

Chadic languages are spoken mainly across Niger, northern Nigeria and northern Cameroon, as well as Chad. The 150 languages are usually classified as either West Chadic – which includes Hausa, by far the largest language by number of speakers and geographical spread – Central Chadic, which includes languages spoken in north-eastern Nigeria and northern Cameroon, and East Chadic for languages spoken in Chad. Various features of grammar, lexis and phonology constitute the basis for identifying Chadic languages as a whole and for the finer classification of them. Tera belongs to Central Chadic; more specifically, to one of its sub-divisions known as Biu-Mandara.

The phonological features that unite Chadic languages are found principally in the consonant, vowel and prosodic systems of words; the prosodic systems include tone and syllable weight (or 'moras') rather than stress. 'Stress ... in Chadic phonological systems generally is a function of the interaction of tone, syllable weight, and intonation and plays no role that is not attributable to those properties' (Schuh 2017: 89).

Chadic consonant systems are, typically, fairly extensive and share sets of pulmonic and non-pulmonic plosives (implosives and ejectives); a relatively large set of fricatives and affricates; 'prosodies' of palatalization and labialization among obstruents as well as phonemically independent approximants [j, w]; a set of nasals with matching pre-nasalized plosives; and a rich range of *r*- and *l*-type articulations. In this respect, Tera is a fine example, as can be seen from the consonant chart below containing no less than 43 consonant phonemes (Tench 2007):

Table 6.1 Tera consonants

	bilabial	labio-dental	alveolar	post-alveolar	palatal	velar	labial-velar	glottal
plosive	p b		t d			k g	k^{w} g^{w}	
implosive	ɓ ɓ^{j}		ɗ			ɠ		
fricative		f v v^{j}	s z	ʃ ʒ		x ɣ	x^{w} ɣ^{w}	h
lateral fric			ɬ ɮ					
affricate				ʧ ʤ				
nasal	m m^{j}		n		ɲ	ŋ		
pre-nasal	^{m}b		^{n}d		^{ɲ}ʤ	^{ŋ}g	^{ŋ}g^{w}	
trill			r					
lateral			l					
approximant				j		w		
glottal approx				ʔj				

/h/ is marginal, occurring mainly in loan words from Hausa and English. NLP (2015) in fact does not include /h/, although Tench (2007) and Magaji (2018) do.

Vowel systems, on the other hand, are relatively simple. Schuh (2017: 49) explains: 'With vowels, it seems preferable to list an inventory of idealized systems and specify the system that a particular language comes close to, with the adjustments needed to fit the language. Here are three such idealized systems that cover most Chadic languages, with some adjustments required for probably all languages.' Table 6.2 displays Schuh's three systems, in which the double vowel length indicates length.

Table 6.2 Schuh's three idealized Chadic vowel systems

	Minimal	Intermediate			Maximal		
	Central	Front	Central	Back	Front	Central	Back
High	/ə/ [i, ɨ, u]	i	ə	u	i, ii		u, uu
Mid (tense)		ee		oo	e, ee		o, oo
Mid (lax)					ɛ, ɛɛ		ɔ, ɔɔ
Low	a, aa		a, aa			a, aa	

The 'adjustments' needed to fit Tera between the intermediate and the maximal systems include contrasts in vowel length and four diphthongs as shown in the chart below (Tench 2007):

Table 6.3 Tera vowels

Front	Central	Back
i, i:	ɨ	u, u:
e, e:, eu		o, o:, oi
	a, a:,	
	ai, au	

See Tench (2007) for illustrations of Tera consonants and vowels. See Tench (2007a, 2008) for the development of standard Tera orthography, endorsed by the local Tera Forum, and reproduced in the *Reading & Writing Nyimatli* booklet published by the Nyamatli Language Project (NLP 2015). The consonant letters are indicated in the chart below matching the phonemic chart above:

Table 6.4 Tera orthographical consonants

p, b		t, d		k, g,	kw, gw	
ɓ, ɓy		ɗ		q		
	f, v, vy	s, z	sh, zh	kh, gh	khw, ghw	h
		tl, dl				
			ch, j			
m, my		n	ny	ng		
mb		nd	nj	ngg	nggw	
		r				
		l				
			y		w	
			ɗy			

Note that the letters <ɓ, ɗ> are familiar to Tera speakers as letters from the Hausa alphabet. The velar implosive /ɠ/ does not occur in Hausa; Hausa's <ƙ> represents a velar ejective and was therefore deemed inappropriate for Tera; <q> was chosen for its similarity in appearance to /g/, but with a backward turning tail in its handwritten form.[2] /ŋ/ and /ᵑg/ are carefully distinguished as <ng, ngg> respectively. Lateral fricatives are now regularly written as <tl, dl> across north-eastern Nigeria.

The orthographic form of /ʔj/ as <ɗy> requires some explanation of a historical nature. The consonants /ʧ, ʤ, ʔj/ are modern forms derived from palatalized /t, d, ɗ/, but in the case of /ʔj/ the alveolar contact was lost and only the glottal element retained. An exact parallel has been described for Hausa; Schuh and Yalwa (1999: 92) describe the development of what they called a 'palatalized glottal stop', which represents, historically, a contraction of the sequence [ɗì:]. In Tera, orthographic *ɗyim* ('water') represents the pronunciation /ʔjim/. The decision to adopt <ɗy> was to help older speakers with their familiarity with the older pronunciation; on the other hand, they were already familiar with <ch, j> from English for the 'new' /ʧ, ʤ/.

The orthography of Tera vowels was a much simpler affair, as shown in this chart:

Table 6.5 Tera orthographical vowels

i, ii	u̲	u, uu
e, ee, eu		o, oo, oi
	a, aa	
	ai, au	

The vowel /ɨ/ is written now as <u̲>; in the orthographies of the 1930s, it was spelled as <ụ>, since a subscript dot was relatively easy to add in handwritten texts, but it became awkward when texts were typed. With later typewriters in the 1990s, underlining a letter was made much more easily, and this strategy was adopted and retained, although nowadays, with computing, many other Chadic orthographies employ the letter <ə>. The other vowels are written as the phonemic symbols suggest, with long vowels written double, as <ii, ee, aa, oo, uu>.

As mentioned above, the prosodic systems of tone and syllable weight operate throughout the range of Chadic languages in words, but not stress. Tone systems are generally very simple and are classified (Schuh 2017: 91–92) as

Two level system: high (H) and low (L)
Three level system: high (H), mid (M) and low (L)
'Terraced' system: high (H) and low (L), and a downstep (D) immediately following a H

Contour tones are often heard on long syllables, but they are usually interpreted as HL (falling) and LH (rising).

Syllable weight operates as a system of timing; in Tera, it is expressed simply as either 'light' or 'heavy' syllables. Light syllables are open syllables (i.e. without final margin) with a short vowel; heavy syllables are either open syllables with a long vowel or closed syllables with any vowel and a final margin. In parallel terminology, a light syllable consists of a single 'mora', whereas a heavy syllable has two 'moras'.

The segmental and prosodic features of Tera word phonology are, accordingly, very typical of the phonological features of Chadic languages. However, this simple inventory, although typical of classic phonemic phonology, does not reflect the richness of Tera word phonology as a Systemic Phonology description does.

We begin with the notion of foot, which because stress has no phonological function has to be construed quite differently from English, German and Welsh.

6.2 The Foot in Tera

As in English, German and Welsh, the rank of foot in the phonological hierarchy has a structure of syllables, which in turn have structures of phonemes, but whereas in those three languages, the nucleus of the foot is a syllable with prominent stress, that cannot be the case in Tera. The foot consists, instead, of a combination of two light syllables, or a single heavy syllable, which may or not be accompanied by a light syllable.

The notion of syllable weight in Chadic languages was first established by Newman (1972). In general, syllable weight is only relevant in languages with contrastive vowel length, although it is itself distinct from vowel length. The 'moraic' foot is required in the phonology of Tera lexical items, but not in grammatical items. In this chapter, we concentrate on the former with only occasional references to the latter. We consider grammatical affixes in the sections **6.7 Lexical Alternations** and **6.8 Verb Morphophonology**.

Syllable structures in regular lexical items in Tera typically begin with an initial consonant, which does not impinge on syllable weight. Syllables are either open or closed: CV, CV:, CVC. In terms of syllable weight, CV is regarded as the 'light' syllable; CV: and CVC are regarded as 'heavy' syllables.

The initial consonant may be any consonant, although, as noted above, /h/ is marginal, confined as it is to a relatively few loan words taken typically from Hausa and English. CV requires a short vowel and is confined to 'light' syllables within polysyllabic items and to a number of grammatical words, whereas CV: and CVC occur as monosyllabic items as well as 'heavy' syllables in polysyllabic items. The system of final consonants for CVC is somewhat restricted as will be shown below.

There are a few lexical items in Tera that, orthographically, take an initial vowel, mainly <a>, but occasionally <i>; they appear mostly as loan words from Hausa. Magaji (2018) lists less than 30 lexical items with initial <a>, and only three with initial <i>, excluding personal names, grammatical items and interjections. Phonetically, however, it is noticeable that, at least in citation form, they begin with a non-phonemic glottal stop [ʔ]; it is treated as non-phonemic because it is an automatic phonetic realization consequent upon the few vowel-initial words, and it is severely restricted to this single point of distribution.

The three syllable types constitute the basis of the syllabic structure of lexical words, both monosyllabic and polysyllabic. Monosyllabic lexical words are either CV: or CVC.[3] (For tone marks, see **6.3 Tone** below.)

CV:	/ɓái/	*ɓai*	'fire'	/ɮa:/	*dla*	'to cut, climb'
CVC	/vat/	*vat*	'four'	/ɓɨr/	*bur*	'to marry'

Disyllabic items follow the same patterns: there are no syllables without an initial consonant and there are no clusters of consonants. Syllable division is marked with /./, in the formulas of the following structures:

CV.CV	/ɓala/	*ɓala*	'to talk'
CV:.CV	/ɓé:la/	*ɓeela*	'baby'
CVC.CV	/ɓurti/	*ɓurti*	'to knead'
CVC.CV:	/ɓolgo:/	*ɓolgoo*	'bone marrow'
CV.CVC	/ɓiláŋ/	*ɓilang*	'beans'
CVC.CVC	/burdol/	*burdol*	'track'

Other polysyllabic items:

CV.CV.CV	/bakurá/	*bakura*	'male goat'			
CV:.CV.CV	/zo:ɓarí/	*zooɓari*	'to boast'	/pu:zari/	*puuzari*	*'to lick'
CV.CV:.CV	/duma:ri/	*dumaari*	'morning'			
CVC.CV.CV	/ɓɨlgaʒi/	*bulgazhi*	'well'			
CVC.CV:.CV	(unattested)					
CV.CVC.CV	/ʛusoŋga/	*qusongga*	'children'			
CV:.CVC.CV	(unattested)					
CVC.CVC.CV	/gùmbaxla/	*gumbakhla*	'tortoise'			
CV.CV.CVC	/ʧiʧiwal/	*chichiwal*	'flag'			
CV:.CV.CVC	/ta:ᵐbɨlam/	*taambu̲lam*	'shallow'			
CV.CV:.CVC	(unattested)					
CVC.CV.CVC	/ʤemkúɗék/	*jemkuɗek*	'hedgehog'			
CVC.CVC.CVC	/ɓolkɨnʤoŋ/	*ɓolku̲njong*	'faded'			
CV.CV.CV.CV	/tolótoló/	*tolotolo*	'turkey'			
CV.CV.CV.CVC	/ʃabagulaŋ/	*shabagulang*	'cattle egret'			
CV.CV.CVC.CV	/makaranta/	*makaranta*	'school'			
etc.						

It is a notable feature of consonant sequences over a syllable boundary that the transition between a syllable-final nasal or other resonant and the initial consonant of the following syllable is close, whereas after a syllable-final obstruent it is often open; for example *ɓakhla* 'to cut across' is, phonetically [ɓaxᵊla]; *shokpa* 'to rinse' [ʃokᵊpa], etc. Pearce (2007) found a very similar phenomenon in Kera, an East Chadic language. She noted that in the sequence of nasal/resonant and a following consonant, the transition was typically 0.1 milliseconds, i.e. virtually a close transition, whereas the transition between an obstruent and a following consonant was typically 0.2 to 0.4 ms, an open transition. This longer transition, however, did not constitute a vowel, which was typically 0.6 to 0.8 ms long. The transition generally took the form of [ᵊ].

This open transition between an obstruent and a following consonant occurs in a small set of 'irregular' lexical items that appear to defy the regular rule of single consonants only at syllable initial and final margins. A sequence of two consonants with open transition was noted in word-initial position in NLP (2015: 9–10); an example is [vᵊnàx] 'to vomit'. NLP decided to spell the word as *vu̲nakh*, noting that because there are only a few of these words, readers would recognize them and not interpret <u̲> as a 'full' vowel. Other examples include

obstruent + obstruent	[tᵊpá]	*tu̲pa*	'to push'
	[pᵊtó]	*pu̲to*	'to continue'
	[ᵑgᵊbùŋ]	*nggu̲bung*	'fool'
	[xᵊxé:tí]	*khu̲kheeti*	'air'
obstruent + sonorant	[bᵊlà]	*bu̲la*	'to write'
	[gᵊmà]	*gu̲ma*	'old (non-human)'
	[vᵊna]	*vu̲na*	'grinding stone'
	[sᵊla]	*su̲la*	'drowsy'

There is a near minimal pair:

[zᵊmà]	*zu̲mà*	'source of water'
[zɨma]	*zu̲ma*	'right (direction)'

The quality of the open transition is noticeably different after /ʃ, ʒ/, being more [i]-like, as might be expected. NLP (2015) decided to spell this front open quality as <i>, again expecting readers to recognize the words and not interpret <i> as a 'full' vowel:

[ʃⁱvan] *shivan* 'guinea fowl'
[ʃⁱlàx] *shilakh* 'broken calabask'
[ʃⁱráx] *shirakh* 'to spit'
[ʒⁱrà] *zhira* 'cauldron'
[ʒⁱráŋ] *zhirang* 'crocodile'

A possible alternative spelling that might be considered in any spelling reform would be to disregard the phonetic quality of the open transition and simply position the two consonants together, as *tpa, pto, nggbung, khkheeti, bla, gma, vna, sla, zma* (as distinct from *zu̱ma*), *shvan, shlakh, shrakh, zhra, zhrang.*

6.3 Tone

The tone system in Tera operates quite independently of the foot; it is borne by the syllable. However, there is an interesting observation that the most frequent pattern of tone sequences is the one that remains steady throughout the foot. Tone is an inherent phonological feature of lexical items although it does not feature extensively with a contrastive function; some examples of the latter appear below.

Tera has a three tone system: H marked as /´/, M (unmarked), L as /`/, as illustrated, initially, with examples of monosyllabic lexical items:

H /lém/ *lem* 'net' /lóŋ/ *long* 'bat'
M /woi/ *woi* 'child' /ɠur/ *qur* 'neck'
L /pòn/ *pon* 'seed' /sàr/ *sar* 'leg'

There are a small number of minimal pairs by tone, but generally speaking, it was found that the 'functional load' of tone in discriminating between lexical items was relatively small; hence the decision not to include tone marks in standard Tera orthography except where necessary to distinguish ambiguous items. Examples of minimal pairs are shown below:

H /ʒí:/ *zhí* 'to smell'
M /ʒi:/ *zhi* 'to swell'/'pestle'/'satisfied'[4]
L /ʒì:/ *zhì* 'to measure, weigh'

H /xí:/ *khí* 'to grind'
M /xi:/ *khi* 'to sink'

M /vi:/ *vi* 'to enter' /ʒum/ *zhum* 'warthog'
L /vì:/ *vi* 'iron' /ʒùm/ *zhum* 'dark'

In the latter two cases, the low tone is not marked orthographically, because the lexical items belong to different word classes and therefore are unlikely to cause ambiguity. No minimal pairs were discovered with a contrast between H and L. Furthermore, Schuh (2017:102) tentatively suggested from an admittedly very small sample that M tone was favoured by a wide margin:

tone	number	% of total	example	gloss
H	14	16.47%	ɓó	'headpad'
M	45	52.94%	ɓō	'cooking pot
L	26	30.59%	bù	'measure'

There are nine potential patterns of tone for disyllabic words, illustrated as follows:

HH	/ʧélém/	*chelem*	'giraffe'	/ʃéɗék/	*shedek*	'hut'
HM	/kúɗum/	*kuɗum*	'hippopotamus'	/tútuŋ/	*tutung*	'dust'
HL	(unattested)					
MH	/likám/	*likam*	'maize'	/lefún/	*lefun*	'cotton'
MM	/doma/	*doma*	'horn'	/kuka/	*kuka*	'baobab'
ML	/ɬugù/	*tlugu*	'knife'	/kɨzàp/	*ku̲zap*	'cloud'
LH	(unattested)					
LM	/màɣam/	Magham	'God'	/gàwu/	*gawu*	'river'
LL	/jùrvù/	yurvu	'fish'	/gàwà/	*gawa*	'guinea corn'

Tench (2007) had no instances of either HL or LH; Schuh (2017: 102) admits that his very few items of HL and LH may well be transcription errors![5] He otherwise suggests that Tera words do not have tone patterns with maximum distance from each other. As with monosyllabic words, there are only few cases of minimal pairs, or near minimal pairs, such as the following:

HM	/ʤímbi/	jímbi	'tiger nut'	/ʃíŋgi/	shínggi	'folktale'
MM	/ʤimbi/	jimbi	'shade, shadow'	/ʃiŋʤi/	shinji	'xylophone'

Schuh's calculation of proportions of tone patterns indicate once again a preference for M tones (2017:102):

Tone	word count	% of total	example	gloss
HH	29	5.84%	kwáxá	'crab shell'
HM	50	10.06%	xúskā	'puff adder'
HL*	5	1.01%	díghì	'honey; bee'
MH	47	9.46%	wānxá	'young woman'
MM	201	40.44%	nyāxā	'saliva'
ML	21	4.23%	nyīxlà	'nonsense'
LH*	1	0.20%	ɗyìví	'castrated goat'
LM	59	11.87%	dàxlā	'quarrel'
LL	84	16.90%	kùʒà	'cough'

(* possible transcription errors; see footnote [5])

By the same reasoning there are 27 potential contrasts for trisyllabic words, illustrated as follows:

HHH	/kélébé/	*kelebe*	'scarf'
	/ándʒíndʒá/	*anjinja*	'star'
HHM	(unattested)		
HHL	(unattested)		
HMH	(unattested)		
HMM	/áŋgori/	*anggori*	'red earth/clay'
HML	(unattested)		
HLH	(unattested)		
HLM	(unattested)		
HLL	(unattested)		
MHH	/ʃabáté/	*shabate*	'kind of fruit' (Hausa: *dinya*)
	/dʒemkúɗék/	*jemkuɗek*	'hedgehog'
MHM	(unattested)		
MHL	(unattested)		
MMH	/malaiká/	*malaika*	'angel' (derived from Hausa *malaika*)
	/bulgaʒí/	*bulgazhi*	'well (noun)'
MMM	/tʃitʃiwal/	*chichiwal*	'flag'
	/mutuka/	*mutuka*	'motor car'
MML	/ajabè/	*ayabe*	'banana' (Hausa *ayaba*)
	/toʃilòm/	*toshilom*	'torch' (English *torch lamp*)
MLH	(unattested)		
MLM	(unattested)		
MLL	/moŋòròm/	*mongorom*	'mango' (Hausa *mangworo*)
	/agàtè/	*agate*	'hat'
LHH	(unattested)		
LHM	(unattested)		
LHL	(unattested)		
LMH	(unattested)		
LMM	/bùnduku/	*bunduku*	'gun' (Hausa *bindiga*)
	/gùmbaxla/	*gumbakhla*	'tortoise'
LML	/tùrmatùr/	*turmatur*	'tomato' (cf Hausa *tumatir*)
	/ɣùrɗoɣùm/	*ghurɗoghum*	'crested crane'
LLH	(unattested)		
LLM	/gìnàrwa/	*ginarwa*	'silver'
	/ʃivùna/	*shivuna*	'namesake'
LLL	/kìr^{m}bìɮìm/	*kirmbidlim*	'beetle'
	/ʒùʒùmì/	*zhuzhumi*	'dawn'

Again, it is clear that not all potential patterns are used, and it should be noted in particular that no combination of H and L is permitted, even when M might intervene. Even so, HHM, HMH, and MLM appear not to be utilized. There are noticeably fewer trisyllabic lexical items in our, admittedly, limited workshop data (see footnote [3]):

HHH	7
HMM	1
MHH	3
MHM	2
MMH	6
MMM	21

MML 2
MLL 5
LMM 4
LML 2
LLM 5
LLL 11

What is also very noticeable are two features: there does indeed appear to be a preference for a 'straight' tone pattern: HHH, MMM, LLL; and the number of items with M tones is considerably higher than items with H and L:

Hs 18
Ms 51
Ls 29

This reinforces Schuh's observation above for a preference for M tones as in mono- and poly-syllables. This is further borne out by the few lexical items with more than three syllables:

MHMH	/tolótoló/	*tolotolo* 'turkey' (Hausa *tolotolo*)
MMMM	/makaranta/	*makaranta* 'school'
	/ʃabagulaŋ/	*shabagulang* 'cattle egret'
	/aɓolaja/	*aɓolaya* 'welcome' (*aɓo* 'come' and *laya* 'safe/gently'. *Aɓolaya* is written on Deba town gate, the local government headquarters of Yamaltu Deba local government the home of Tera language speakers meaning 'come safe.')
	/abakuru/	*abakuru* '(a kind of) peanut cake'

Tone-spreading is the phenomenon of the tone of one syllable determining the tone of neighbouring syllables. Pearce (2007) gives an example of tone-spreading in the East Chadic language Kera, where the tone of a 'heavy' syllable determines the tone on the preceding 'light' syllable. Schuh (2017: 128), on the other hand, states that tone-spreading is typical of certain West Chadic languages, in which it is the consonants that 'facilitate' a certain tone, e.g. voiced obstruents facilitating the spreading of a L tone, whereas voiceless obstruents facilitate the spreading of a H tone. All the examples given in these two sources (i.e. Pearce and Schuh) are two-tone languages.

It is unclear whether tone-spreading is a feature of Tera, which is a Central Chadic language, and has three tones. It is clear from the above examples that the voice of obstruents, for example, does not determine the tone of the syllable. There appears to be sufficient variety of voiced and voiceless consonants, close, mid and open vowels, and pulmonic and implosive mechanisms with all tones and patterns to suggest that tone spreading is not an important feature in the prosodic systems of Tera. The tone system can therefore be shown in the following network:

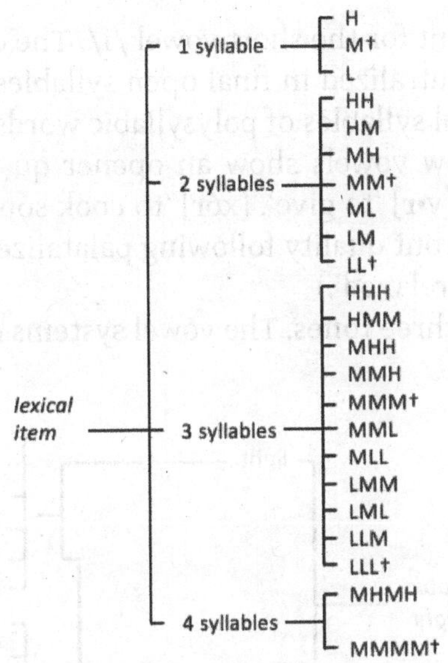

Figure 6.1 System network of tones in lexical items in Tera; † indicates the most frequent patterns

There is a strong tendency for a foot to maintain a 'straight' tone pattern, and for the mid tone to dominate, but there is sufficient variability to prevent establishing a phonological correlation between the foot and tone patterns.

Tones are features of syllables and are expressed through syllable peaks, principally vowels, to which we now turn.

6.4 Vowel Systems

There are basically two vowel systems: one for light syllables and another for heavy syllables. Light syllables in Tera consist of an obligatory onset consonant and a short vowel, but no final margin consonant. The short vowels, as presented in **6.1** above, are:

Table 6.6 Tera short vowels

i	ɨ	u
e		o
	a	

Heavy syllables consist of an onset consonant with either a short vowel plus obligatory final consonant, or a long vowel with optional final consonant. The long vowels are:

Table 6.7 Tera long vowels

i:		u:
e:, eu		o:, oi
	a:,ai, au	

There is no long equivalent for the short vowel /ɨ/. The contrast between equivalent short and long vowels is neutralized in final open syllables; in (lexical) monosyllables, the vowel is long, but in final syllables of polysyllabic words, the vowel is short.

(Phonetically, the non-low vowels show an opener quality in closed syllables, e.g. [ʧít] black', [ɮɛp] 'to plait', [v•r] 'to give', [xɔ́r] 'to cook soup', [jɔ́p] 'to sink'. The vowel /a/ tends to show a closer front quality following palatalized consonants, e.g. [ɓʲæx] 'to tear', [mʲǽsi] 'eight', [vʲæ̀x] 'relaxed'.)

All vowels take all of the three tones. The vowel systems of Tera can be displayed in a network as follows:

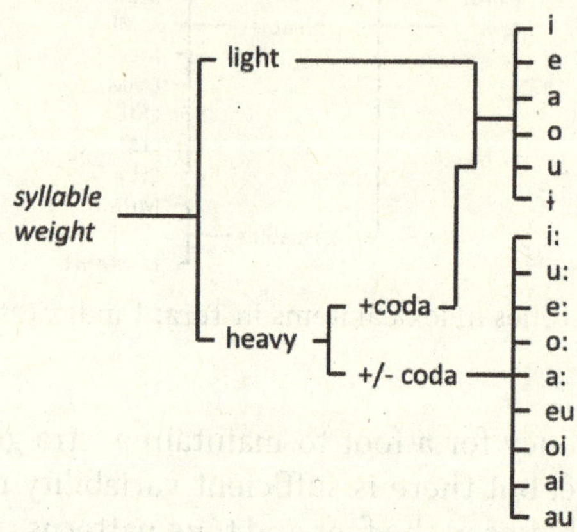

Figure 6.2 System network for vowels in light and heavy syllables in Tera

6.5 Syllable-initial Margin Systems

We turn now to the deployment of Tera phonological resources in the margin systems of syllables. Our first consideration is the syllable-initial margin system.

Tera consonants have been introduced already, and, without exception, all consonants appear in syllable-initial margins at the beginning of words. However, there are a number of phonotactic constraints to the vowels that can follow. All consonants are followed by /a/, although the historically derived post-alveolar affricates from palatalized alveolar stops /ţ, d, ɗ/ rarely take any vowel other than /i, e/; however, it is an indication of their new recently developed phonemic status that a number of words do now appear with /ʧ, ʤ, ʔj/ (<ch, j, ɗy>) followed by one or more of /a, o, u, ɨ/; examples:

/ʧaxi/	*chakhi*	'to prop up' (Magaji[6])
/ʧɔ̀rɔ̀/	*choro*	'forge'
/ʤàtà/	*jata*	'dappled (horse)' (Magaji)
/ʤù/	*ju*	'to stand up'
/ʔjáxɮúm/	*ɗyakhdlum*	'tasteless' (Magaji)
/ʔjót/	*ɗyot*	'bitter'

Generally speaking, the phonotactic constraints on vowels after syllable-initial /ţ, d, ɗ/ were historically complemented in the system by palatalized forms (marked *) before /i, e/:

*/tʲ, dʲ, ɗʲ/ + /i, e/
/t, d, ɗ/ + any other vowel.

There are also similar phonotactic constraints following /n, ^{n}d/. Neither Magaji nor NLP record any lexical item with /n, ^{n}d/ before /i, e/ and only the grammatical item, *ndi* ('with') as an instance of an exception to this constraint. On the other hand, there are plenty of examples of /ɲ, ^{n}dʒ/ before /i, e/; but there are also some examples before /a/ and other vowels; examples:

/ɲaxɬí/ *nyakhtli* 'young man'
/^{n}dʒa:ri/ *njaari* 'coarse sand, gravel'
/^{n}dʒòŋ/ *njong* 'six'

Again, historically, there was complementary distribution of vowels after these consonants:

*/^{n}dʲ, ^{n}ɗʲ, nʲ/ + /i, e/
/n/ + any other vowel.

A similar relationship exists between the alveolar sibilant fricatives /s, z/and their post-alveolar counterparts /ʃ, ʒ/. There are no instances of /s/ followed by /i, e/,[7] but there are plentiful instances following /ʃ/. However, there are instances of /ʃ/ followed by /a, o, u/, including (segmental) minimal pairs, e.g. *saka* 'prayer' and *shaka* 'to weave'. In an almost parallel fashion, Magaji (2018) has no instance of /z/ followed by /e/, and only three of /z/ followed by /i/: *zi* 'to pour', *zi* 'to tell' and *zimat* 'catfish', but plentiful instances of /ʒ/ followed by /i, e/. As with /ʃ/, /ʒ/ is followed by a whole range of vowels: /i, e, a, o, u, ɨ/, producing a number of (segmental) minimal pairs, e.g. *zi*, as above, and *zhi* 'to smell'/ 'stirring stick'; *za* 'to drink' and *zha* 'break'.

Here is, therefore, another historical case of complementary distribution of vowels:

*/sʲ, zʲ/ + /i, e/
/s, z/ + any other vowel.

To conclude with other cases of palatalization, only cases with voiced consonants have been noted among labial articulations, and even these are confined to the following examples. Magaji and NLP record:

/ɓʲáx/ *ɓyakh* 'to tear'
/vʲaŋ/ *vyang* 'red'
While Magaji records:
(/mijási/) *miyasi* 'eight'
NLP has:
/mʲa:si/ *myaasi* 'eight'

Magaji's spelling *miyasi* might well provide a clue to older forms with open transition, with /j/ determining the form of the transition as [^{i}].

The palatal approximant /j/ <y> itself has historically tended the follow the same phonotactic pattern as palatalized consonants, with plentiful examples with a following

/i, e/, but also /a/ [æ]. However, there are now a few examples of /j/ with /o, u/ following, e.g.

/joɓi/ 'to dye'
/jurvu/ 'fish'

but here are no examples of /ɨ/ following /j/.

A similar, though much more limited, case appears with labialization. Labialized consonants are followed exclusively by /a/:

/kʷ/: /kʷáɗá/ *kwaɗa* 'chieftainship'
/gʷ/: /gʷaŋ/ *gwang* 'ten'
/ᵑgʷ/: /ᵑgʷana/ *nggwana* 'hard baobab seed'
/xʷ/: / xʷa:ti/ *khwaati* 'opening' (*khwaati kiba* 'window', i.e. an opening in a room)
/ɣʷ/: /ɣʷaɗi/ *ghwaɗi* 'to hit'

The labio-velar approximant /w/ similarly has plentiful examples with a following /a/, but also with /o, u/, but none with a following /i, e/[8]; like /j/, there are no examples of /w/ followed by /ɨ/.

It might also be noted that implosive consonants follow the patterns of their pulmonic counterparts, although /ɠ/, the voiced velar implosive <q> is restricted to /a, u, ɨ/ following, with just one exception: *qilis* 'charcoal'. Pre-nasalized forms follow the patterns of their plain counterparts. Laterals and the trill /r/ take the full range of vowels following. /h/ as the newest addition to Tera consonants is generally followed only by /a/:

/háŋkal/ *hankal* 'gently' (from Hausa)
/harmɨndi/ *harmu̲ndi* 'harmony' (from English)
/hausa/ *Hausa*

We are now in a position to set up a hierarchy of phonotactic restrictions between initial consonants and immediately following vowels. We will simply refer to short vowels, not only because long vowels and diphthongs are relatively less frequent, but also because their initial phonetic features conform to the pattern of the phonetic features of short vowels.

One category of initial consonants has an obligatory vowel following: /h/, all labialized consonants and labial palatalized consonants (/ɓʲ, vʲ, mʲ/) are all followed only and always by /a/.

A second category concerns mainly non-lateral alveolar obstruents and those consonants developed from their 'historical' palatalized forms, /ʧ, ʤ, ⁿʤ, ʔj/. The latter tended mainly to take /i, e/ as their following vowels, on phonetic grounds, but have acquired other following vowels as Tera vocabulary has developed, which demonstrates their more recently acquired phonemic status. On the other hand, /t, d, ɗ, ⁿd, s, z/ tended to take all vowels except /i, e/, but equally now there are occasional cases with those vowels. Similarly, the historically parallel case of complementary distribution of vowels after /n/ and /ɲ/ is also giving way. Also /j/ has had a strong tendency to be followed only by /i, e, a/, but there are now a few examples with other vowels following; and likewise /w/ with its strong tendency to be followed only by /a, o, u/ has a few instances with other vowels. One other case of a strong tendency concerns /ɠ/, which traditionally has been restricted to /a, u, ɨ/ but now has at least /i/ following as well.

The third category consists of all the other consonants, which take an unrestricted set of following vowels: /p, b, ɓ, k, g, ᵐb, ᵑg, f, v, ʃ, ʒ, x, ɣ, m, ŋ, l, ɬ, ɮ, r/, although there are occasional gaps that seem to have no phonological or phonetic explanations: there does not appear to be a word beginning <dlo ..> or <ngge ..> even though *tlogha* 'to answer' and *gege* 'beard' exist.

The system of initial consonants can be displayed according to their phonotactic status as restricted, unrestricted and partially restricted as follows (orthographical representation is shown in brackets):

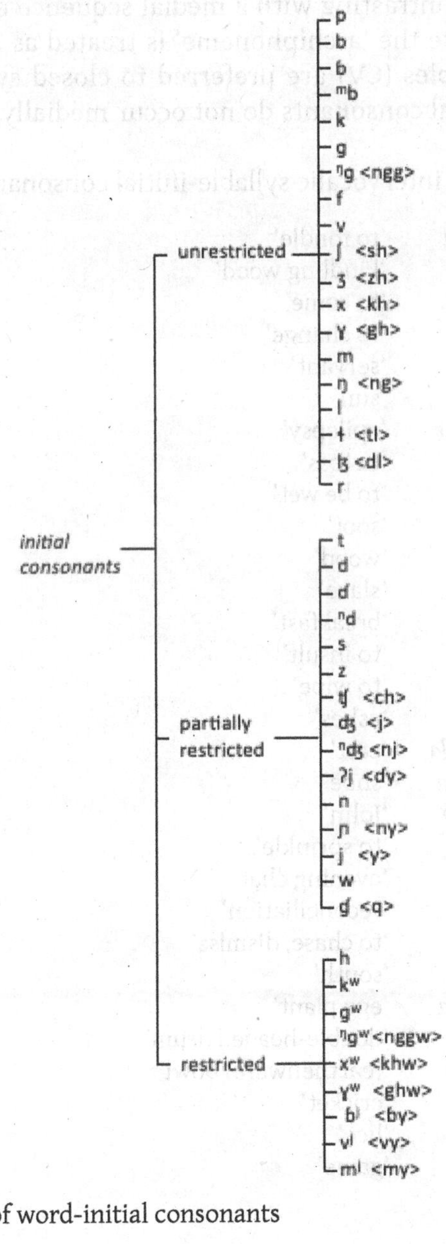

Figure 6.3 System network of word-initial consonants

The network above displays the system of initial consonants and their phonotactic constraints at the beginning of words. A similar network would display syllable-initial consonants in intervocalic position; in a CVCV and other similar patterns with a single consonant in the intervocalic position, the consonant is judged to initiate the following syllable, as described above under **6.2 The Foot in Tera**. However, two points must be noted: first, a potential contrast between an intervocalic pre-nasalized obstruent and a medial sequence of nasal + obstruent is ‘neutralized’, and is here treated as if the nasal element constitutes the final margin of one syllable and the obstruent as the initial margin of the following syllable, on the phonetic grounds that the nasal element has the same articulatory length as a typical nasal phoneme. Moreover, in the case of /ɲ/ potentially contrasting with a medial sequence of /n/ + /j/, the contrast is neutralized; in this case the ‘archiphoneme’ is treated as /ɲ/ on the phonological grounds that open syllables (CV) are preferred to closed syllables (CVC). Secondly, the restricted set of initial consonants do not occur medially, except /h/ in the name *Yohana*.

Examples of legitimate intervocalic syllable-initial consonants follow

/p/	/papurá/	*papura*	‘to fondle’
/b/	/^{n}dʒabí/	*njabi*	‘kindling wood’
/ɓ/	/aɓó/	*aɓo*	‘to come’
/t/	/pata/	*pata*	‘to change’
/d/	/fuda/	*fuda*	‘servant’
/ɗ/	/fuɗa/	*fuɗa*	‘sun’
/ʔj/	/muʔjur/	*muɗyur*	‘epilepsy’
/k/	/^{m}buki/	*mbuki*	‘to toss’
/g/	/puga/	*puga*	‘to be wet’
/ɠ/	/ɠɨɠɨr/	*ququr*	‘soot’
/f/	/ɠúfa/	*qufa*	‘wood’
/v/	/ma:va/	*maava*	‘slave’
/s/	/pasi/	*pasi*	‘breakfast’
/z/	/pɨzi/	*puzi*	‘to insult’
/ʃ/	/páʃá/	*pasha*	‘to wipe’
/ʒ/	/pɨʒit/	*puzhit*	‘ashes’
/x/	/doxaɬa/	*dokhatla*	‘east’
/ɣ/	/paɣàm/	*pagham*	‘shoe’
/h/	/johánà/	Yohana	‘John’
/ʧ/	/piʧirá/	*pichira*	‘to sprinkle’
/ʤ/	/piʤí/	*piji*	‘evening chat’
/m/	/koma/	*koma*	‘reconciliation’
/^{m}b/	/ko^{m}ba/	*komba*	‘to chase, dismiss’
/n/	/koná/	*kona*	‘south’
/^{n}d/	/ʧí:^{n}da/	*chiinda*	‘egg plant’
/^{n}ʤ/	/ka^{n}ʤau/	*kanjau*	‘double-headed drum’
/ɲ/	/ɣaɲà/	*ghanya*	‘(earthenware) bowl’
/ŋ/	/ʒaŋa/	*zhanga*	‘cricket’
/^{ŋ}g/	/ʒa^{ŋ}ga/	*zhangga*	‘lice’
/l/	/palam/	*palam*	‘game’

/ɬ/	/paɬa/	*patla*	'father'
/ɮ/	/paɮa/	*padla*	'to pat'
/r/	/piri/	*piri*	'to blow (horn, etc.)'
/w/	/ɗawar/	*ɗawar*	'high ground'
/y/	/ajim/	*ayim*	'ring'

6.6 Syllable-final Margin Systems

The syllable-final margin system at the ends of words is much smaller than the syllable-initial systems, as the phonotactically restricted items do not occur finally; there are no cases of words ending in either labialized or palatalized consonant forms, including /ʧ, ʤ, ʔj/, or in /ɲ, j, w/, or pre-nasalized obstruents, or /ɣ,[9] ʃ, h/.

On the other hand, resonant consonants frequently feature in word-final position, especially /l, r/ and plain nasals; examples:

/l/	/xál/	*khal*	'to step on'
/r/	/xar/	*khar*	'hand'
/m/	/ɣùm/	*ghum*	'mouse'
/n/	/xalan/	*khalan*	'ownership'
/ŋ/	/gwaŋ/	*gwang*	'ten'

Less common final consonants are obstruents; examples:

/p/	/rap/	*rap*	'two'			
/b/	/kab/	*kab*	'to sow'			
/ɓ/	/ʃíɓ/	*shiɓ*	'to wash'			
/t/	/ʧít/	*chit*	'black'			
/d/	/^{ŋ}gɨ̀d/	*nggud*	'to fall'			
/ɗ/	/^{ŋ}gɨɗ/	*ngguɗ*	'to look'			
/k/	/tɨk/	*tuk*	'to listen'			
/g/	/^{n}dɨg/	*ndug*	'to stop'			
/f/	/^{n}dʒif/	*njif*	'person'	/ruf/	*ruf*	'to bend'
/v/	/^{n}dʒiv/	*njiv*	'road'			
/s/	/más/	*mas*	'to rest'			
/z/	/kàz/	*kaz*	'spear'	/xɨz/	*khuz*	'to shave'
/ʃ/	/pɨʃ/	*push*	'to sprinkle'			
/ʒ/	/pɨ̀ʒ/	*puzh*	'to sharpen'			
/x/	/ɗɨx/	*ɗukh*	'to pound'			
/ɬ/	/^{ŋ}géɬ/	*nggetl*	'to detach'	/^{n}dʒeɬ/	*njetl*	'to be arranged one after the other'
/ɮ/	/ɲè:ɮ/	*nyeedl*	'to fill'			

There do not appear to be any phonotactic restraints between vowel and final margin. Two categories of word-final consonants can be established purely on the ground of frequency and shown in a network as (frequent) resonants and (less frequent) obstruents:

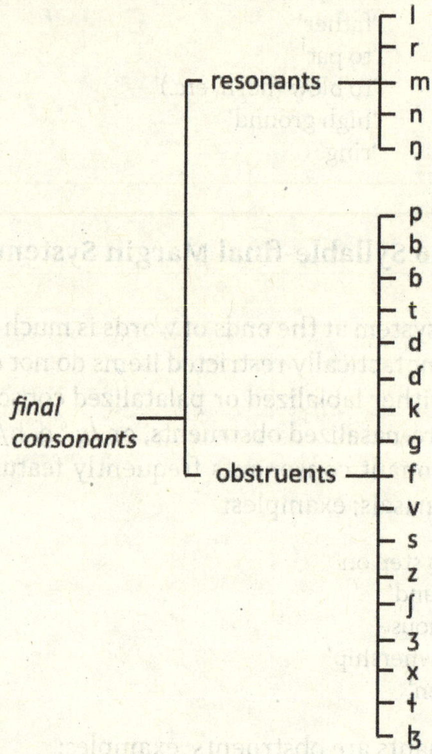

Figure 6.4 System network for word-final consonants

The network above displays the system of final consonants at the end of words. A similar network would display final consonants in closed syllables in word-medial position, i.e. as the final margin before a following syllable with an initial consonant, as in, for instance, a CVC.CV pattern. Examples follow:

/l/ /kultàn/ *kultan* 'bark (of tree)'
/r/ /kɨrsi/ *kursi* 'to hesitate'
/m/ /kɨmda/ *kumda* 'to swear'
/n/ /kɨ^{n}dil/ *kundil* 'clay jug'
/ŋ/ /ɗaŋtá/ *ɗangta* 'to sieve'

Less common syllable-final consonants are obstruents, excluding /ɣ/ and, so it seems, /p, ɗ, v, ʃ, ʒ, ɬ, ɮ/ :

/p/
/b/ /dabti/ *dabti* 'clay for pottery, building'
/ɓ/ /dɨɓtí/ *duɓti* 'sap, resin'
/t/ /kutkum/*kutkum* 'to be low'
/d/ /kudkum/*kudkum* 'short, shallow'
/ɗ/
/k/ /rɨkna/ *rukna* 'dirty'
/g/ /dagla/ *dagla* helmet, to defend'
/f/ /raftiki/ *raftiki* 'friend'
/v/

/s/ /xuski/ *khuski* 'man'
/z/ /ʔjɨzki/ *dyu̲zki* 'to, insult'
/ʃ/
/ʒ/
/x/ /pixta/ *pikhta* 'fan'
/ɣ/ /ʔjeɣlem/ *dyeghlem* 'to refuse out of polite consideration'
/ɬ/
/ɮ/

This leaves a reduced system network for the less common syllable-final consonants in word-medial position:

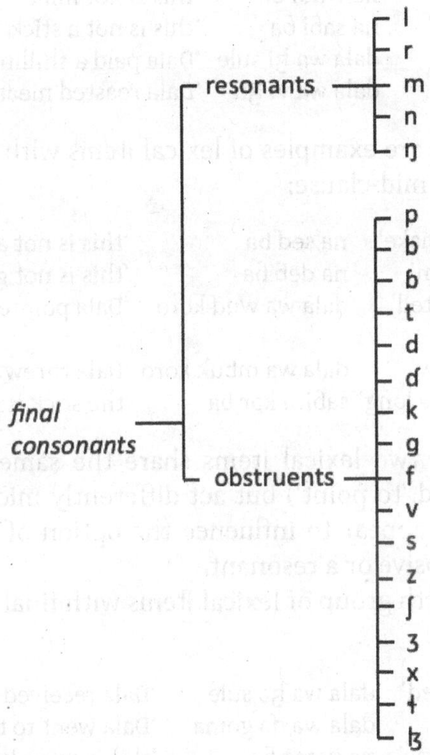

Figure 6.5 Partial system network for syllable-final consonants in medial position in basic words

This system is re-visited in **6.8 Verb Morphophonology** where gaps are filled with verbal suffixes. Incidentally, there do not appear to be any phonotactic restrictions between nucleus and final margin.

6.7 Lexical Alternations

There are a number of issues concerning the phonology of lexical items in their morphological variations and in syntactic context. Perhaps the most famous case is that of alternating forms that involve a final /-i/. Newman (1968) first drew attention to these alternations; Odden (2005: 287–290) presents Newman's case simply and elegantly, so his presentation is taken as the basis for this description. (His transcription of the vowel spelled <u̲> is /ə/, rather than /ɨ/; no tones are provided.)

Generally speaking, lexical items keep their 'citation' forms wherever they occur in clauses and sentences; the following examples (op cit) are typical:

na ruf	'this is a baboon'	na ruf ɓa	'this is not baboon'
tin zoɓ	'she is a slob'	tin zoɓ ɓa	'she is not a slob'
na boŋ	'this is white'	na boŋ ɓa	'this is not white'

Here are examples with final /-i/ that likewise maintain their 'citation' form:

na wuɗi	'this is milk'	na wuɗi ɓa	'this is not milk'	(NLP, Magaji: wuɗyi)
na[10] saɓi	'this is a stick'	na saɓi ɓa	'this is not a stick'	
dala wa ɮi	'Dala paid'	dala wa ɮi sule	'Dala paid a shilling'	
dala wa vi	'Dala roasted'	dala wa vi ɮu	'Dala roasted meat'	

However, thirdly, there are examples of lexical items with final /-i/ in citation form that lose their final vowel mid-clause:

na seɗi	'this is a snake'	na seɗ ɓa	'this is not a snake'	(Magaji: su̲ɗi)
na deɓi	'this is gum'	na deɓ ɓa	'this is not gum'	
dala wa wuɗi	'Dala pointed'	dala wa wuɗ koro	'Dala pointed at the donkey'	(Magaji: waɗi)
dala wa mbuki	'Dala threw'	dala wa mbuk koro	'Dala threw at the donkey'	
saɓira kəri	'the stick is long'	saɓira kər ɓa	'the stick is not long'	

It will be noticed that two lexical items share the same segmental combination, namely /wuɗi/ ('milk' and 'to point') but act differently mid-clause. Also, the type of final consonant does not appear to influence the option of alternation, whether it a voiceless plosive, an implosive or a resonant.

However, there is a fourth group of lexical items with final /-i/ in citation form with an alternation to /ə/ (/ɨ/):

dala wa ɮi	'Dala received'	dala wa ɮə sule	'Dala received a shilling'
dala wa ɗi	'Dala went'	dala wa ɗə goma	'Dala went to the market'
na pərsi	'this is a horse'	na pərsə ɓa	'this is not a horse'
dala wa kədi	'Dala pulled'	dala wa kədə koro	'Dala pulled a donkey'

Other common verbs show the same alternation: *shi* ~ *shu̲* ('to do'); *ghi* ~ *ghu̲* ('to shoot'); *zi* ~ *zu̲* ('to say'). Odden (op cit) argues, from this fourth group, that these lexical items have an underlying 'base' form with final /-ə/, which converts to /-i/ in citation form and that disappears before a suffix with an initial vowel; for example, the definite marker *-a*, and the imperative marker *-u*:

persa	'the horse'
ɗu	'go!'
kədu	'pull!'
mbuku	'throw!'

He then maintains that the lexical items in the third group also have an underlying 'base' form with final /-ə/, which also disappears, but before a consonant. However, the weakness of his argument is that he has to resort to inventing hypothetical forms, for there is no evidence of */seɗə, deɓə, wuɗə, mbukə/ in the language. It is simpler to acknowledge a subset of lexical items that alternate their final /-i/ either a) by deleting their final vowel mid-clause, or b) by deleting it before a vowel or converting it to /-ə/ before a consonant.

It would be advisable for any future dictionary project to specify the alternations of such words:

deɓi ~ deɓ 'gum'
ɗi ~ du 'to go'
dli ~ dlu 'to receive'
ghi ~ ghu 'to shoot'
kudi ~ kudu 'to pull'
kuri ~ kur 'long'
mbuki ~ mbuk 'to throw'
pursi ~ pursu 'horse'
seɗi ~ seɗ 'snake'
shi ~ shu 'to do'
wuɗi ~ wuɗ 'to point'
zi ~ zu 'to say'

It might be observed that the forms *du, dlu, ghu, shu, zu* with final /ɨ/ (or /ə/) appear to defy the foot rule that a foot must contain a heavy syllable, since /ɨ/ cannot be long; this may be explained away in either of two ways: either 1) these forms constitute the second syllable of the verbal group following *wa* 'past' marker, which together constitute a foot; or 2) because these forms are never final in a clause, they constitute a light syllable belonging to the following foot.

The loss of final /i/ produces words with final /ɗ/ that was not otherwise allowed, see **6.6 Syllable-final Margin Systems**. This alters the system network for word-final consonants.

This subset is also noticeable for one other diachronic effect (Newman 1968; Odden 2005: 289–290); historical palatalization has not affected the alveolar obstruents of this subset. This is evident in the immediate list above: *ɗi* has not become **ɗyi*; *kudi* has not become **kuji*; *pursi* has not become **purshi*, etc. In other words, the phonology of this subset is slightly different from the phonology of other lexical items in respect of modern 'palatalized' forms.

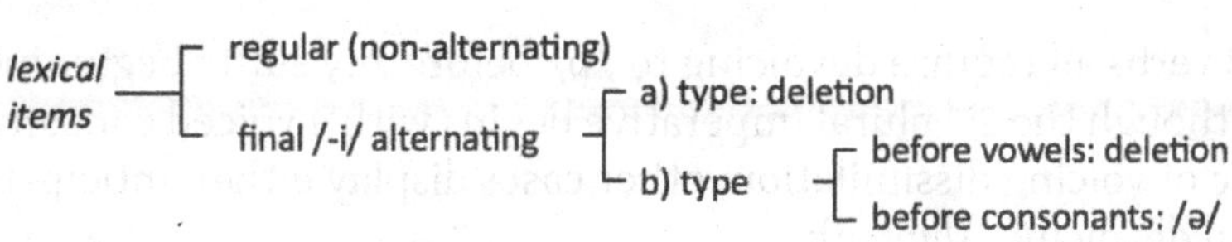

Figure 6.6 System network of lexical alternations

6.8 Verb Morphophonology

This description of verb morphology relies entirely on Crozier (2010), which was based on the data of 238 common verbs provided by Babayo Mahdi. The morphological variations are displayed in Table 6.8 below and show, basically, six categories of verbs:

1. those ending with a nasal, e.g. /wun/ *wun* 'to bake'
2. those ending with a bilabial obstruent, e.g. /ʃíɓ/ *shiɓ* 'to wash'
3. those ending with a non-nasal alveolar/postalveolar consonant, e.g. /ᵑgɨɗ/ *nggu̲ɗ* 'to look'; /lát/ *lat* 'to spread'; /mas/ *mas* 'to rest'; /taɬ/ *tatl* 'to sew'
4. those ending with a velar obstruent, e.g. /ʃax/ *shakh* 'to share'
5. those ending with /r/, e.g. /ɓɨr/ *ɓu̲r* 'to marry'; /dàr/ *dar* 'to taste'
6. those ending with a vowel, e.g. /pa/ *pa* 'to bury'

It will also be seen that certain suffixes remain constant whatever category of verb they are attached to; namely *-ma*, *-ki*, *kandi*, *-kandang*. Other suffixes display variations according to the final consonant of the verb. Final consonants themselves show phonological processes in some cases. All suffixes take the same tone of the citation form of a verb.

Table 6.8 Morphological variations of Tera's 6 categories of verbs

Verb form	perfect	2 sg	2 pl imper	past imper	progress	partic-ularity	partic definite	gerund	result[11]
1 *wun*	-i	-u	-ma	-ki	-di	-kandi	-kandang	-dang	-dan
2 *shiɓ*	-i	-u	-ma	-ki	-ti	-kandi	-kandang	-tang	-tan
3a *nggu̲ɗ*	-i	-u	-ma	-ki	nggu̲ti	-kandi	-kandang	-ang	-an
lat	-i	-u	-ma	-ki	la:ti	-kandi	-kandang	la:tang	la:tan
3b *mas*	-i	-u	-ma	-ki	ma:si	-kandi	-kandang	-ang	-an
3c *tatl*	-i	-u	-ma	-ki	ta:tli	-kandi	-kandang	-ang	-an
4 *shakh*	-i	-u	-ma	-ki	-ti	-kandi	-kandang	-tang	-tan
5a *ɓu̲r*	-i	-u	-ma	-ki	-ti	-kandi	-kandang	-tang	-tan
5b *dar*	-I	-u	-ma	-ki	da:ri	-kandi	-kandang	da:rang	da:ran
6 *pa* 'to bury'	-ø	-u/-o	-ma	-ki	-ri	-kandi	-kandang[12]	-rang	-ran

Category 1 contains verbs that exhibit no change in their form, whatever suffixes follow; hence, Crozier takes that category as providing the basic form of the suffixes themselves.

Category 2 verbs all require devoicing to /p/ before any suffix beginning with a consonant, even though the 2nd plural imperative begins with a voiced consonant /m/. This latter is a case of voicing dissimilation; other cases display either anticipatory assimilation or mutual devoicing (*shiptan*):

shiɓ /ʃíɓ/ /ʃíɓi ʃíɓu ʃípma ʃípkí ʃíptí ʃíptaŋ ʃíptan/

Category 3 verbs all accept the same form of suffixes, as shown above, but they divide over processes to their final consonants. Category 3a verbs end with alveolar plosives, which all require /ɗ/ before *-i*, and *-u*, /d/ before *-ma*, devoicing before the *-k* suffixes and before progressive *-i*, and 'participles' *-ang*, *-an*, avoiding a doubling of the consonant /t/. However, monosyllabic verbs with /-at/ lengthen the vowel as well as avoiding a doubling of /t/; in this case, the heavy syllable with a long vowel has a grammatical function.

ngguɗ /ᵑgɨɗ/ /ᵑgɨɗi ᵑgɨɗu ᵑgɨdma ᵑgɨtki ᵑgɨti ᵑgɨtaŋ ᵑgɨtan/
lat /lát/ /láɗi láɗu ládma látki lá:ti lá:taŋ lá:tan/

Category 3b end with sibilants, both alveolar and postalveolar; they are not subject to any processes, except the lengthening of the vowel and skipping potential /t/ in suffixes; again, the heavy syllable with a long vowel has a grammatical function.

mas /mas/ /masi masu masma maski ma:si ma:saŋ ma:san/

Category 3c verbs end with a lateral consonant, both resonant and fricative; the lateral fricatives become/l/ before *-ma* and *-ki* and lengthen the vowel and skip potential /t/ in suffixes (like Category 3b); and again, the heavy syllable with a long vowel has a grammatical function.

tatl /taɬ/ /taɬi taɬu taɬma taɬki ta:ɬi ta:ɬaŋ ta:ɬan/

Category 4 verbs end with a velar obstruent consonant; final fricatives maintain friction before vowel suffixes, are voiced before *-ma* and lose their friction before /-t, -k/.

shakh /ʃax/ /ʃaxi ʃaxu ʃaɣma ʃakki ʃakti ʃaktaŋ ʃaktan/

Category 5 verbs end with /r/; some (5a) are attached with the same suffixes as to Category 4 verbs.

ɓu̲r /ɓɨr/ /ɓɨri ɓɨru ɓɨrma ɓɨrki ɓɨrti ɓɨrtaŋ ɓɨrtan/

Others (5b) follow the example of *lat* above, with lengthening of the vowel and the elision of /t/; and once again, the heavy syllable with a long vowel has a grammatical function.

dar /dàr/ /dàri dàru dàrma dàrki dà:ri dà:raŋ dà:ran/

Category 6 verbs end with a vowel in their citation form. Perfect *-i* is elided, 2nd singular

imperative *-u* undergoes various changes: to *-o* for all non-close vowels, elided with /u/, and front vowels are reduced to *y* before either /u/ or /o/.

pa /pa/ /pa po pama paki pari paraŋ paran/
vi /vi/ '*enter*' /vi vʲu vima vaki vari varaŋ varan/
ge /ge/ '*swim*' /gé gʲo gema geki geri geraŋ geran/
pu /pu/ '*rub*' /pu pu puma puki puri puraŋ puran/
ko /kó/ '*sweep*' /kó kó kómá kókí kórí kóráŋ kórán/

(It is tempting to regard the basic forms of the 'gerund' and 'result' suffixes as *-rang* and *-ran*, since they are not influenced by preceding consonants; the /d/ of *-dang*, *-dan* for Category 1 verbs could then be regarded as a hardening after nasals that are voiced, and the /t/ of *-tang* and *-tan* for Category 2 and 4 verbs as a hardening with mutual devoicing, and the elision of /r/ after 'fellow' alveolar articulations.)

The phonological system of verb morphology differs from monomorphemic word phonology in two respects. First, any initial consonant before /i, e/ becomes palatalized, not just / ɓʲ, vʲ, mʲ, ʔj, ʃ, ʒ, ʧ, ʤ/ with 2nd singular imperative *-u, -o*.

Secondly, there is a fuller incidence of final consonants in closed syllables in word-medial position, i.e. as the final margin before a following syllable with an initial consonant, as in, for instance, a CVC.CV pattern, as a result of consonant-initial suffixes; these are marked by the symbol + in the examples below.

/p/	/ʃíp+kí/	*shipki*	'washed'
/b/	/dabtí/	*dabti*	'clay for pottery, building'
/ɓ/	/dɨɓtí/	*duɓti*	'sap, resin'
/t/	/kutkum/	*kutkum*	'to be low'
/d/	/kudkum/	*kudkum*	'short, shallow'
/k/	/rɨkna/	*rukna*	'dirty'
/g/	/dagla/	*dagla*	'helmet, to defend'
/f/	/raftiki/	*raftiki*	'friend'
/v/	/ⁿʤiv+ku/	*njivku*	'roads'
/s/	/xuski/	*khuski*	'man'
/z/	/ʔjɨzki/	*ɗuzki*	'to insult'
/ʃ/	/pɨ́ʃ+má/	*pushma*	'sprinkle (2nd plural imperative)'
/ʒ/	/pɨ̀ʒ+mà/	*puzhma*	'sharpen (2nd plural imperative)'
/x/	/pixta/	*pikhta*	'fan'
/ɣ/	/ʔjeɣlem/	*ɗyeghlem*	'to refuse out of polite consideration'
/ɬ/	/taɬkandi/	*tatlkandi*	'something sewn'
/ɮ/	/ɓɨɮkandi/	ɓudlkandi	'something forged'

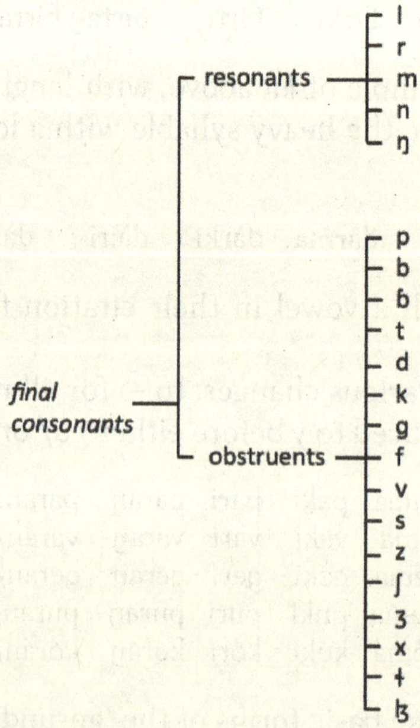

Figure 6.7 System network for syllable-final consonants in word-medial position including verb suffixes

This requires yet another system network for syllable-final consonants in word-medial position that takes into inflected verbs account.

6.9 Phonology of Ideophones

Passing reference was made in Chapter **1.4 Phonology and Words** to primary and secondary onomatopoeia, the latter also known as 'sound symbolism', which refers to culture-specific attempts to represent sensations rather than natural sounds. Sound symbolism requires book-length examination in its own right and has not featured greatly in this present study. One reason for that is that generally a language uses its own regular phonological resources, no different from 'plain' lexical items. (This does not include interjections like *brrr*, etc., which additionally utilize phonetic (i.e. non-phonological) articulations.)

Tera, like many African languages, has a large stock of words that symbolically represent sensations, known as ideophones. Magaji (2018) has approximately 3,240 Tera entries, of which no less than 6% are identified by her as ideophones. There are four general categories of ideophones with the following associations:

- shape, size and surfaces (e.g. smooth, shiny)
- physical and moral conditions (e.g. fever, sleepy)
- intensive expression (e.g. very warm, boastful)
- actions and positions as a result of actions (e.g. strolling aimlessly, cross-legged)

The reason for drawing attention to them is that a number of phonotactic constraints in standard Tera word phonology are 'loosened' in the phonology of ideophones.

There are three main phonological structures for Tera ideophones: duplicating compounds, disyllables with assonance (repeated vowels) and trisyllables with assonance; there are far fewer instances of rhyme and consonance (repeated consonants). Duplicating compounds are most numerous with intensive expressions (35 out of 38 items) and actions and positions (26 out of 39 instances); examples:

ɓangɓang	held tightly
ɓeuɓeu	very sour
ɗumɗum	warm
genegene	taking a long time to eat
guɗak-guɗak	gulping
keɗen-keɗen	moving furtively, stealthily

Assonance is very common among ideophones depicting shape, size and surfaces (45 out of 53 instances); examples:

keleɓeng	small and flat
kuɗkhum	very short, shallow
lu̲ɓu̲ndu̲ng	greasy, sticky with dirt

Physical and moral conditions have a wider range of structures; examples:

ɓalɓal fever
damtaran loose, misaligned, helpless
k̲ur̲ung quiet and worried, flaccid, limp

A full study of Tera ideophones would be a fruitful task for the future. The phonology of ideophones is slightly different from standard word phonology: word-initial /s/ does not precede /e/, nor /w/ precede /i/, and word final /ɣ/ (<gh>) does not occur, but Tera ideophones include

sekerkitek small and round
wilwil sharp, pointed
zhaghzhagh[13] joy

6.10 Conclusion

The phonology of Tera is quite different from the three European languages described above, although the **ranks** of the phonological **hierarchy** match. The foot for lexical items relates to syllable weight rather than stress. However, free-standing grammatical items have their own separate syllable weight characteristics, which need to be researched further. Tone appears as a prosodic feature of syllables and is shown in a **system network**. The consonant systems require fewer networks even though the inventory of them is more complicated; there are no clusters of consonants within syllables and the final margins are simpler than those of the initial margins, even when taking verb suffixes into account. Initial margins have strong phonotactic control over following vowels. Also, there are basically only two systems for the vowels: in light and heavy syllables. Nevertheless, the **polysystemic** principle applies throughout, including separate systems in lexical alternations, verb morphology and ideophones.

Hypothetical 'underlying' forms have been avoided by relying solely on actual **surface data**. We have noted historical changes in the development of Tera word phonology that display its **creative potential**.

This description is not complete, since the morphology of word classes besides verbs needs investigating, but there is evidence that syllable weight can have a grammatical function in morphology. Nevertheless, the descriptive apparatus of word phonology within a SFL perspective is shown to be hugely beneficial in displaying the richness of the phonology of Tera words.

Postscript

The purpose of this book has been to explore the possibilities of extending the reach of Systemic Functional Linguistics, by embracing a basic component of language that has not been credited with the effort and thought that has been expended on lexicogrammar, intonation and a wide range of discourse interests. In one sense, this lack of interest in word phonology is understandable in that options in meaning are not readily recognized in consonants and vowels and such like.

The intention was to see whether the principles and practices of SFL might apply at the level of the word in phonological terms as well as lexicogrammatical. It is clear that phonological systems at word level would not yield insights of potential meaning; after all, we are all well aware of the arbitrary nature of the relationship between *signifié* and *signifiant*, although investigations in onomatopoeia across cultures offer intriguing possibilities.

This primary intention of attempting to adopt the **architecture** of SFL to word phonology has been presented here and it has also highlighted the strengths of the approach and contrasted them with other theoretical attempts to account for phonological data and features. Those highlights are briefly documented in the following final few paragraphs.

SFL lays great store on the concept of **function** as a basis for explaining the structures and choices in a language. The primary function of phonology is simply to provide lexicogrammar with forms to distinguish all its units; that is its principal raison d'être, whether it is rhythm for groups and phrases, intonation for clauses, clause complexes and larger units of discourse, or phonemes, syllables and feet (and other rhythmic units) for humble words. As has been claimed several times, there can be no lexicogrammar without phonology.

Because the lexicogrammar provides the starting point, Systemic Phonology takes *word* as a starting point, rather than a set of phonemes; hence its top-down approach with the foot as the phonological parallel to *word* as a lexicogrammatical unit. Feet have structures of syllables, which in turn have structures of phonemes; certain types of phonemes have certain functions in syllables, and certain types of syllables have certain functions in feet. In this way, a **hierarchy** of ranks of units is established in phonology with mutual relationships of structure and function. Systemic Phonology also ventures into allophonic details since they are peculiar to each language.

In many introductory textbooks in linguistics, there is a tendency to introduce phonology first as if it was basic to the rest of language. That is unhelpful. Language is a resource for meaning and communication; meaning should take pride of place when introducing a study of language and then comes the 'embodiment' of meaning in its spoken and written forms. Phonology is a servant to lexicogrammar.

This book has attempted to explore the concepts of function and system in the phonology of the word in four quite different languages. **Systems** display what a language engages from the total range of phonetic material and commandeers for establishing units of meaning. For instance, English, German and Welsh all engage the foot as a unit at the top of the word phonology hierarchy; in very broad terms, English engages a wide variety of foot structures with a considerable amount of change in complex words; German engages a slightly narrower range of structures but with a very conspicuous distinction between regular vocabulary and 'irregular' loan words and borrowings; Welsh has a relatively tight range of structures and a very tight obligation of position in a word. Tera does not have feet in the usual sense, but the equivalent unit is built of heavy and light syllables. Tera does not engage stress, but tone in syllables and has a very limited range of syllable structures, whereas English, German and Welsh each have a very wide range. They also have relatively complex vowel systems and a consonant system comprising around twenty items, whereas Tera has a relatively simple vowel system, but a consonant system that is more than double. Allophonic variation among Tera vowels corresponds to phonemic opposition in English; the distribution of consonants in English and German is profoundly different; phonotactic rules in Welsh are much more significant than they are in the other languages. And so the differences in systems can be enumerated.

Furthermore, a language employs numerous systems at different points in the phonology of words; hence the importance of the **polysystemic** principle in Systemic Phonology, rather than attempting to establish a single monolithic inventory.

Systemic Phonology eschews artificial, so called 'underlying', forms that have no real existence. Throughout SFL, descriptions are based on **actual text**, and that is the case in word phonology too. 'Underlying' forms have no real psychological reality, but are constructions that certain linguists create to establish a particular theory. Systemic Phonology represents people's linguistic competence in actual performance, and this undergirds a person's **creativity** with language, even in phonology.

Systemic Phonology is intentionally **non-universalistic**. It recognizes that each language engages with the total potential of the range of human speech in its own way, in the same way that people of different language communities perceive the world around them in different ways. In the same idiosyncratic spirit, the studies in this book have not followed a standard format of presentation, but each study has progressed in such a way that suits the phonological characteristics of each language. It has not attempted to produce either a contrastive or a comparative study of phonology between the four languages; it has simply investigated the viability of Systemic Phonology.

This book is just the start of an interesting exercise. Other minds will enlarge upon and integrate these ideas more succinctly in the future, with fresh, innovative thinking (Matthiessen 2021; Fawcett 2022), but what is needed above all are descriptions of the phonology of words in the vast number of languages across the world, to test these ideas and formal structures and provide fresh insights in to how the languages of the world organize their word phonology – and so, expand the statement on Systemic Phonology that appears in **1.6** (and Tench 1992: 15).

Notes

Chapter 1

1. Tone group, or tone unit, is otherwise known as an intonation unit; the advantage of the latter term is that the intonation unit contains choices of tonality and tonicity as well as tone – all three systems of intonation.
2. See Hedberg et al. (2014) and Dehé and Braun (2019) for some recent corpus investigations using ToBI.

Chapter 2

1. *strength* for some speakers with epenthetic /k/: /'strɛŋkθ/, see below 2.7, p. 37; strictly speaking not a monomorphemic word, since it is *strong* + *th*, but see Chapter 3, 3.3.
2. The term *rhyme* is often used to refer to the sequence of nucleus and syllable-final margin.
3. 'Fortis' is a term that refers to a high level of muscular tension in the articulator and at the larynx; IPA has no specific symbol for it, but Ladefoged and Maddieson (1996: 56) employ an asterisk [*] for a similar characteristic in Korean, e.g. /p*/.
4. See further under *Rounding* (p. 52).

Chapter 3

1. It must be noted that *quicker* often now acts as the adverb: *he ran quicker than anybody else.*
2. This cluster is identical to the /-lst/ of *whilst*, but is included at this point for the sake of completeness.

Chapter 4

1. Transcription questions are dealt with later (pp. 92–93 and 95–100).
2. I am grateful to Prof. Dr. Petr Rösel, Mainz University, for his help and advice at this point.
3. Als Lehnwörter werden Wörter aus fremden Sprachen bezeichnet, die lautlich und der Form nach an die eigene Sprache angeglichen wurden. In dieser Hinsicht nicht angeglichene Übernahmen sind Fremdwörter. [Words from foreign languages are designated *Lehnwörter* ('loan words'), which are assimilated to the sound and form of the language. In this respect, non-assimilated transfers are *Fremdwörter* ('foreign words').].
4. However, words of Latin origin with final -ie have it as unstressed, e.g. *Familie* /fa'mi:ljə/; *Materie* /ma'te:rjə/.
5. However, words of Latin origin with final -ik have it as unstressed, e.g. *Klinik* /'kli:nɪk/; *Logik* /'lo:gik/; *Arsenik* /aʀ'zɛnɪk/. (See further, below, under *4.1.3 Shifting Word Stress.*)
6. However, many words of French origin retain a French final nasalized vowel, e.g. *Abonnement* /abɔnə'mã/; *Arrangement* /arã:ʒə'mã/.)

7. Umgangssprachlich wird man heute die anfangsbetonte Version vorziehen. Die Stammbetonte klingt etwa „offiziell". [Colloquially people today prefer the initial stressed version. Stress on the stem sounds somewhat "official".]

Chapter 5

1. They themselves also cite Morris-Jones (1913).
2. Evans and Thomas (1953) spell it as *saets*.
3. This designation will be revised in due course; see below *Final tertiary stressed in regular polysyllables.*
4. Evans and Thomas (1953) has *starts*, with a combination of three consonants: /r+t+s/.
5. Evans and Thomas (1953) accepts the two forms *ewythr* and *ewyrth*, but only one form of *dieithr.*
6. See Clee, G (2017: 54–56) for a succinct explanation of orthographical vowel accents in modern Welsh orthography: ^ = long vowel where spelling would suggest a short vowel; ′ = short stressed vowel rather than an unstressed; ` = short vowel where spelling would suggest a long vowel; ¨ = stressed monophthongs before another vowel.
7. *nes* /nɛs/ = 'until', whereas /neːs/ = 'nearer'.
8. *gwaell* gwaːɬ can also be *gwäell* gwa(ː).ɛɬ without change of meaning.
9. *eu* is an exceptional spelling for /ei/.
10. Note that colloquial pronunciations of *ei, eu, ein, eich* tend to become /i, i, ən, əχ/.
11. In modern orthography, final /-ʧ/ is spelled as <-tsh>, replacing older <-ts>, *starts.*
12. Please note footnote 6 above for the function of orthographical accents in modern Welsh spelling.

Chapter 6

1. i.e. 'The letters of the Nyamatli language'.
2. Note that *Reading & Writing Nyimatli* (NLP 2015: 14) erroneously describes this consonant as equivalent to the Hausa ejective <ƙ>.
3. Data and glosses are from Nyimatli Language Project workshops, unless credited otherwise, e.g. Schuh (2017), Magaji (2018).
4. Mid tone on *zhi* yields these homophones, with identical tone as well as consonant and vowel.
5. We can confirm that they are in fact errors: HL is ML dighì 'honey; bee' ; LH is LL ɗỳlvì 'castrated goat'.
6. See note 3.
7. But see 6.9 Phonology of ideophones.
8. But see 6.9 Phonology of ideophones.
9. But see 6.9 Phonology of ideophones.
10. This appears to have been misspelt on Odden (2005: 287).
11. The labels of the verb suffixes may best be interpreted as follows: 2 sg/pl imper = singular and plural imperatives; progress = progressive/continuous; particularity = nominalization (e.g. *a doing*); partic definite = definite nominalization (e.g. *the doing*); gerund similar to 'present participle'; result similar to 'past participle'.
12. To simplify the illustrative examples in the six categories, *-kandi, -kandang* will be omitted, as Crozier (2010) does, since any phonological processes follow the pattern before *-ki.*
13. See Musa (2018: 23).

References

Abercrombie, D.T. 1967. *Elements of general phonetics*. Edinburgh: Edinburgh University Press.

Aitchison, J. 2003. *Words in the mind: An introduction to the mental lexicon*. 3rd edition. Oxford: Blackwell Publishing.

Arwel, R. 2016. *Welsh language project in Chubut: 2016 annual report*. Cardiff: British Council Wales.

Awbery, G. 1984. Phonotactic constraints in Welsh. In Ball, M.J. and Jones, G.E. (eds), *Welsh phonology*, 65–104. Cardiff: University of Wales Press.

Awbery, G. 2009. Welsh. In Ball, M.J. and Müller, N. (eds), *The Celtic languages*, 2nd edition, 359–373. New York: Routledge.

Ball, M.J. and Jones, G.E. 1984. *Welsh phonology*. Cardiff: University of Wales Press.

Ball, M.J. and Williams, B. 2001. *Welsh phonetics*. Lampeter: The Edwin Mellen Press.

BBC. 2014. Viewpoint: The Argentines who speak Welsh. 16 October 2014.

Bell, E. 2016. *Phonemic vowel length in Welsh-Spanish bilingual speech*. Poster. University of Arizona.

Berry, M. 1975. *An introduction to systemic linguistics*. Vol 1: *Structures and systems*. London: Batsford.

Berry, M. 1977. *An introduction to systemic linguistics 2: Levels and links*. London: Batsford.

Bithel, J. 1952. *German pronunciation and phonology*. London: Methuen.

Bloomfield, L. 1933. *Language*. New York: Holt and Company.

Brazil, D. 1975. *Discourse intonation I*. English Language Research: Birmingham University.

Brazil, D. 1978. *Discourse intonation II*. English Language Research: Birmingham University.

Brazil, D. 1985. *The communicative value of intonation in English*. English Language Research: Birmingham University.

Butler, C. 1985a. *Theory and applications*. London: Batsford.

Butler, C.S. 1985b. *Systemic linguistics: Theory and applications*. London: Batsford.

Chomsky, N. and Halle, M. 1968. *Sound patterns of English*. New York: Harper & Row.

Clee, G. 2017. *Cwrs ynganu*. Pontypridd: University of South Wales.

Coleman, J. 2005. *Introducing speech and language processing*. Cambridge: Cambridge University Press.

Coloma, G. 2018. Argentine Spanish. *Journal of the International Phonetic Association* 48(2): 243–250.

Coupland, N. and Garrett, P. 2010. Linguistic landscapes, discursive frames and metacultural performance: The case of Welsh Patagonia. *International Journal of the Sociology of Language* 205: 7–36.

Crozier, D. 2010. Nyimatli verb morphophonology. Paper presentation. Jos: Jos Linguistic Circle.

Davies, M. 2012. *To the ends of the earth*, edited by Gwen Emyr. Caernarfon: Bwthyn.

Dehé, N. and Braun, B. 2019. The prosody of rhetorical questions in English. *English Language and Linguistics* 24(4): 607–635.

Downing, A. and Locke, P. 2004. *English grammar; a university course*. Abingdon: Taylor & Francis.

Duden. 2015. *Das Aussprachewörtherbuch*. 7th edition. Berlin: Duden.

Eberhard, D.M., Simons, G.F. and Fennig, C.D. (eds). 2019. *Ethnologue: Languages of the world*. 22nd edition. Dallas, TX: SIL International. Available at: http://www.ethnologue.com

Evans, H.M. and Thomas, W.O. 1953. *Y geiriadur newydd. The new Welsh dictionary*. Llandebie: Llyfrau'r Dryw.

Fawcett, R. 2022. *An integrative architecture for Systemic Functional Linguistics and other theories of language*. Sheffield: Equinox.

Fontaine, L. 2013. *Analysing English grammar: A systemic-functional introduction*. Cambridge: Cambridge University Press.

Gimson, A.C. 1962. *An introduction to the pronunciation of English*. London: Edward Arnold.

Gimson, A.C. 1989. *An introduction to the pronunciation of English*. 4th edition. London: Edward Arnold.

Gimson, A.C. 2014. *Gimson's pronunciation of English*. 8th edition, revised by Cruttenden, A. London: Edward Arnold.

Griffiths, B. and Jones, D.G. 1995. *Geiriadur yr Academi*. Cardiff: Gwasg Prifysgol Cymru.

Goldsmith, J. 1976. *Autosegmental phonology*. PhD thesis. Massachusetts Institute of Technology.

Goldsmith, J. 1990. *Autosegmental and metrical phonology*. Oxford: Blackwell.

Goldsmith, J. 1999. *Phonological theory: The essential readings*. Oxford: Blackwell.

Guierre, L. 1970. *Drills in English stress-patterns*. London: Longman.

Gussenhoven, C. 2004. *The phonology and tone and intonation*. London: Hodder Arnold.

Hall, C. 1992. *Modern German pronunciation*. Manchester: Manchester University Press.

Halle, M. and Mohanan, K.P. 1985. Segmental phonology of modern English. *Linguistic Inquiry* 16(1): 57–116.

Halliday, M.A.K. 1961. Categories of the theory of grammar. *Word* 17: 242–292.

Halliday, M.A.K. 1967. *Intonation and grammar in British English*. The Hague: Mouton.

Halliday, M.A.K. 1970. *A course in spoken English: Intonation*. London: Oxford University Press.

Halliday, M.A.K. 1975. *Learning how to mean*. London: Edward Arnold.

Halliday, M.A.K. 1985. *An introduction to functional grammar*. London: Edward Arnold.

Halliday, M.A.K. 1992. A systemic interpretation of Peking syllable finals. In Tench, P. (ed.), *Studies in systemic phonology*. London: Pinter.

Halliday, M.A.K. 2002. *On grammar*, edited by J.J. Webster. London: Continuum.

Halliday, M.A.K. and Greaves, W.S. 2008. *Intonation in the grammar of English*. London: Equinox.

Halliday, M.A.K., McIntosh, A. and Strevens, P. 1964. *The linguistic sciences and language teaching*. London: Longmans, Green & Co.

Halliday, M.A.K. and Matthiessen, C.M.I.M. 2004. *An introduction to functional grammar*. 3rd edition. London: Routledge.

Hannahs, S.J. 2009. Welsh svarabhakti: Sonority sequencing and foot structure. *Journal of Celtic Linguistics* 13: 21–44.

Hannahs, S.J. 2013. *The phonology of Welsh*. Oxford: Oxford University Press.

Harris, Z.S. 1951. *Methods in structural linguistics*. Chicago, IL: University of Chicago Press.

Hayes, B. 1982. Extrametricality and English stress. *Linguistic Inquiry* 13: 227–276.

Hedberg, N., Sosa, J.M. and Görgülü, E. 2014. The meaning of intonation in yes-no questions in American English: A corpus study. *Corpus Linguistics and Linguistic Theory* 10: 1–48.

Hudson, R.A. 1974. Systemic generative grammar. *Linguistics* 139: 5–42.

International Phonetic Association. 1999. *Handbook of the International Phonetic Association*. Cambridge: Cambridge University Press.

Iosad, P. 2017. The phonologisation of redundancy: Length and quality in Welsh vowels. *Phonology* 34: 121–162.

Jespersen, O. 1932. *Lehrbuch der Phonetik*. 2nd edition. Leipzig: Teubner.

Jideonwo, I.A. 2004. *Let's develop Nyimatli language*. Lagos: Community Development Project.

Johnson, I. 2009. How green is their valley? Subjective vitality of Welsh language and culture in the Chubut Province, Argentina. *International Journal of the Sociology of Language* 195: 141–171.

Johnson, I. 2010. Tourism, transnationality and ethnolinguistic vitality: The Welsh in the Chubut Province, Argentina. *Journal of Multilingual and Multicultural Development* 36(6): 553–568.

Jones, G.E. 1984. The distinctive vowels and consonants of Welsh. In Ball, M.J. and Jones, G.E. (eds), *Welsh phonology*. Cardiff: University of Wales Press.

Jones, R.O. 1976. Cydberthynas Amrywiadau Iaith a Nodweddion Cymdeithasol yn y Gaiman Chubut – Sylwadau Rhagarweiniol. *Bwletin y Bwrdd Gwybodau Celtaidd* XXVII: 51–64.

Jones, R.O. 1984. Change and variation in the Welsh of Gaiman, Chubut. In Ball, M.J. and Jones, G.E. (eds), *Welsh phonology*, 237–261. Cardiff: University of Wales Press.

Kelly, J. 1992. Systems for open syllabics in North Welsh. In Tench, P. (ed.), *Studies in systemic phonology*. London: Pinter.

Kohler, K. 1999. 'German'. In International Phonetic Association, *Handbook of the International Phonetic Association*. Cambridge: Cambridge University Press, pp. 86–89.

Ladd, D.R. 1996. *Intonational Phonology*. Cambridge: Cambridge University Press.

Ladd, D.R. 2008. *Intonational Phonology*. 2nd edition. Cambridge: Cambridge University Press.

Ladefoged, P. and Maddieson, I. 1996. *The sounds of the world's languages*. Oxford: Blackwell.

Liberman, M. 1979. *The intonational system of English*. New York: Garland.

Magaji, M. 2018. *Tera-English-Hausa dictionary*. Potiskum, Yobe: Ajami Graphics.

Martens, C. and Martens, P. 1961. *Phonetik der Deutshen Sprache*. München: Max Hueber Verlag.

Matthiessen, C.M.I.M. 2021. *Systemic Functional Linguistics Part 1: The collected works of Christian M.I.M. Matthiessen Vol 1* (edited by K. Teurya, C. Wu and D. Slade). Sheffield: Equinox.

Mayr, R. and Davies, H. 2011. A crossdialectal acoustic study of the monophthongs and diphthongs of Welsh. *Journal of the International Phonetic Association* 41(1): 1–25.

Morris-Jones, J. 1913. *A Welsh grammar*. Oxford: Clarendon Press.

Moulton, W.E. 1962. *The sounds of English and German*. Chicago: University of Chicago Press.

Musa, R.I. 2018. Alternation of the velar phonemes of the Tera language. *International Journal of English Language and Linguistics Research* 6(1): 22–30.

Newman, P. 1964. A word list of Tera. *Journal of West African Languages* 1(2): 33–50.

Newman, P. 1968. The reality of morphophonemes. *Language* 44(3): 507–515.

Newman, P. 1970. A grammar of Tera. Berkeley: University of California Publications in Linguistics 57.

Newman, P. 1980. Tera. In Kropp Dakubu, M.E. (ed.), *West African Data Sheets*, vol 2. Ter1-5. Leiden: West African Linguistic Society and African Studies Centre.

Nyimatli Language Project (NLP). 2015. *Reading & writing Tera (Nyimatli)*. NLP: Nyimatli Forum.

O'Brien, M.G. and Fagan, S.M.B. 2016. *German phonetics and phonology*. Yale: Yale University Press.

O'Grady, G. 2010. *A grammar of spoken English discourse*. London: Continuum.

O'Grady, G. 2013. *Key concepts in phonetics and phonology*. Basingstoke: Palgrave Macmillan.

Odden, D. 2005. *Introducing phonology*. Cambridge: Cambridge University Press.

Palmer, F.R. (ed.). 1970. *Prosodic analysis*. London: Oxford University Press.

Pearce, M. 2007. Iambicity in Kera. *Selected Proceedings of the 37th Annual Conference on African Linguistics*, edited by Doris L. Payne and Jaime Peña, 66–76. Somerville, MA: Cascadilla Proceedings Project.

Pierrehumbert, J. 1980. *The phonology and phonetics of English intonation*. PhD thesis. Massachusetts Institute of Technology.

Pierrehumbert, J. and Hirschberg, J. 1990. The meaning of intonational contours in the interpretation of discourse. In Cohen, P., Morgan, J. and Pollack, M. (eds), *Intentions in communication*. Massachusetts Institute of Technology.

Pike, K.L. 1947. *Phonemics: A technique for reducing languages to writing*. Ann Arbor: The University of Michigan Press.

Pike, K.L. 1955. *Language in relation to a unified theory of the structure of human behavior*. 3 volumes. Ann Arbor: The University of Michigan Press.

Pike, K.L. 1962. Practical phonetics of rhythm waves. *Phonetica* 8: 9–30.

Pike, K.L. and Fries, C.C. 1949. Coexistent phonemic systems. *Language* 25(1): 29–50. Reprinted in Brend, R.M. 1972. *Kenneth L Pike: Selected writings*, 51–73. The Hague: Mouton.

Rees, I.W. 2018. Length and quality in Welsh mid vowels: New evidence from mid Wales. *Journal of Celtic Linguistics* 19: 157–208.

Rees, I.W. 2021a. Hispanicization in the Welsh settlement of Chubut Province, Argentina: Some current linguistic developments. In Perez, D. and Sippola, E. (eds), *Postcolonial language varieties in the Americas. Koloniale und Postkoloniale Linguistik / Colonial and Postcolonial Linguistics. KPL/CPL)*, Vol. 18, 239–269. Berlin/Boston: De Gruyter.

Rees, I.W. 2021b. The Welsh in diaspora: Patagonia. In Morgan, W.J., Bowie, F. and O'Connell, J. (eds), *Social anthropologies of the Welsh: Past and present*. The Royal Anthropological Institute's Country Series (Series Editor: Dr David Shankland). Canon Pyon: Sean Kingston Publishing.

Roach, P. 2000. *English phonetics and phonology*. 3rd edition. Cambridge: Cambridge University Press.

Sanchez-Stockhammer, C. 2018. *English compounds and their spelling*. Cambridge: Cambridge University Press.

Sapir, E. 1933. La réalité psychologique des phonèmes. *Journal de Psychologie Normale et Pathologique* 30: 247–265. English version published in 1949 as: The psychological reality of phonemes. In David G. Mandelbaum (ed.), *Selected writings of Edward Sapir in language, culture, and personality*, 46–60. Berkeley: University of California Press.

Saussure, F de. 1916. *Cours de Linguistique Générale*. Compiled by Charles Bally and Albert Sechehaye. Paris: Payot.

Schuh, R. 2017. *A Chadic cornucopia*, edited by Paul Newman. //escholarship.org/uc/item/5zx6z32d

Selkirk, E. 1982. The syllable. In van der Hulst, H. and Smith, N. (eds), *The structure of phonological representations*. Part II. Dordrecht: Foris.

Stankiewicz, E. (ed.). 1972. A *Baudouin de Courtenay anthology: The beginnings of structural linguistics*. Bloomington and London: Indiana University Press.

Tench, P. 1976. Double ranks in a phonological hierarchy. *Journal of Linguistics* 12: 1–20.

Tench, P. 1990. *The roles of intonation in English discourse*. Frankfurt aM: Peter Lang.

Tench, P. (ed.). 1992. *Studies in systemic phonology*. London: Pinter.

Tench, P. 1996a. *The intonation systems of English*. London: Cassell.

Tench, P. 1996b. Intonation and the differentiation of syntactical patterns in English and German. *International Journal of Applied Linguistics* 6(2): 223–256.

Tench, P. 1997. The fall and rise of the level tone in English. *Functions of Language* 4(1): 1–22.

Tench, P. 2003a. Processes of semogenesis in English intonation. *Functions of Language* 10(2): 209–234.

Tench, P. 2003b. Non-native speakers' misperceptions of English vowels and consonants: Evidence from Korean adults in UK. *International Review of Applied Linguistics* 41: 145–173.

Tench, P. 2007a. Illustrations of the IPA. *Tera. Journal of the International Phonetic Association* 37(2): 227–234.

Tench, P. 2007b. A new orthography in Tera. Available at: www.paultenchdocs.co.uk

Tench, P. 2008. Phonological competence in the design of a new orthography. Available at: www.paultenchdocs.co.uk

Tench, P. 2011. *Transcribing the sound of English*. Cambridge: Cambridge University Press.

Tench, P. 2014. Towards a systemic presentation of the word phonology of English. In Bowcher, W.F. and Smith, B.A. (eds), *Systemic Phonology; recent studies in English*. Sheffield: Equinox.

Tench, P. 2017. The phoneme and word phonology in systemic functional linguistics. In Bartlett, T. and O'Grady, G. (eds), *The Routledge handbook of Systemic Functional Linguistics*. London: Routledge.

Tench, P. and Miller, J. 1980. Aspects of Hausa intonation, 1: Utterances in isolation. *Journal of the International Phonetic Association* 10: 45–63.

Thompson, G. 1996. *Introducing functional grammar*. London: Arnold.

Trubetzkoy, N.S. 1958/1967. *Grundzüge der phonologie*. 4th edition. Göttingen: Vandenhoeck & Ruprecht.

Wängler, H.-H. 1967. *Grundriss einer Phonetik des Deutschen*. Marburg: N. G. Elwert Verlag.

Wells, J.C. 1990. *Longman pronunciation dictionary*. Harlow: Longman.

Wells, J.C. 2006. *English intonation: An introduction*. Cambridge: Cambridge University Press.

Wiese, R. 2000. *The phonology of German*. Oxford: Oxford University Press.

Williams, B. 1989. *Stress in modern Welsh*. PhD thesis, distributed by Indiana University Linguistics Club.

Young, D.J. 1980. *The structure of English clauses*. London: Hutchinson.

Young, D.J. 1992. English consonant clusters: A systemic approach. In Tench, P. (ed.), *Studies in systemic phonology*. London: Pinter.

Author Index

Subject Index